PELICAN BOOKS

A 525

A HISTORY OF MODERN FRANCE

VOLUME TWO

A HISTORY
OF MODERN FRANCE

BY ALFRED COBBAN

VOLUME TWO

From the First Empire to the Fourth Republic

1799–1945

PENGUIN BOOKS

Penguin Books Ltd, Harmondsworth, Middlesex
U.S.A.: Penguin Books Inc., 3300 Clipper Mill Road, Baltimore 11, Md
AUSTRALIA: Penguin Books Pty Ltd, 762 Whitehorse Road,
Mitcham, Victoria

—

First published 1961
Reprinted 1962, 1963

—

Copyright © Alfred Cobban, 1961

—

Made and printed in Great Britain
by The Whitefriars Press Ltd,
London and Tonbridge
Set in Monotype Baskerville

CONTENTS

INTRODUCTION

EVERY author knows that the preface is the last part of a book to be written, which is why this one appears only with the publication of the second and last volume. The opportunity has been taken of the re-issue of both volumes to correct a number of small mistakes. I am indebted to those reviewers and other readers who drew my attention to some of these. The first object of the introduction is to explain what this history of modern France is not. It is not a strict narrative history, following the course of events year by year. Hence tables of dates have been added to assist the reader. It is not intended to be a text-book giving the facts, all the facts, and nothing but the facts necessary for passing an examination in French history. I have not attempted to spread the history evenly if thinly over the whole period. On the contrary I have concentrated attention where events are densest and most significant, and passed more rapidly over those periods and aspects which seem of less interest, even if this has meant neglecting much repetitive political manoeuvring. Again, the details of foreign relations, in peace and war, are passed over rather slightly. Of course, not all omissions are necessarily deliberate. In some cases they are the result of lack of information. This is particularly so in respect of economic history, for the results of research in this field are still hardly adequate even for a broad picture.

Such gaps constitute one of the major difficulties in compiling the appendices on Further Reading. These are not intended as anything more ambitious than their title suggests: they represent a rather arbitrary choice and obviously exclude many important works. While the eighteenth-century bibliography was not difficult to compile, the nineteenth-century one is frankly patchy and inadequate. At least some of my debts are reflected in these lists. There should be added an acknowledgement of what I have learned in supervising the work of those students who have researched on subjects from this period for their doctoral theses in my seminar during recent years. The justification for my treatment of the Girondins can now be found in Michael Sydenham's *The Girondins* (Athlone Press, 1961). An analysis of the membership and motivation of the revolutionary mobs, which has finally eliminated the picture drawn by Taine, is given by George Rudé in *The Crowd in the French Revolution* (Clarendon Press, 1959). The lack of influence of Rousseau's political writings before 1789, and their ambivalence after, is shown by Joan Macdonald in a study now being prepared for the press of their influence during the Constituent Assembly. An analysis of the application of the Civil Constitution of the Clergy in the diocese of Lisieux by Winifred Edington, part of which has been published in French periodicals, revealed, among other things, the acute financial problems it involved. J. P. McLaughlin traced the growth of French annexationist policy from the beginning of the Revolution, and recently J. F. Murley has completed the first detailed account of the circumstances out of which the Revolutionary War between France and Great Britain arose. The counter-revolution has always been a neglected field of study, at least by serious historians. J. A. Johnson, writing a revealing study of the rôle of Calonne in the counter-revolution, found the origin of its cleavages in the ministerial rivalries of the *ancien régime*; N. F. Richards traced the attitude of the British government in respect of the French monarchy from 1789 to 1802; and the research of Harvey Mitchell, which has partly been published in journals, revealed the actual connexion of the comte d'Antraigues with the famous and mysterious Dropmore Bulletins, and also showed how near the Republic came to being overthrown at the time of Fructidor. Turning back to the *ancien régime*, the struggle of the factions for the succession to Fleury, which was only known in general terms, has been subjected to a valuable examination by Evelyn Cruickshanks. G. J. de C. Mead's analysis and survey of the intendants of eighteenth-century France and J. Bosher's account of the efforts to eliminate the internal customs dues will both, I believe, when they are published, add considerably to our knowledge of French administration in the eighteenth century; as, in a different field, will a study by Nora Temple of the government of French towns in the eighteenth century, with special reference to Auxerre and Avalon. Echoes from most of these theses, on the points mentioned, will be found in Volume I. Another debt which I must also express is to Mrs Audrey Munro for coping so efficiently and patiently with my handwriting in this and other books she has typed for me.

The final problem that presented itself in writing this history was how and where to conclude. Partly for lack of space, my treatment of the twentieth century has been confined mainly to an outline of political developments; and I have chosen to finish at what is admittedly a rather artificial date, 21 October 1945, when the Third Republic formally came to an end.

University College London   A. COBBAN

I

THE FIRST EMPIRE

1. FRANCE IN 1799

THE pattern of French society, and even its physical setting, received so strong an imprint in the eighteenth century that the mark of that age still remains in many aspects of national life the dominant characteristic of France. In its provincial capitals, the solid eighteenth-century quarters, well-planned enclaves, or graceful urban extensions in a semi-rural setting, still recall the memory of a more elegant age. In Paris, when the older buildings were swept away under the Second Empire and even the street plan modernized out of recognition, the eighteenth century survived in the great town-houses scattered from the Chaussée d'Antin through the faubourg Saint-Honoré to the Seine, and by way of the place de la Concorde across the river to the faubourg Saint-Germain. Under Louis XV, Paris, pushing outwards, had swallowed up the limits traced by Charles V in the fourteenth century and their western extension of 1631 under Louis XIII. The hated wall of the Farmers General, built in 1785 as a customs barrier with imposing monumental gates, took in a vast new area, stretching round the western and northern heights of Passy, Chaillot, Belleville, and Ménilmontant, including – south of the river – the faubourgs Saint-Victor, Saint-Marceau, Saint-Jacques, and Saint-Germain, and curving back round the Champ de Mars. At the end of the eighteenth century much of this new territory was not yet built up; within the barrier, beyond the Bastille and the Temple in the East, were fields and scattered houses with their gardens. In the West the Champs Élysées were woodland crossed by roads and wandering paths, and the Champ de Mars a huge open space. Paris proper still huddled together within the boulevards that marked the site of its former fortifications, a solid agglomeration of high, closely-packed, terraced houses separated by winding, narrow streets and alleys, noisy with street cries, busy with passers-by, crowded and dangerous with carriages and wagons of all kinds, strewn with rubbish and filth lying about in heaps or carried along in the torrents of water pouring after a storm down the wide gutters, across which pedestrians could only pass dry-shod by little plank bridges. After a decade of revolution the house-fronts were dilapidated, their plaster falling, paint-work peeling, and shreds of posters flapping in the wind. At night, when there was no moon, an occasional *lanterne*, jutting out from the wall, shed a feeble and after 1789 a rather sinister light in these dark canyons. For all the fine architecture of the classical age, and the palatial *hôtels* of the wealthy, urban amenities were rare. Voltaire, in 1749, had called for such improvements as fountains to supply pure drinking water, roads adequate for the traffic of a great capital, and worthy public buildings, especially theatres. The narrow and squalid streets of Paris, he declared, should be widened, and fine buildings which were concealed from sight by a huddle of houses freed from their squalid surroundings. It was a century later before his hopes for Paris began to be realized, and then to the artistic taste of the Second Empire instead of that of the age of Louis Quinze.

Paris, at the end of the eighteenth century, was still in some respects an homogeneous city. Though there were faubourgs like Saint-Antoine and Saint-Marceau, inhabited mainly by small masters and their journeymen, and new wealthy quarters like the faubourg Saint-Germain, in much of older Paris the homes of the well-to-do, of the middling people and of the poor existed under the same roof. It might almost be said that class stratification was vertical, the rich and the poor entering by the same door, the former to mount by a short and broad staircase to the impressive apartments of the first floor, the latter to climb high up by ever narrowing stairs till they reached the attics in the mansard roof.

From Paris and the provincial capitals already radiated out the network of great roads that so impressed Arthur Young, as did the lack of traffic on them. The new industrial regions of France have witnessed many changes since the eighteenth century, but the great ports were already considerable cities. They still glory in their eighteenth-century quarters, while to many smaller towns and villages, scattered up and down the length and breadth of the country, alteration has come only slowly and imperceptibly. It was from the provinces that was drawn, then as now, much of the busy, scurrying population of the ant-heap of Paris, and many a Parisian, his fortune made or lost and his active life over, withdrew to pass his declining years in the quiet town or village of his childhood, along with the men who had been boys when he was a boy, who had not stirred from their native soil and who were the millions of France. Perhaps 600,000 lived in Paris at the end of the eighteenth century. The total urban population of France must have been well under two millions. Probably some 95 per cent of France's 26 millions lived in isolated farms, hamlets, villages, and small country towns. Mountain and forest still covered, as they do today, large tracts of country, though under pressure of rural over-population farming had pushed into marginal land on moor and hill-top that has since been abandoned. Agriculture, little influenced by the new methods developed in eighteenth-century England, followed its routine of the Middle Ages. Industry was still largely domestic.

In all these fundamental respects it matters little whether we are writing of 1789 or 1799. The Revolution did not materially add to or subtract from the basic resources of France, though it altered the use that was, or could be, made of them. What France had that still endowed her, at the end of the eighteenth century, with a potentially greater strength than any other country, was the largest population in Europe under a single government, apart from Russia, and even that had only just caught up with France. The application of the steam engine to industry was hardly yet a factor in national strength; and this apart, France had a technical skill and equipment second to none. The Revolution had freed her from the trammels of the *ancien régime*. Paris, which for some five years had tried to rule France, had been disciplined with the aid of the armies drawn from the unpolitical rural millions. All was ready for a great general to concentrate the newly released forces into a great centralized despotism and direct them into a bid for world empire.

2. FROM CONSULATE TO EMPIRE

CENTURIES do not usually end so punctually as the French eighteenth century did with the year 1799; though in another sense, as I have suggested, the France of the *ancien régime* still survives. For both its sudden conclusion and its persistence the chief responsibility must be attributed to Bonaparte. With his sense of realism, executive capacity, and ruthless strength of will, he wrote finis to the doubts and feuds of the revolutionaries, and imposed, out of the materials to hand, a new-fashioned framework on France, which was to last in its essentials to the present day. For the very reason that it was an artificial superstructure, which bore the weight of the state without ever being consciously shaped to the society on which it was arbitrarily imposed, it prevented the natural growth of institutions which might otherwise have taken place. This is, of course, wisdom after the event. When Bonaparte was brought to the chief office in the republic, though there was a general feeling that a new period had opened, the politicians who had effected the *coup d'état* did not appreciate what they had done, any more than those who had overthrown Robespierre five years earlier.

On the morrow of *brumaire* Bonaparte himself had only taken the first step, though a long one, on the path to Empire. He had yet to show that he was more than a successful general and to consolidate by the arts of politics what he had staked out a claim to by those of war. The original proposals for the new constitution came from that self-appointed Solon of the Revolution, Sieyes. Given a third opportunity to demonstrate his genius at making constitutional bricks without straw, he framed a system of legislative bodies ingeniously devised to remove all effective political power from the sovereign people without attributing it to anyone else. In the best revolutionary tradition he was proposing to set up an imposing machine of government without providing any motive power to work it. The central position in the whole complicated system was to be occupied by a Conservative Senate, and if we ask how this was to be created we come to the heart of the matter: it was to be nominated, in effect, by Sieyes. The executive power, on the other hand, was to be entrusted to a Grand Elector with powers so carefully cabined and confined that he could do nothing by himself: this rôle was reserved for Bonaparte. We can hardly be surprised that for the third time Sieyes' plans proved abortive. His proposal for drawing the teeth of democratic sovereignty by attributing the right of voting to electors nominated from above – 'authority must come from above and confidence from below', to quote his new-style formula for democracy – suited Bonaparte well enough, as did the various devices for preventing the legislative chambers from exercising any real power. But Bonaparte was determined that he himself, as First Consul, should have effective and undivided executive authority. Even the other two Consuls were to be little more than rubber stamps. The result of his revision of the constitutional proposals was that whereas the age of divine-right monarchy had ended in 1789, the age of dictatorship began in 1799. Sieyes, who had written the birth-certificate of the Revolution, also signed its death warrant. He accepted, soon after, a large estate from Bonaparte, and confined himself henceforth to drawing-room politics. In a popular vote on the Constitution, which was in effect a plebiscite for or against General Bonaparte, the people performed what was to become its customary role in dictatorships in exemplary fashion: 3,011,007 voted for and 1,562 against.

The politicians of Paris did not immediately acknowledge the finality of *brumaire*. No sooner was Bonaparte installed in power than they began to intrigue against him. For his part, the First Consul set about consolidating his position by winning over, through the personal charm which he had at his command, as well as by material favours, men of all parties, revolutionary or royalist, so long as they were willing to forget their principles in his service. All the arts of popularity and propaganda were put to work. The propertied classes, old and new, saw in Bonaparte a saviour of society. A mixture of clemency and force pacified the rebellious departments of the West. The outlines of a new administrative structure for France were drawn up and – more important – put into effective operation. A peace offensive – and peace the French people now ardently longed for, gone the warlike passions of the early nineties – was launched by personal letters from the First Consul to George III and the Emperor; but peace, he was careful to tell the French people, could only come after victory. This was also necessary if he was to be able to put an end to the political intrigues of Paris and consolidate his personal authority.

The military situation was unpromising. When the year 1800 began the remnants of the defeated French army of Italy were still hanging on in Genoa in imminent danger of starvation, and their final collapse would open the door into France. Therefore, leaving Moreau in charge of an offensive on the Rhine, Bonaparte hastily gathered an army at Dijon and descended on Italy by way of the Great St Bernard. The campaign which followed was confused and unplanned. Important documents which might have revealed too much about it were destroyed by Bonaparte subsequently, and his own dispatches are a tissue of lies, so that it is difficult to know exactly what happened. The decisive clash of the French and Austrians at Marengo on 14 June 1800 took Bonaparte by surprise, with his army scattered. He was saved by the return, in the nick of time, of the division he had sent off under Desai. It was a soldiers' battle, won by the staunchness of the Guard and the dash of Desai, who was killed in the fighting. Bonaparte, in a dispatch from the battle-field, provided for him a romanticized death: a dead man could be no rival. By the battle of Marengo Lombardy was regained and France relieved from the threat of an Austrian invasion. Meanwhile Moreau had advanced through Bavaria, occupied Munich, and in December, after routing the Austrians at Hohenlinden, was within fifty miles of Vienna.

Bonaparte had not waited for the completion of the German campaign to return to Paris, where, he knew, his enemies, Carnot prominent among them, were counting on defeat or at least a stalemate in Italy to enable them to overthrow the Consulate. Instead, hot on the heels of the news of Marengo, Bonaparte came spurring across France to pluck the fruits of victory. The Guards, who had served him so well, were brought back hurriedly to enter Paris with their general on the morning of the Quartorze Juillet, so that their entry could coincide with the celebration of the fête of the Bastille. The faubourg Saint-Antoine, where Robespierre had once been the idol, turned out its *sans-culottes* in their thousands to hail the triumph and welcome the victor.

Peace with victory was now within reach. The Holy Roman Emperor, threatened by French armies advancing from southern Germany on Austria itself and from northern Italy on Venetia, acknowledged defeat. By the treaty of Lunéville, in February 1801, French possessions on the left bank of the Rhine, from Switzerland to the sea, and the French satellite states – the Cisalpine and Ligurian Republics in northern Italy, the Helvetic Republic in Switzerland, and the Batavian Republic of the Dutch – were recognized. The hereditary princes of the Empire who lost territory on the left bank of the Rhine were to be compensated within Germany, and France as a party to the Treaty was to participate in the process of territorial redistribution. This was to open the door to large-scale French intervention in the Holy Roman Empire.

Now only England remained in the way of complete

pacification. To ensure her isolation Bonaparte negotiated an agreement with Russia, and conciliated Spain by the grant of the duchy of Tuscany to the Bourbon Duke of Parma. Under Russian leadership the Armed Neutrality was formed to oppose British attacks on neutral shipping, but the assassination of Paul I of Russia, and the bombardment of Copenhagen, dislocated it. In Egypt the isolated French army had been forced to capitulate by a British expeditionary force. These, however, were peripheral events. Faced with the bankruptcy of their European policy, Pitt and Grenville resigned and a new British government was ready to conclude peace with France. The negotiations were long and difficult, but slowly and reluctantly Great Britain gave up a large part of her conquests: it is true they had mainly been at the expense of former allies and not of France. In March 1802 the Treaty of Amiens was signed; Bonaparte had achieved peace for France and could proceed to collect the fruits of victory.

The change from Consulate to Empire was to be effected with the aid of victories abroad and plots at home. Marengo was followed, on 24 December 1800, by an attempt to blow up Bonaparte on his way to the opera. The attempted assassination was the work of a group of royalists under the Vendean leader, Georges Cadoudal, but the First Consul seized the opportunity to eliminate the unreconciled Jacobins, whom he regarded as his more dangerous opponents. Many of them were sent to rot to death in Guiana or the Seychelles.

The signature of the Treaty of Amiens enabled Bonaparte to secure the passing, by a majority of $3\frac{1}{2}$ millions to eight thousand, of a new plebiscite making him Consul for life. The next step followed fairly soon after. Cadoudal, who had taken refuge in England after the failure of his plot in 1800, organized a new attempt on Bonaparte's life in 1803, possibly with the connivance of Windham among the British ministers. Moreau, whose victory at Hohenlinden had been deliberately played down by Bonaparte to enhance his own glory, and Pichegru, returning secretly from

England where he had taken refuge since his failure to over-throw the Directory, were also implicated. The conspiracy was discovered before it could be put into effect. Cadoudal and his group of desperate men were arrested and executed; Pichegru was imprisoned in the Temple and found strangled one morning. According to the official theory he had committed suicide, as enemies of dictators are apt to do. Moreau, against whom the evidence was weaker, and whose victories were too recent for him to be disposed of so easily, was allowed to go into exile.

Bonaparte now decided that the royalists must be taught a lesson, as the Jacobins had been. The young duc d'Enghien, the last of the Condés, was seized on territory neighbouring France, brought back over the frontier and shot as an *émigré* in foreign service. There was nothing to link him with the plot of Cadoudal: it was an exemplary murder. As a Corsican perhaps Bonaparte regarded it as a legitimate exercise of the right of vendetta, his own life having undoubtedly been threatened by royalist plots. The much-publicized Cadoudal conspiracy also provided an appropriate atmosphere for the final transmutation of the First Consul into the Emperor. The Senate, duly prompted, passed the necessary legislative measures and the subsequent plebiscite, now *de rigueur*, gave popular sanction by 3,572,329 votes against 2,579 to the establishment of an hereditary Empire. This was perhaps less of a shock to republican sentiment than one might think, because, as early as 1789, the term empire had been in use to describe the French state, as a means of avoiding the word monarchy without falling into that of republic. The religious sanction was the one thing lacking, Napoleon felt, to make him a real Emperor. It could be provided. Pius VII was prepared for what to a less holy-minded man might have seemed an humiliation, if it could be regarded as a further step to win France back to the fold, and agreed to perform the cere-mony of crowning Napoleon in Notre-Dame. There were many difficulties to be smoothed out but – except that the Pope, or according to the version at the time of the divorcee

Josephine herself, insisted that Napoleon should go through a religious ceremony of marriage with her, which he did in strict privacy – in most matters the Emperor had his own way. Anointed by the Pope, Napoleon himself placed the crown on his own head. The day was 2 December 1804.

3. NAPOLEONIC FOUNDATIONS OF THE NINETEENTH CENTURY

When he became First Consul Napoleon Bonaparte was only thirty years old, but already marked as a man of destiny. The impecunious son of what passed for a gentle family in Corsica, after the French conquest he went with government assistance to the school at Brienne and then to the École Militaire, whence he emerged as sub-lieutenant of artillery. The Revolution was the time, the army was the career, for an ambitious young man. Short, but thin and muscular, he had good looks, though little notice should be taken of portraits in which he is already the Byronic hero of the coming romantic movement. He had tremendous energy and a powerful and disciplined memory. He could work continuously for long periods, with only snatches of sleep. In order not to disturb his habits, says his police official, Réal, he had taken care not to form any. He had a thirst for glory, fed partly on the writings of the pre-romantics but more on the history of the great conquerors of the ancient world, Caesar and Alexander, for this was also the period of the classical revival. Although he read Rousseau and was not uninfluenced by the ideals of the Enlightenment, his contribution to the legal code which bears his name showed a natural preference for the more conservative and less enlightened ideas of the *ancien régime*. Politically his bent was towards despotism untrammelled by divine right. His experience of the Revolution had left him with a deep contempt, not unmixed with fear, for the people. For politicians he had the dictator's natural aversion. He was not without humane instincts, and was capable of kindness in private life, to say nothing of the charm which he could turn on at will; but such qualities vanished when they stood in the way of his success. Even early in his career, before overweening egoism had quite mastered him, when military considerations demanded it he was entirely ruthless. There is no evidence that bloodshed mattered a scrap to him, or that he ever thought, as a Marlborough or a Wellington did, of economizing in the lives of his soldiers. The mass attack on which he relied depended on not counting the cost in dead and wounded. A French Colonel describes him riding, as was his custom, over the field of Borodino after the battle, rubbing his hands and radiant with satisfaction as he counted five dead Russians to every one French corpse. I suppose, the Colonel adds sardonically, he took the bodies of his German allies for Russians. Such nobility as might have been given, even to the career of a military despot, by the service of some end, although a mistaken one, was lacking. Apart from his own personal glory, the only other ambition he had at heart was to found a dynasty. When, in his last campaign, he might have saved much for France by abandoning his dream of Empire, he was incapable of such moderation, or even realism. After all this, to say that he was an adventurer is an anti-climax; but it is not irrelevant or unimportant. Coming from islanders whose social institutions were the *banditti* and the *vendetta*, he carried the same standards into a country where the Revolution had already shown how uncertain were the conquests of the Enlightenment. For fifteen years France and Europe were to be at the mercy of a gambler to whom fate and his own genius gave for a time all the aces. He always cheated at cards and his carriage had diamonds concealed in its lining in case of hurried flight.

The short intermission from continual war that the Treaty of Amiens inaugurated gave Bonaparte the opportunity to establish the bases of a new government. As soon as he became First Consul he began the task of reconstruction. The simulacrum of representative institutions was preserved as a sop to revolutionary tradition, with an advisory Senate, a Legislative Body which could vote but not speak, and a Tribunate which could speak but not vote. Since the last, powerless as it was, did not invariably say just what the Emperor wanted, it was reduced in membership to fifty, divided into sections, and finally, in 1807, abolished. The Legislative Body, chosen by the Senate and composed mostly of obscure former revolutionaries, was then ungagged but remained a passive register of the Emperor's will. The Senate, including many of the great names of the period, at first sight looks a more substantial body, with real legislative powers; but for all their distinction, its members were a mere collection of nominees, serving only to give dignity to their master's decisions.

If we turn from the legislative to the executive, even the façade of limitation on the will of the Emperor disappears. The reorganization of the ministries had mostly been effected during the Revolution. Foreign Affairs, War, and Marine, to which was attached Colonies now that France had lost them all, remained as before 1789. The Keeper of the Seals became the Minister for Justice. The most important changes were the result of amalgamating, and then subdividing on more logical grounds, the Contrôle Général and Maison du Roi, out of which emerged the Ministry of Finances and the Ministry of the Interior. Finally, like all dictators, Bonaparte required a Minister of Police. A State Secretariat was also set up, through which the First Consul controlled and coordinated the policies of his ministers.

Over the Police the ex-terrorist Fouché, later, when titles were handed round, to become the duc d'Otranto, reigned, with the assistance of a choice collection of scoundrels gathered from the police of the *ancien régime* and the underworld of the Revolution. At Foreign Affairs Tallyrand was indispensable. Berthier at the War Office was an invaluable chief of staff. Lucien Bonaparte, the first Minister of the Interior, though efficient showed signs of independence which could not be tolerated, least of all in a brother, and was soon dismissed. Finances were entrusted to Gaudin, formerly a high official of the Contrôle Général. There was, of course, no first minister, and the ministers never constituted a cabinet. The Emperor consulted them individually, took their advice or gave them their orders as it pleased him, like an *ancien régime* monarch. Louis XIV had at last found a successor and France was again ruled by the *bon plaisir* of an autocrat, but one enfranchised from the bonds of aristocratic and provincial privilege and controlling a new-fashioned and far more efficient administrative machine.

At the centre of the new administrative structure was the Council of State. Napoleon, for all his seizure of arbitrary power, was no mere vulgar dictator imposing unconsidered decisions on a servile nation. An expert himself in the matter of war, he knew the value of experts. He was also, at least when he first came to power, conscious of his own limitations and of his need for a body of specialists who, without possessing political power, could provide him with the advice he needed in all fields of government. The Council of State was intended, in the first place, as the means of his own political education. It was also to draw up laws and administrative regulations and expound them to the legislative bodies: it was in fact the real legislative organ. The Councillors of State took the place of the masters of requests and councillors of the *ancien régime*, from whom the *intendants* and higher officials had been recruited. They formed a permanent corps whence Napoleon could draw *missi dominici* for the varied tasks of imperial government. The sections into which the Council was divided supervised the various fields of government and provided him with a means of checking and controlling the actions of his ministers. The importance he attributed to the Council was well shown in his advice to the former *parlementaire* and constitutional monarchist, Roederer, one of Bonaparte's associates in the *coup d'état* of *brumaire*, not to accept a nomination to the Senate but rather to enter the Council of State. 'In that', the First Consul said, 'there are great things to be done; from that I will draw my ambassadors and ministers.' The advice, as was inevitable with Bonaparte, was not disinterested. He was counting on the Council of State, more than on any other of his administrative bodies, to draw into his service able men from all fields and from all points on the political scale, except the most intransigent republicans and royalists. Former magistrates and high officials of the *ancien régime* sat side by side with men who had made their mark in the struggles of the Revolution, generals of the revolutionary armies with civilian technicians and scientists.

What was to be ultimately the greatest achievement of the Council of State, the creation of a system of administrative law, was as yet a minor activity; but as well as its major rôle in the central government it exercised an unlimited supervision over local administration and all public establishments, and gradually filled in the details of the administrative and financial system sketched out under the Consulate. From its creation in 1800 to 1813, 58,435 separate cases were brought up for examination in the general assembly of the Council; the number dealt with annually rose from 911 in 1800 to 6,285 in 1811. While the Council of State formed the ideal instrument for an absolute régime, its work was far too valuable for any subsequent government to dispense with its services. Though under Napoleon it was no more than an instrument without any independence, the Council of State developed in due course a tradition and an *esprit de corps* of its own and became the unshakeable corner-stone of the French bureaucracy. In the absence of an effective parliamentary system it provided, along with the administrative substructure, the ferro-concrete framework of government, which was to enable French society to survive and emerge comparatively unchanged from so many political upheavals. At the same time, and for this very reason, it also stood in the way of the creation of effective parliamentary institutions. Through the Council of State and his other administrative institutions, the shadow of Napoleon continued to darken the following century. He had given France, when she needed it after the stresses of the Revolution, a steel corset on which she was to become dependent and from which she was to emancipate herself only slowly and painfully and never completely.

The system of centralized bureaucracy called for the creation of machinery of local administration which could carry the will of the government at Paris into the most remote communes. Administrative centralization, as de Tocqueville pointed out, was not an invention of Napoleon. The modern prefect can trace his ancestry back to the intendants of Louis XIV and Richelieu, and even to the *sénéchaux* and *baillis* of the Middle Ages; but the element of continuity, though important, must not be exaggerated. The *ancien régime* still retained too many medieval relics for the writ of the central government to run unchallenged and unimpeded throughout the provinces. The great achievement of the Revolution, for good or ill, had been to make a *tabula rasa*, administratively speaking, of France. The system of democratic councils with which the Constitutional Assembly endowed, as by a stroke of the pen, its new administrative divisions, could not survive the strains of the Revolution. Already under the Committee of Public Safety a big step had been taken in the direction of the restoration of central control. Under the Directory the local authorities became increasingly weak and corrupt, though the more exaggerated accounts of Directorial decay are perhaps the work of Bonapartist propaganda. However, an official report of 1799 declared, 'The pillage of public funds, attacks directed on public officials, the inertia of a great number of them, the assassination of republicans – such is unfortunately the picture which several departments present.' The picture had at least some truth in it and was perhaps more generally true than was admitted.

Bonaparte and his advisers, in 1800, had no doubt what was wrong: it was the attempt, still surviving in theory, to govern the departments and communes by a system of elected councils. In the basic law on local government of the year VIII the elective principle was eliminated from the appointment of all local officials. Local councils still survived in name, it is true, but their functions were reduced to microscopic proportions. As Chaptal, wealthy proprietor and scientist, ennobled before 1789, and the successor to Lucien Bonaparte at the Ministry of the Interior, put it, 'These popular councils are placed, so to speak, to one side of the line of executive action: they do not hamper in any way the rapid progress of the administration.' In fact adequate precautions were taken to ensure that they should not do so. They were not allowed to meet for a longer period than fifteen days in the year; their chief function was to give their approval to the distribution of taxation between the various *arrondissements*, towns, and villages of the department. All administrative authority in the department was placed in the hands of a prefect, appointed from Paris, with sub-prefects under him. The latter were generally local men and often former revolutionaries, but a job was a job. They had no independent authority. The first list of prefects included many Jacobins who had rallied to Bonaparte, as well as former *ancien régime* officials. The prefects, unlike the sub-prefects, were never local men. There has been much discussion whether they were mere passive agents of the central government. They probably possessed less independence than the former intendants; but since, even now, instructions took eight days to reach Toulouse from Paris, and the newly invented system of telegraphs was only used for important communications, mostly military, detailed control of the prefects' actions was obviously difficult. Lucien Bonaparte in a circular of the year VIII said, 'General ideas must come from the centre. I note with regret that some of you, with praiseworthy intentions doubtless, concern yourselves with the interpretation of the laws. ... It is not this that the government expects of its administration.' That the prefects were the officers of a central government and subject to the same kind of obedience as was expected of officers of the army was made quite clear by putting them into uniform. It was a dignified one – blue coat, white waistcoat and breeches, silver thread on collar, cuffs, and pockets, a *chapeau français*

ornamented with silver, red scarf with silver fringes, and a
sword – but one wonders what an intendant would have
said if he had been expected to wear a uniform. STOP

The first task of the prefects was that of economic restoration. In a note of 1800 Bonaparte wrote, 'The 36,000
communes in France represent 36,000 orphans, heirs of the
old feudal rights, which have been abandoned or pillaged
for ten years by the municipal guardians of the Convention
and the Directory.' Now the communes were to be taught
that they had a master and a more efficient one than the
medley of *ancien régime* authorities. This is not to say that
the prefects could afford to ride rough-shod over all local
feeling. Under the Empire the local notabilities re-emerged
as the dominant interest and the prefects and sub-prefects
found it wise to remain on friendly terms with them, for
their mutual advantage. Of the general ability of the prefects and the valuable work they did in restoring administrative good habits to the departments there can be no
question. Taine once expressed the regret of not having had
the experience of serving for a year as secretary to one of
Napoleon's prefects.

The prefects had other tasks besides that of promoting
the economic well-being of their departments. They had to
collect favourable votes for the plebiscites: the success with
which they performed this duty foretold their future political
rôle. Gradually, as the war pressed increasingly heavily on
French life, its requirements came to dominate the activities
of the prefects. They drew up lists of conscripts, authorized
exemptions, sought out deserters, confiscated horses for the
army, looked after troops in passage, and guarded prisoners
of war. As early as 1801 a prefect is found complaining that
the enforcement of conscription occupies one-third of the
employees of his prefecture and that these are barely
sufficient. Continually increasing military demands bore so
heavily on the departments that by 1814 their financial
resources had been exhausted.

In the later years of the Empire the personnel of the
administration underwent considerable changes. Especially

from 1809 onwards, Napoleon, with the weakness of a new man for real gentlemen, tended to appoint former nobles to office. A host of *émigrés* flocked back to take up good jobs, to introduce more easy-going methods into the prefectures, and leave the real work to their secretaries-general. From 1810 all prefects were given the title of count or baron and ordered to assume coats of arms. Many were now secret royalists, ready to accept the Emperor's pay while he was in power, but prepared to desert him with cynical haste in 1814. During the Hundred Days the prefects exhibited what would be a comic, if it were not equally a cowardly and treacherous anxiety to be on the winning side. Official adulation of the Emperor was carried to extreme lengths. A prefect of the Pas-de-Calais, formerly officer of the Royal Normandy regiment, apostrophized his department, when it was about to receive a visit from the Emperor, thus: 'You are about to see him, that Napoleon, proclaimed so justly the greatest of men in the greatest of nations ... *Dieu créa Bonaparte et se reposa.*' As soon as Napoleon lost power the same official addressed his devotions with equal fervour to the duc de Berry, only to renew his loyal protestations to the Emperor when he returned from Elba. Among those with a genius for guessing which way the cat was going to jump and getting there in advance, the prize must be held by M. de Jessaint, prefect of the Marne uninterruptedly from 1800 to 1838. The fact is that the prefectoral system was an immensely powerful instrument in the hands of the central government, but its power was entirely derivative. While the *régime* was strong at the centre the prefects could guarantee to control the rest of the country; but a *coup d'état* in Paris could shatter the whole fabric, for no element capable of standing by itself existed in the provinces. The prefectural system, for all its merits, combined the vices of excessive rigidity and excessive instability. It was to be in no small measure responsible for the alternation of revolution and reaction that marked the history of nineteenth-century France.

Besides creating a unified administrative machinery,

Napoleon laid down the legislative basis on which it was to operate. The idea of reducing the varied laws of France to a uniform, written code was inherited by the Revolution from the *ancien régime*. The work had been begun by the *Ordonnances* drawn up under Colbert and d'Aguesseau. The revolutionary Assemblies set up committees to complete the work of codification, but they were never able to catch up with the mass of their own legislation. In 1800 Bonaparte appointed a committee of distinguished lawyers to draw up a civil code, and gave them five months to do it in. After their draft code had been discussed in the Council of State, the First Consul himself being present at about half of the meetings though of course he had not the legal knowledge to make a serious contribution to them, it was submitted to the legislative bodies, where criticism was so hostile that it did not obtain final acceptance until 1804. The criticism to which the Code was subjected, though it infuriated Napoleon, was largely sound. His rôle was not to frame the Code but to see that the lawyers came to a conclusion, good or bad, without further delay. For some of the worst features he was personally responsible. Such were the deterioration in the legal status of women, who were allowed no control over the family property and could not acquire, sell, or give property without their husband's consent; the reintroduction of confiscation as a legal penalty; and the use of the fiction of civil death. The First Consul's influence was also responsible for the tightening up of the laws of marriage and divorce and the restoration of paternal authority in the family. The great gains of the Revolution, however, were maintained: equality before the law, the principle of religious toleration, the abolition of privileges and seigneurial burdens. Property rights were strictly maintained and there was particular emphasis on the interests of the small owner. Property was to be inherited equally by all legitimate children at death, except for a certain disposable proportion: to this provision has been speculatively attributed the limitation of families in nineteenth-century France. Perhaps the most important feature of the Civil

Code was that all its 2,281 articles could be contained in a single fairly small volume. It was to be the most effective agency for the propagation of the basic principles of the French Revolution that was, or perhaps that could have been, devised. It was carried by the French armies through Europe and thence spread across the world. There followed in France a Code of Civil Procedure, cumbersome and mostly copied from *ancien régime* rules, a Commercial Code, and a severe and arbitrary Criminal Code, which was all the same a model of enlightenment compared with the barbarous laws that still prevailed in Great Britain.

The Revolution had in nothing failed so completely as in its finances. The first step towards their rehabilitation was taken by Gaudin, head of a division in the Contrôle Général before the Revolution and after the 18 *brumaire* Minister of Finances, when he removed the assessment and collection of direct taxation from the control of local authorities and formed a central organization charged with the task. France, however, has never been able to draw the major part of its revenue from the wealthy, and the new rich were no more willing to pay for the privilege of being governed than had been the old privileged orders. All indirect taxes had been abolished by the Constituent Assembly, though the Directory re-introduced them on playing cards and tobacco. Napoleon revived the tax on salt, brought back the hated *droits* on wines and cider, and created a *régie* for their collection. The Directory had also re-established local *octrois*; these were greatly extended under the Empire and the central government took an increasing proportion of them.

In 1800 was founded another of the great and permanent creations of the Consulate, the Bank of France. Though with semi-public functions, this was a private bank, its shareholders represented by a general assembly of the 200 most important, who elected the 15 regents and 3 censors. The Bank, like the other Napoleonic institutions, was to remain a power in France throughout the régimes which followed.

In 1802 the French budget was balanced, but this was only a temporary success. The existence of private and military funds under the direct control of the Emperor prevented the imperial budgets from ever being more than paper exercises, with little relation to the facts. No institutional reforms could put the country on a sound financial basis in time of continual war; and there was never sufficient confidence in the permanence of the régime for the government to draw, as Great Britain did to such a great extent, on loans. Moreover, Napoleon had a profound suspicion of them. He had to fall back, just like the *ancien régime*, on expedients, and live from hand to mouth. And like the Revolution he exploited the conquered countries, to such an extent that it might almost be said that war was a financial necessity for France.

Yet another of the loose ends left by the Revolution for Napoleon to cut and tie up in his own fashion was the problem of a religious settlement, and this also was largely, if not essentially, an administrative question. Whether religious differences still remained, in 1799, a source of danger to France, or whether the increasingly tolerant *modus vivendi* reached by the Directory could have survived, is a much disputed point on which agreement is unlikely to be reached; but it can be agreed that religious persecution during the Revolution had not merely failed to destroy the hold of the Roman Catholic religion on the people, it had strengthened religious feeling and played some part in promoting a religious revival. The more moderate policies of the Directory were perhaps more dangerous to the Church than active dechristianization. The secularization of education – a circular of the year VIII ordered teachers in the central schools to avoid 'everything that pertained to the doctrines and rites of all religions and sects whatever they may be' – may be regarded as initiating a struggle that was to continue to the present day.

The Catholic Church had certainly something to gain in this respect from the renewal of State support. There were also powerful inducements to the State to abandon its policy of religious neutrality and secularization. The complete pacification of the Vendée and Normandy would undoubtedly be greatly facilitated if the support of the clergy could be gained. This would also powerfully aid in the assimilation of the Belgic provinces and other newly acquired territory where the Catholic religion was strong. Bonaparte himself was aware of the sentimental appeal of a vague kind of Rousseauist religiosity, though one can hardly envisage him as a disciple of the Savoyard vicar. Religion, like every other ideal, was to him a means to an end, his own power. Sayings attributed to him represent truly his essential attitude – 'Religion is a kind of inoculation which by satisfying our love of marvels guarantees us against charlatans and sorcerers'; 'Society cannot exist without inequality of wealth, and inequality of wealth cannot exist without religion.' Walking in the park at Malmaison he is alleged to have said, listening to the bells, 'What an impression that must make on the simple and credulous. . . . How can your philosophers and ideologues answer that? The people must have a religion and that religion must be in the hands of the government.'

The Vatican, for its part, despite its denunciations of the Revolution, was prepared to make considerable concessions to regain official recognition in France. The new Pope, Pius VII, elected in 1800, a simple and holy monk with little knowledge of the world, was not violently hostile to the Revolution, and papal agents had been sent secretly to Paris as early as September 1800. The victory over Austria and the Peace of Lunéville in February 1801 made it desirable to come to terms with a France which now controlled all northern Italy. Secretly instituted negotiations were concluded in July 1801. To minimize the inevitable resistance of the strong anti-clerical elements in the legislative bodies, Bonaparte waited until the Peace of Amiens had been concluded before he announced the Concordat, in April 1802. Characteristically, having secured an agreement, he proceeded to distort it in his own interest by means of the issue of Organic Articles. Even so, many of the former revolutionaries exhibited open hostility to the Concordat and Fouché issued a mocking circular. By the Concordat the Vatican agreed to the institution of a new episcopate which should contain a proportion of bishops from the Constitutional Church, recognized the alienation of Church lands as permanent, and accepted the payment of clerical salaries by the State. Catholicism was described as 'the religion of the great majority of citizens', and its practice was to be free and public so long as it conformed to such police regulations as were required by public order. By the supplementary Organic Articles Bonaparte tried to turn the Concordat into the instrument of a new and stronger Gallicanism. No Papal bull was to be published, nor any Papal representative to function in France, without the permission of the government. The bishops were placed under the close control of the prefects and the lesser clergy lost the considerable independence of episcopal authority they had formerly enjoyed. Subsequent concessions to religious opinion included the suppression of the official ten-day cult, already practically dead, the restoration of Sunday as the day of rest for officials, and of the Gregorian calendar; children were to be given only saints names or those of the great figures of antiquity; the payment of salaries was extended to all clergy and the actual salaries were increased; religious orders reappeared in France, with official sanction for women's orders and for male missionary orders, while others, such as the Jesuits, were tolerated by official connivance; primary, though not higher education, was restored to the control of the clergy.

Despite all these concessions the Vatican was not quite happy about the bargain it had concluded. The Pope protested against the Organic Articles and only consecrated the bishops Bonaparte had chosen from the Constitutional Church after two years' delay. On the face of it the Concordat was a great victory for Bonaparte and a masterstroke of policy. The Emperor was able henceforth to use the clergy as an instrument of government. They celebrated his victories with Te Deums, published his imperial proclamations from their pulpits, delivered patriotic sermons, stimulated conscription, and promoted loyal sentiments. An Imperial Catechism was issued for the purpose of 'binding by religious sanctions the conscience of the people to the august person of the Emperor'. A national fête was created for the day of the Assumption which was also Napoleon's birthday and turned out conveniently to be the Saint's day of a newly discovered St Napoleon. Yet with all this he failed to obtain any permanent religious sanction for his rule. In the last years of the Empire the barely concealed royalist sentiments of most of the clergy undermined the loyalty of the people and prepared the way for his fall.

The religious revival, of which the first great manifesto was Chateaubriand's *Génie du Christianisme* in 1802, would have come about without Napoleon. The Concordat, by pushing Gallican principles farther than ever before, and this in the interests of no divine-right sovereign, did much to discredit Gallicanism and strengthen the ultramontane tendency in the French Church. It also reduced the lower clergy to a position of total dependence on their bishops, and made the bishops themselves much more dependent on the Papacy than formerly. The act by which the Pope, in agreement with Napoleon, deposed the whole episcopate of France, including many lawfully appointed and consecrated bishops, marked a great step forward in the assertion of papal authority. The thirty-seven *ancien régime* bishops who were excluded from their sees by the Concordat kept the allegiance of a small group of the faithful who founded what was called *la petite Église*. The injury to vested interests and nice consciences, and the elevation of a dozen somewhat grisly constitutional bishops, was a cheap price to pay for such a great extension of papal authority. The ultimate result was immensely to strengthen the influence of the Vatican in France. Napoleon had won for himself an unreliable and temporary ally, and he had bequeathed to his successors a Church which would henceforth never willingly be the junior partner of the State. The intermittent struggle between Church and State which bedevilled French politics for the following century and a half was as much the inheritance of the Napoleonic Concordat as of revolutionary anti-clericalism.

That hierarchical conception of society which made it easy for Napoleon to come to terms with the Roman Church, so long as he imagined that he had safeguarded his own position at the apex of the pyramid, was applied also, though less appropriately, to the organization of the Protestant churches. Their pastors became salaried officials and like the curés took an oath of loyalty. Their synods and consistories were chosen from the wealthier adherents of the faith and controlled by the secular authorities. Louis XIV had failed to extirpate French Protestantism, Napoleon succeeded in domesticating it.

While Napoleon restored official recognition to the Roman Catholic Church, he had no intention of returning the control of education they had possessed under the *ancien régime* to the ecclesiastical authorities. But he needed a system of education to provide administrators and technical experts for the service of the State. The Revolution had destroyed the old system of education but created nothing to put in its place apart from a limited number of Central Schools, which were neither sufficiently traditional in their curriculum, nor sufficiently authoritarian in their discipline, for Bonaparte's taste. They would produce, he thought, liberals and ideologists, for neither of which was there room in the Napoleonic state. Bonaparte himself expounded the basic principles of his theory of education: 'So long as children are not taught that they must be republican or monarchist, catholic or irreligious, etc. ... the State will not be a nation, it will rest on insecure or vague foundations. ... In a properly organized state there is always a body destined to regulate the principles of morality and politics.' Defending the law of 1802 on education, presented to the Legislative Body, ironically enough, by Fourcroy, a leading chemist, another of Bonaparte's necessary experts, Roederer, declared that Latin must be restored to its primacy and quasi-monopoly in the educa-

tional system. There followed an almost complete return
to the syllabus and methods of the *ancien régime*, which lasted
with little change until the reforms of 1865. The Central
Schools were replaced by *lycées*, boarding-schools with a
semi-military uniform and discipline and military training
from the age of twelve.

In these the new *élite* of France was to be formed with the
aid of some 6,000 national *bourses*, of which rather more than
a third were reserved for the sons of officials and officers.
They led on to the specialized schools of law, medicine, and
pharmacy, the *école militaire spéciale* and the famous *école
normale*, founded in 1808 to prepare for service in schools
and universities 300 young men chosen by competitive
examination. These were to provide the technical experts
needed by the Empire. On a lower level, secondary schools,
established by municipalities or individuals, gave the
education needed for commercial or minor administrative
posts. At the bottom, the primary schools were left to the
initiative of the communes and the teaching Orders, and
were still too few to bestow even a modicum of literacy upon
more than a small fraction of the population. The educational system was placed, by a law of 1808, under the control of a single imperial university. The whole structure
formed a rigid hierarchy, under a Grand Master nominated
by and responsible to the Emperor. An imposing bureaucratic apparatus centred in Paris was charged with regu-
lating the educational life of France down to the smallest
detail. If, today, the Rector of a university cannot appoint
his secretary, dismiss a cleaner, or modify an academic
course without reference to Paris, it is in obedience to the
dead hand of Napoleon.

In the *lycées* religion was kept, by Napoleon's prescrip-
tion, to the 'necessary minimum'. Primary education, on
the other hand, he was content to leave in the hands of the
Church. Under the influence of its Grand Master, Fontanes,
the University was increasingly subjected to clerical influence. The schools run by priests prospered at the expense
of the state *lycées*. Even before his fall the instrument created

by Napoleon to dragoon the mind of France was escaping from his control, and the conflict between secular and clerical education, which was to be one of the dominant themes in the history of the following century, was emerging.

Where the task was simply one of repression, the success of the Napoleonic system was less qualified. The press became a mere instrument of imperial propaganda, and papers which were not sufficiently docile soon disappeared. A censorship controlled the publication of books. Theatres were put under the Ministry of Police and reduced in Paris to eight. Even in the midst of a desperate war, at Moscow in October 1812, Napoleon could concern himself with drawing up the regulations for the Comédie-Française, a gesture illustrating less his interest in the promotion of the drama than his determination to ensure that every medium for the expression of opinion remained under strict control.

The First Empire was hardly the milieu from which literature was likely to emerge, and very little did. The mock-heroics of *Ossian*, translated in 1801, suited the Emperor's literary taste. The romantic melancholy of Chateaubriand's *Atala* and *René*, Mme de Staël's assertion, in *Delphine* and *Corinne*, of woman's right to happiness, but also of the unhappiness that is the fate of superior persons, Joseph de Maistre's theocratic ideals, had no appeal to him. Of these authors only Chateaubriand stayed under Napoleon's rule. Most of the writing of the Empire falls into the category of journalism or propaganda rather than literature.

In painting also the Empire has little to its credit. Fragonard, when he died in 1809, had long been an anachronism. David was capable of magnificent portraits, but he was prepared to serve Napoleon as faithfully as he had served the Jacobins and wasted his talents on huge, neo-classical, historical set pieces. In such a painting as his *Sabine Women interrupting the battle between Romans and Sabines*, every figure, down to the smallest child, is posed in a rhetorical attitude, consciously playing a part on the stage of history, just like David's own contemporaries of the

Revolution and Empire. The whole scene is as moving as the waxworks of Mme Tussaud which also date from the same period. A more poetical spirit is infused by Prud'hon into his classical compositions: the Empress Josephine reclines in reverie and classical *déshabillé* on mossy rocks amid a romantic landscape. But most of the painting of the period is frank propaganda. David rearranges the Coronation of Napoleon to order, as he had already done the Tennis-court Oath. Napoleon's charger rears up as his master with an heroic gesture points the way across the Alps to a stage army in the background. The baron Gros paints huge battle scenes to the glorification of the Emperor and his Marshals. He was perhaps the most successful of the official painters of the Empire until he committed suicide.

Napoleon himself was represented *ad nauseam*, the hero leading the charge across the bridge at Lodi, presenting the eagles to his legions, riding his chariot in a Roman triumph or apotheosized as a classical deity, sparing the conquered on the battlefield or subjecting the proud, visiting the victims of plague, rousing by his very presence the spirit of devotion in the wounded and dying. It is quite clear that the French painters of the period and Goya – of course, a painter on a different scale of magnitude – were not illustrating the same war. But it would be a mistake to judge the political success of Napoleon's artists by their artistic merits. Their influence in the formation of the Napoleonic legend and in creating and perpetuating a romantic attitude to war is not to be underestimated. More important for the history of art is the group of young men – Ingres, Vernet, Géricault – which was appearing in the last years of the Empire.

The decorative taste of the Empire was luxurious and heavy, adding Egyptian and Etruscan motives to the influence of the now triumphant classical revival. The provincial cities were not important enough to receive much imperial attention, and there the eighteenth century largely survived, but considerable steps were taken towards the spoiling of Paris. Napoleon required a grandiose setting for the capital of his Empire, and of course a classical one. Triumphal arches – such as the Étoile and the Carrousel – were *de rigueur*. For public buildings the correct thing was temples; so we have the temple of Finance – the Bourse with its sixty-four Corinthian columns, the temple of religion – the Madeleine, the temple of the laws – the palais Bourbon, all heavy pastiches and all equally unsuited to the purposes for which they were intended. The proportions of the place Vendôme were ruined by sticking in its middle, in place of the destroyed royal statue, a monstrous column, in imitation of that of Trajan. To enable the Napoleonic monuments to be seen, the process of driving long straight roads through Paris, which was to be carried much further under the Second Empire, was begun. Unlike the lath and plaster erections of the Revolution, the buildings of the Empire were made to last – unfortunately, for they embody too well the Emperor's chief aesthetic rule: '*Ce qui est grand est toujours beau.*'

Literature and art could not be expected to flourish in the hard climate of the Empire. Speculation about society was even less likely to be encouraged. In 1803 Napoleon suppressed the Academy of Moral and Political Sciences. On the other hand the natural and mathematical sciences have usually seemed able to accommodate themselves quite happily to absolutism. Apart from the guillotining of Lavoisier as a Farmer General, the Revolution and Empire did nothing to check scientific progress. The older generation of mathematicians and physicists such as Lagrange, Laplace, whose name is identified with the theory of nebulae, Monge, mathematician and accomplice of Bonaparte, and the botanist Lamarck, overlapped with younger men – Cuvier, who brought geology and palaeontology to the aid of zoological studies, Ampère, the founder of electromagnetism, and the astronomer Arago. In psychology, Destutt de Tracy and Cabanis continued the materialist theories of Condillac.

All this – art or science – is incidental or irrelevant to the history of the Empire. Napoleon's peculiar and lasting achievement was the work of the Consulate – that administrative reorganization, which, in perspective, can be seen as bequeathing not only to France but to much of the rest of the world, the most powerful instrument of bureaucratic control that the Western world had known since the Roman Empire. It was not a framework for the kind of society that the idealistic liberals of 1789 had imagined themselves to be inaugurating, nor should we treat the Napoleonic system, as it often has been treated, as the mere logical sequel to the *ancien régime* and the Revolution, and Napoleon simply as the heir of Louis XIV and the Committee of Public Safety. This is to underestimate the scope of his achievement. The Grand Monarch did not leave an imprint on French institutions that can be compared with the heritage of the Emperor. His immediate successors might repudiate his work, they could not undo it, and the Napoleonic state was long to outlive its author and the ends to which he had directed it.

4. THE NAPOLEONIC EMPIRE: RISE

THE Consulate was more important in the history of France, though not of Europe, than the Empire. What remains is a ten-years wonder, the history of conquests as dazzling as they were ephemeral, of armies marching and counter-marching from Lisbon to Moscow, and peace a brief breathing-space between wars. If we ask, as the Greeks would have done, what was the end of the Napoleonic state, the answer must be war. In war it had begun, war remained its *raison d'être*, and by war it was to end.

The Treaty of Amiens could not in the nature of things be more than an armistice, but it provided an opportunity for extra-European policies to be developed by Bonaparte. With France's position in Europe consolidated, he looked to the restoration of her overseas empire. Louisiana and the Spanish port of St Domingo had been gained from Spain; and the colonies which had been conquered by Great

Britain during the Revolutionary War were restored to France, which thus had in 1802 a larger colonial domain than in 1789. The position was less favourable than it might seem, but to understand the reason for this we must briefly look back over developments in the West Indies since 1789.

The Revolution had at first seemed a golden opportunity for the wealthy planters of the French Antilles, the Grands Blancs, in the name of self-government (the usual demand of those who want to oppress others) to relieve themselves of the control of the authorities in Paris. At the same time, to prevent the liberal ideas of the Constituent Assembly from being applied to the colonies, a number of big colonial proprietors had formed in Paris, in June 1789, a club to defend their interests, called from its meeting-place the club Massiac. On the other side, the Société des Amis des Noirs rallied anti-slavery opinion. The liberal tendency was the stronger in the Assembly, and it was joined to a belief in centralized control. The principle that the colonies are an integral part of France was first enunciated by the Revolution in a decree of March 1790; it was repeated in August 1792 and again in the Constitution of the year III. The extension of civic rights was much slower and more reluctant. In May 1791 coloured men who were sons of a free father and mother were given the vote. This was only some 5 per cent of the whole black or mulatto population, but both white and black now began to take up arms. In an attempt to restore peace the Legislative Assembly gave political rights to all free men, and sent over to St Domingo, in September 1792, commissaires and 6,000 troops to enforce its policy. The planters resisted and their leaders signed a treaty temporarily delivering the islands to the British, in return for military and naval assistance. The commissaires, in desperation, proclaimed the enfranchisement of all blacks who would join them. Meanwhile, in July 1793, the Convention had abolished the slave trade, and in February 1794 was to vote the abolition of slavery. In the confused triangular struggle of English, French, and coloured that followed, the chief victor was the yellow fever. But by 1798 the great Negro general Toussaint-Louverture was undisputed ruler of St Domingo; while in Guadeloupe a revolutionary commissaire with the aid of the Negroes had driven out a British force of occupation.

The legislation of the Revolution had, in spite of everything, made important reforms, but the French colonists, supported by Bonaparte, had no intention of accepting them. The Constitution of the year VIII laid it down that the colonies should be ruled by special laws; in 1802 they were placed under executive regulations and exempted from legislative control. The department of the Colonies in the Ministry of the Marine, staffed with *ancien régime* officials from whom Bonaparte took his advice, willingly abandoned all the reforms of the Revolution. The French trading monopoly was restored in the West Indies. Slavery was re-established where it had been abolished, Negroes were excluded from France, and mixed marriages prohibited. It is reasonable to suppose that the influence of the creole Josephine reinforced Bonaparte's native illiberalism in his dealings with the colonies. In the lesser islands small military expeditions from France restored French authority without difficulty. St Domingo, where Toussaint-Louverture had established an autonomous authority with himself as Governor though recognizing French suzerainty, presented a more difficult problem. To solve it Bonaparte despatched an army of 30,000 under General Leclerc, with instructions to gain the confidence of the Negroes and arrest their leader. Toussaint was seized and sent to France, where he died within a year in prison, to be remembered in one of Wordsworth's greatest sonnets. The removal of the one Negro leader with authority and statesmanship intensified the ferocity of the servile war against France. Those of the French who were not killed by the Negroes were exterminated by disease, and the pearl of the Antilles passed for ever out of French possession.

Louisiana was lost in a different way. Officially annexed in March 1803, it was sold to the United States in December. The remaining scattered colonies fell to English naval expeditions in the course of the following years. The loss of the first French Empire, begun in 1763, had been completed by Bonaparte. He was too much a man of the *ancien régime* to be really interested in colonies save as pawns in the military struggle, and his imagination turned more easily to the East than to the West. There, the army he had left behind in Egypt, defeated by a British expeditionary force in 1801, had capitulated; but Napoleon's eyes still saw the Mediterranean as the route to India, where French agents were hard at work. His troops remained at Leghorn and Ancona on the west and east coasts of Italy; treaties were concluded with Tripoli and Tunis; Algiers, after the pillage of a French ship, was threatened with attack; French diplomacy was active at Constantinople; and a French agent, Sébastiani, was sent on a mission to Syria and Egypt. All this, while perfectly within French rights, was not likely to reassure her recent enemies.

Military movements on the Continent were also a source of alarm to Great Britain. French control over the satellites was strengthened. In Italy, Piedmont was divided into six departments and its army amalgamated with the French; the Ligurian Republic became a French military division; and Bonaparte appointed himself president of the Cisalpine republic. In the north, French troops continued to occupy the Dutch ports. By an Act of Mediation the Swiss cantons were re-organized and French control was established over the Alpine passes. Italians, Swiss, and Dutch were all called on to furnish contingents of conscripts for the French army.

None of these measures, except the retention of troops in Holland, was an infringement of the Treaty of Amiens. The new *casus belli* was to arise in the Mediterranean, where Great Britain had undertaken by the Treaty of Amiens to restore Malta to the Knights of St John, but on second thoughts, despite her treaty obligation, could not bring herself to abandon such a valuable strategic position. British intransigence was encouraged by secret negotiations with Russia, also alarmed at the evidence of Bonaparte's interest in the Near East. On 30 January 1803 the *Moniteur* published Sébastiani's report on his tour there, in which he seemed to be putting forward, in language referring to the British in terms of contempt, proposals for a French reconquest of Egypt.

Why did Bonaparte, although he toned down the report slightly, publish such a provocative document at a moment when – though we need not attribute any noble dreams of permanent peace to him – he was not yet ready for a renewal of war? The answer seems to lie in the natural incapacity of a dictator for understanding the politics of a parliamentary country. The vulgar and immoderate personal attacks of the British press, which he attributed to the inspiration of the British government, drove him to fury; and the language of the parliamentary opposition led him to believe that the country was too divided by political conflicts to react strongly to his provocations. British opinion, on its side, had now overwhelmingly decided that Bonaparte was merely using the peace as an armistice during which to prepare for further aggression. The British government was determined to obtain further securities. Bonaparte, who had given hostages to fortune overseas and had not yet rebuilt French naval strength, was also suspicious of the reliability of his Russian alliance. He therefore temporized and even offered concessions. A British ultimatum on 23 April insisted on the continued occupation of Malta for ten years, the cession of the neighbouring island of Lampedusa to Great Britain, the evacuation of Holland by French forces, and the recognition of the Italian satellites only on condition of compensation for Sardinia and Switzerland. This was in effect a repudiation of the terms of Amiens. Bonaparte offered more concessions but the British government would be satisfied only by the integral acceptance of its ultimatum. Failing this, negotiations were broken off and the war renewed in May 1803, after fourteen months of uneasy peace.

The Treaty of Amiens had not contained the conditions of a lasting peace. Bonaparte was not prepared permanently to accept a situation in which Great Britain outweighed France in naval power and in overseas empire; Great Britain, for her part, did not regard French military hegemony in Europe as compatible with her own security. War was inevitable in these circumstances: the problem was how it could be waged, how the land and the sea power could measure their strength against one another. The British could seize French shipping and mop up the French colonies again one by one; but they could only intervene in Europe by means of alliances. Bonaparte's problem on the other hand was to find some means of bringing his far greater military power to bear directly against England. His solution was the Boulogne Camp and invasion across the Channel.

All through the wars of the eighteenth century plans for the invasion of England had accumulated in the dossiers of the French ministries. Bonaparte put these into practice on an unprecedented scale. No attempt was made to conceal his preparations. The Bayeux tapestry was brought to Paris for exhibition as a reminder of a previous successful invasion of England from France. By the summer of 1804 there were six to seven hundred invasion barges and a Grand Army of over 100,000 men gathered on the coast at Boulogne. A year later they were still there. The French admiral Villeneuve's manoeuvre to entice the British fleet to the West Indies had failed to produce that temporary French control of the Channel which was necessary for the invasion. The battle at Trafalgar, into which Villeneuve was driven by Bonaparte's reproaches, brought about the destruction of the French and Spanish fleets and guaranteed British control of the seas for the rest of the war. But even before the battle Napoleon had – he believed temporarily – abandoned his invasion plan and struck camp at Boulogne.

Russia, which had decided on war with France, and Austria, under pressure from Russia and alarmed at the growth of French power in Italy and Germany, joined Great Britain to form the Third Coalition in July 1805. By the end of August the Grand Army was marching across southern Germany in seven columns. By agents and informers Napoleon already knew exactly the dispositions of the Austrians. He fell on the incompetent Austrian general, Mack, at Ulm and routed him. The Russian allies, with another Austrian army, barred the French advance at Austerlitz where, on 2 December, in turn they were overwhelmed. Twice defeated, Austria concluded a humiliating peace at Pressburg.

Prussia, alarmed at the continual growth of French power in Germany, which it had so far done much, passively and even actively, to promote, now belatedly took to arms – the most highly polished, as well as the most antiquated, in Europe – in 1806, to be humiliatingly crushed at Jena in November. Russia, which alone remained of the European allies, was defeated in the bloodiest and most hard-fought battles Napoleon had so far been engaged in, at Eylau and Friedland, in 1807.

The sequel was the meeting of Napoleon and Alexander on the raft at Tilsit, on 25 June 1807, when Napoleon dictated the terms of peace. Prussia was reduced to a mere torso. Russia had to make major concessions in the Near East, abandoning the Ionian Islands to Napoleon, evacuating the Turkish provinces of Moldavia and Wallachia on the Danube, accepting the Continental System, and, if Great Britain did not agree to Russian mediation, concluding an alliance with France. Napoleon was master of Europe west of the Russian border. The frontiers of France were extended to the Rhine in the north-east and to take in Piedmont, Parma, Genoa, and Tuscany in Italy. They were bordered by a glacis of satellite states – the former Batavian Republic, now the Kingdom of Holland, under his brother Louis; the Confederation of the Rhine, with Bavaria, Württemburg, Baden, and other states, and the electorate of Saxony promoted to be a kingdom; the kingdom of Westphalia, formed out of the territories of the deposed rulers of Brunswick and Hesse-Cassel, with the subsequent addition of part of Hanover, placed under Napoleon's younger

brother, Jerome; Prussian Poland, formed into the Grand
Duchy of Warsaw, under the King of Saxony; the Helvetic
Republic; the Kingdom of Italy, based on Lombardy-
Venetia and stretching down the coast of the peninsula
through the eastern part of the Papal States to Ancona,
with the privilege of having Napoleon himself as its king,
crowned in 1805 with the iron crown of Lombardy at
Milan, his step-son, Eugène Beauharnais, being Viceroy.
The western half of the Papal States, surrounded by
French power, still had a precarious and short-lived independence; but to the south the Kingdom of Naples – not
of the Two Sicilies, for sea-power and a British force under
General Stuart which won the small but significant battle
of Maida in 1806, kept the French armies on the landward
side of the Straits of Messina – was given in 1806 to Joseph
Bonaparte, who was succeeded, when he was transferred to
the throne of Spain, by Murat, not so much in his capacity of
cavalry general as in that of husband of Caroline Bonaparte.
Napoleon had done well by his clan. This was not to be the
farthest limit of his empire, but already Russia and Austria
were the only continental powers not dominated by him.

How was it that France, which under Louis XIV had
known no such success, which since Fleury had had no luck
in its foreign policy and known hardly anything but
defeat, within fifteen years had acquired the hegemony of
Europe? The military genius of Napoleon is part of the
answer; the improved weapons, which he inherited from
the reforms of the later years of the *ancien régime*, another
part. But neither leadership nor material would have won
victories without the men, the armies which had grown out
of the ragged battalions of the Republic. What the Revolution had bequeathed to Napoleon was a large body of
veterans, by now all really professional soldiers, many of
them trained in the army of the line before 1789 and all
blooded in the battles of the Republic. Young men of
adventurous spirit, ability, and ambition from all ranks of
society, seeking the quickest path to advancement, furnished
the officers. The wars of the Revolution provided a supply,

though a wasting one, of able generals. The masses that were required to be poured into and amalgamated with these cadres to fill out the armies of the Empire were provided by conscription. Although there were many exemptions and evasions, between 1800 and 1812 Napoleon raised well over a million men from France; a week at the depot to equip them and give them a rudimentary notion of military discipline, and they could be sent to the front, to be fused with trained men and learn the art of war on the field of battle. The brutal punishments which were regarded as necessary to discipline in British and other armies had been abolished by the revolutionaries. *Esprit de corps*, honours, and the spirit with which Napoleon inspired his soldiers from top to bottom, were a better substitute.

To picture a French army, using French resources, as conquering Europe, would, however, not be correct. From the beginning of the Revolutionary War the French armies had lived off the country, and as their wars were always, until 1813, fought on foreign soil, the main burden did not fall on France. The numbers of men raised from France, though large by *ancien régime* standards, were not excessive. Up to 1812 the annual average works out at some 85,000, and this from a France which was steadily expanding its frontiers. As well as Piedmontese, Belgians, Dutch, and inhabitants of some German states, which were subjected to the laws of conscription when they were annexed, levies were raised from the satellite states. The army that invaded Russia in 1812 had contingents from every nation of Europe: of its 700,000 men only a third were French.

It was in moving the huge bodies of men he commanded across the map of Europe and concentrating them on the chosen field of battle that Napoleon showed his greatest military genius. The battle engaged, solid columns were flung at the enemy, a method that was costly in lives but the most efficient way of using masses of half-trained or untrained conscripts; it was successful until it met the concentrated fire of the English regiments of the line.

The most important factor of all in the Napoleonic

conquests was the result of a technical change. The art of war seems to progress through alternate periods in which the defence and the offensive predominate. At the end of the eighteenth century the mobility of armies was greatly increased; the French were the first to exploit this and Napoleon was the first great master of the new techniques. Improved road surfaces, light field-guns, organization of armies in divisions, moving along different roads and therefore able to live off the country and dispense with cumbersome baggage-trains, the concentration of artillery fire and infantry attack – these methods, learnt from the military theorists of the *ancien régime*, especially Guibert, author of the *Essai général de tactique* of 1772, were put into practice by Napoleon, with such effect that by 1807 all Europe, except Russia, was at his feet.

After Tilsit it might have been thought that Napoleon would rest on his laurels, content with his unchallenged military supremacy. The capacity for accepting a limit to his ambition was against his nature, but we need not resort simply to an explanation in terms of personal character; the perpetuation of war was in the nature of his régime, but in a more subtle way. England remained unconquered and after Trafalgar could apparently only be conquered by a restoration of French sea-power to the level at which it could challenge and defeat the might of the British navy. With the resources of France and all the satellite states to draw on, one might have thought that the creation of a new navy would not have been beyond Napoleon's power. If he chose another way of attack it was not, perhaps, because he recognized the restoration of French naval strength as impossible, but because he believed implicitly that this other way, while ensuring the collapse of British power equally, and perhaps more expeditiously and certainly, possessed also other and inherent attractions which made it desirable in itself. The Continental System was a device for bringing Great Britain to her knees, but it was also, quite apart from this, a method of increasing and consolidating the wealth and therefore the greatness of

France. Moreover the Continental System was not invented out of nothing by Napoleon: it was a development of the policies of the Republic and the *ancien régime*.

The use of economic weapons in the struggle for power was not new. The revolutionaries had used them in their war against Great Britain. The hated commercial treaty of 1786 was annulled immediately after the declaration of war in 1793. All British goods were excluded from France; all shipping entering French ports had to be French or that of the country from which the goods came. 'Let us decree', cried Barère, 'a solemn navigation act and the isle of shop-keepers will be ruined.' As early as 1795 there was a proposal to use the alliance with Dutch naval power to exclude British trade from the Continent. Napoleon did not have to invent the Continental System; as in so many other fields, he found an idea already in existence and merely applied it with his own method and whole-heartedness. It was generally believed that British power rested on her naval strength and her subsidies – the guineas of Pitt; and both these on the profits she derived from trade. To destroy that trade by cutting off its markets would ruin her finances and rob her of her power as effectively as if every port in the British Isles were sealed: thus could the sea power be blockaded from the land.

This, however, is only one side of the Continental System. There was also the thought that what England lost France could gain, taking the place of her rival as the great industrial nation of Europe, and drawing in by her exports the wealth that would be barred to England. The Treaty of Amiens gave Napoleon the respite he needed to begin his policy of Bonapartist Colbertism by injecting a stimulus into French industry. His efforts were vigorous and at first not unsuccessful. Schools were set up for technical training, prizes offered for inventions, industrial fairs organized, Jacquard's machine for silk weaving was brought into use. Great French chemists, Lavoisier, Fourcroy, Berthollet, discovered new methods of dyeing, bleaching, and tanning. Industrialists and technicians visited the factories of Great

Britain, and British machines and workers were imported into France, where they were put into operation with the aid of government credits and patronage. The French industrialist, Richard Lenoir, by 1810 had six cotton spinning mills with 3,600 workers in Normandy. Ternaux, a wool manufacturer of Sedan, employed 24,000 workers. Between 1788 and 1812 the number of looms increased from some 7,000 to 17,000 and the workers from 76,000 to 131,000. Such details, however, must not be allowed to give the impression of rapid industrial progress. The Revolution and the Empire may have provided a stimulus in some directions, but it is doubtful whether the pace had in fact increased. By 1815 French industry, it is estimated, was at the level of mechanization reached in Great Britain by 1780. Domestic labour was still the norm. Little workshops, with a master man and a few *compagnons*, working from one to five looms, still overwhelmingly predominated even in the textile industry. The small scale of industry is revealed by a few figures: 452 mines with 43,395 workers, 41 ironworks with 1,202, 1,219 forges with 7,120, 98 sugar refineries with 585. At Marseille the soap industry had 73 workshops and 1,000 workers. The industrial revolution in France, of which there were notable signs before 1789, was progressing very slowly. The energy of the nation had been diverted first to civil strife and then to conquest.

The authoritarian and hierarchical spirit of the Emperor, as well as the victory in the Revolution of the men of property, was reflected in the labour laws of the Empire. In 1803 was introduced the *livret*, a kind of passport and police visa, which every worker had to possess and in which were recorded all his changes of employment, reasons for leaving each job, and wages. It was kept by the employer and without it a worker could not be employed and would be regarded as a vagabond. Strikes were vigorously prohibited under severe penalties. The *compagnonnages* only survived clandestinely. Working conditions were miserable, though there seems to have been a modest rise in real wages up to 1810 and a fall after this.

Napoleon, like his predecessors, was chiefly interested in power, and in prosperity only as a means to power. His commercial policy was therefore at the service of his political ends. His conquests gave him ample opportunity to exclude British trade from the Continent, beginning with the occupation of Hanover in May 1803, which enabled him to close the mouths of the Elbe and the Weser. These measures, along with the prohibition of, or heavy duties on, colonial produce, increased the cost and diminished the supplies of raw material for French industry. This policy was intensified and systematized by the Berlin Decrees of 1806. By the Milan Decrees of December 1807 any ship which had called at a British port, paid a duty to Britain, or even been examined at sea by the British, was made a lawful prize. The result was in effect to exclude neutral shipping, on which Europe now depended for its supplies from overseas, from ports under French control. The British Orders in Council, blockading all French ports, were imposed more effectively by a fleet which swept the seas, and by raiding privateers. French privateers, the most successful of whom was the famous Surcouf, took a heavy toll of British shipping, at a rate of nearly 450 losses a year; but a high percentage of British exports (from 25 to 42 per cent, and re-exports (71 to 83 per cent) continued to go to the Continent. In the attempt to prevent this, Napoleon organized an army of customs officials round the coasts of Europe. The extent to which the Continental System dictated the aggressions of the Empire, such as the invasion of the Iberian peninsula, has perhaps been exaggerated; but annexations were at least influenced by the needs of the System. Napoleon's aim was, in his own words, to close every port from the Sound to the Hellespont to British shipping.

To portray the Continental System, as it has been portrayed, as an attempt to create a great pan-European economic union, is to attribute to Napoleon a degree of enlightenment in the pursuance of his ends which dictators do not usually possess. It if had been this the System might conceivably have aroused less resentment in the rest of Europe. On the contrary, it was, as I have already said, a device not only for defeating England, but also for ensuring French economic supremacy. The economies of the other nations were subordinated and geared to that of France. His object, Napoleon declared in 1810, was to encourage the export of French goods and the import of foreign bullion. Thus, new frontiers in Italy, with high customs barriers between them, were devised to enable French industrial products to capture the Italian market. The Grand Duchy of Berg, centred on the Ruhr valley, already a growing industrial area, was cut off from its markets in the Netherlands and the Baltic by high tariffs. The export of Italian textiles to southern Germany was prohibited. Raw silk from Piedmont was directed to Lyon and away from the silk workers of Lombardy by means of tariff adjustments. French manufactures could be exported freely into Holland, but Dutch goods had to pay customs dues to enter France.

As has already been indicated, these efforts to turn France into the great industrial nation of Europe failed. The loss of colonial raw materials was incompatible with their success, though desperate efforts were made to improvise substitutes. The growing of woad was promoted in the south-west of France, where its production had flourished in the Middle Ages, to replace colonial indigo; chicory provided a substitute for coffee and beet for the sugar cane. Attempts were made to introduce the growing of cotton in southern Italy, but the cotton industry languished for lack of raw materials. The substitutes had at the time only mediocre success.

The decisive factor in Napoleon's attempt to create a French industrial empire was that he was not merely setting land power against sea power, but land communications against sea communications, at a time when transport by water was immeasurably cheaper than transport by land. If the rivers of Europe had flowed in a different direction the prospects might have been brighter, but the great strategic roads that were driven across France and stretched out to the French Empire could not materially diminish the cost of land transport. Despite all Napoleon's efforts, French foreign trade under the Empire never regained the level it had reached in 1789. In Bordeaux, wrote the American consul in 1808, grass was growing in the streets and at the great quays a mere handful of vessels with cargo swung in the tide.

When the economic crisis of 1811–13 burst on Europe, though the contemporary crisis in Great Britain would suggest more general causes, Europe naturally attributed it to the Napoleonic system. In France itself, at Mulhouse 40,000 workers out of 60,000 were unemployed, and 20 to 25,000 at Lyon. Napoleon, who had learnt during the Revolution to fear starving urban mobs, modified and opened loop-holes in his economic legislation, and this was the effective end of the real enforcement of the Continental System, though it had already broken down largely in practice. Round the coastline of Napoleonic Europe, from Gotenburg in Sweden, Heligoland, Gibraltar, the Balearics, Malta, after their capture in 1809 the Ionian Isles, a flood of contraband goods seeped into Europe. Smuggling became one of the most remunerative and by no means the least numerous of professions. It was conducted sometimes by official subterfuge, sometimes by force of arms. Administrators and generals, and the customs officials themselves, made a regular trade of corruption. Against universal smuggling the Napoleonic machine of repression that had been created was powerless. When confiscated goods were ordered to be burnt, valueless rubbish was destroyed in their place. Smuggling became so much an organized trade that smuggled goods were even insured against seizure. The rate at Strasbourg on illicit goods destined for France was 30 per cent. Napoleon himself connived at the infringement of his own laws. He wrote to his brother Louis to fix the point where English smugglers were to land to purchase Dutch gin: what was essential, he believed, was that they should be made to pay in bullion and not in goods. But at

Hamburg, English clothing and shoes were being bought for the French army.

It was only after the economic crisis of the latter years of the Empire that Napoleon had recourse to the organized breach of the Continental System by the method of licences. Since Great Britain was doing the same, an interchange of goods developed between the two countries at war. French ships were allowed to trade with England under a neutral flag; unfortunately, once outside Napoleon's clutches they generally stayed outside, to swell the merchant marine in British service. The licences were, of course, expensive, and there were heavy duties on the imported goods, so that fiscal motives were not absent from Napoleon's mind. Finally, the opposition that his economic policies had always aroused in the rest of Europe spread to France. The commercial and industrial classes began to detach themselves openly from a régime the burden of which went on increasing and the benefits diminishing.

Empire and military glory were in the end as incompatible with economic progress as the political chaos of the Revolution had been. And the Emperor himself, if he had started as the heir of the Revolution, was turning in his social policy into something more like the restorer of a pseudo-*ancien régime*. The creation of the Legion of Honour in 1802, against the advice of many of his supporters, was an early sign of his anti-egalitarian tendencies. Once he was Emperor he needed a Court, the nucleus of which was provided by the six Grand Dignitaries of the Empire – Grand Elector Joseph Bonaparte, Grand Constable Louis, Arch-chancellor of State Eugène de Beauharnais, Grand Admiral Murat, Arch-chancellor Cambacérès, and Arch-treasurer Lebrun – four relations plus the former second and third consuls. For the ceremonies of the new court a series of Grand Officers of the Crown, drawn from the *ancien régime*, provided the correct tone. Mme Campan was there to explain to the Ladies of Honour and the Empress how Marie-Antoinette used to do things. A whole gamut of titles, from duke to chevalier, was recreated and made hereditary on the granting of an appropriate entail. Sons of ministers, councillors of state and the like, and the nephews of archbishops, became counts. Prefects were barons or counts. Altogether Napoleon created over 3,000 nobles. Of course, a real noble was even better. Those among the *ancien régime* nobility who rallied to the imperial banner were singled out for favour. They came increasingly to dominate the Court and the administration as the Empire reached its zenith.

5. THE NAPOLEONIC EMPIRE: FALL

IN 1807, after Tilsit, there was a reorganization of the ministries, in which Talleyrand lost the Ministry of Foreign Affairs, though he was made a Grand Dignitary. He had already decided that Napoleon's ambition would bring him to ultimate ruin, and having served him well and gained a huge fortune by the acceptance of bribes, he was now secretly negotiating with Napoleon's enemies. He had never believed in the wisdom of the humiliation of Austria. In the course of 1808 Talleyrand and Fouché, when Napoleon was absent in Spain, began to make plans for the choice of a successor, who was apparently to be Murat. Napoleon did not remain in ignorance of this. When he returned he dismissed Talleyrand with a torrent of abuse; but the ex-bishop, ex-revolutionary, ex-minister of Foreign Affairs, ex-Grand Chamberlain, continued to haunt the Court like a vulture of ill omen biding his time. Fouché, former terrorist and regicide, minister of police since 1799, and a particular friend of Josephine, had been useful to Napoleon as a link with the revolutionaries, but subsequently established a position also as a kind of patron to many royalists. During the Revolution, while a leader of the anti-religious party, he had protected priests, especially members of his old order of the Oratory. His contempt for the Concordat was unconcealed, not for lack of a clerical capacity for dissimulation but from a natural independence of mind. He was the least servile of all Napoleon's servants and the humanest minister of police a dictator ever had. But when, in 1810, Napoleon discovered that Fouché had been engaging for the past year in secret negotiations with England, his dismissal was inevitable. Though Talleyrand and Fouché waited to be dismissed – and it is a sign of their confidence that they feared no more – it is evident that they had deserted Napoleon by their own choice and were preparing for a future in which they foresaw his inevitable defeat. It was an ominous sign. Their successors, often former royalists, were men of inferior calibre and untried loyalty. Whereas at first Napoleon had gathered round him a collection of the ablest men in France, his later appointments were increasingly influenced by favouritism and Court intrigue. He now wanted flunkeys, says Chaptal bitterly, not advisers.

Intolerance of criticism was only one sign of the degeneration that was beginning to come over the Emperor, both physically and mentally. His decline may be said to have begun even before the Empire had reached its height. His aggressions were increasingly irrational. Thus the Pope had not realized the nature of the relationship which Napoleon assumed to have been created by the Concordat. 'So far as the Pope is concerned', he wrote, 'I am Charlemagne'; if the Pope did not behave he would be reduced to the status of bishop of Rome. For military purposes, French troops had already occupied the Adriatic coastline of the Papal States and the port of Ancona. In 1809 the Papal States were annexed to the French Empire and the Pope was arrested and carried off to captivity. His subsequent refusal to collaborate with Napoleon, though inconvenient, especially because it prevented the filling of vacant sees in France, had surprisingly little practical result.

The French intervention in Spain was to have more momentous consequences. Under Godoy, Prince of the Peace, an adventurer who had made the Queen his mistress, Spain had become a French satellite. To extend French control over the whole peninsula, a joint Franco-Spanish army invaded Portugal in 1807. Napoleon, however, was not satisfied with the aid he was getting from Spain. Under direct French rule, he believed, this backward and priest-ridden nation could be modernized and so contribute far more to the strength of the French Empire. The sordid intrigues which followed in the Spanish Court need not delay us. In May 1808 the King and Queen and the heir Ferdinand were summoned to Bayonne and by threats made to sign away their rights over Spain. Godoy was imprisoned, regretted only by the infatuated Queen and a few other mistresses. Joseph Bonaparte, brought from the throne of Naples, was put on that of Madrid.

Even before Joseph entered his new capital, where he was able to stay on this occasion only for eleven days, a spontaneous insurrection all over Spain had imperilled some 150,000 French troops dispersed over the whole peninsula. In July one force had to capitulate at Baylen and in August another, beaten at Vimiero by a hurriedly dispatched British expeditionary force under Wellesley, signed the Convention of Cintra and was shipped back to France. Joseph and the remaining French troops withdrew behind the Ebro. All this was unprecedented. If allowed to succeed it might set a fatal example. The veteran corps of Victor, Mortier, and Ney were called from Germany and a great French army was assembled under Napoleon on the Ebro. The Spaniards were routed and driven back. A small British force under Moore retreated to Corunna and was evacuated by sea. Joseph was reinstated in Madrid. However, the diversion effected by Moore's army had drawn back the French forces from their triumphal sweep through the peninsula. After this Napoleon returned to Paris and never came to Spain again. During the remainder of the wars of the Empire, Wellington from his base in Portugal, and the Spanish guerrillas, were to tie down a large French army permanently. In Napoleon's winter campaign of 1808 he had over 300,000 men in Spain; in the spring offensive of 1810 the number rose to 370,000; in the crisis of the Empire in 1812 there were 290,000 and in 1813 still 224,000. The wastage by battle and disease was heavy all through. If it was a side-show it was a very expensive one: henceforth Napoleon was to have to fight on two fronts.

The French reverses in Spain may have played some part in the resurgence of Austria, which had remained un-reconciled to the humiliation of Austerlitz and had since been reorganizing her military forces. A hard-fought campaign from April to July 1809 ended in another Austrian defeat, at Wagram; but Napoleon's position was still not secure. The Tyrol had revolted, Venetia had been captured by the Austrians, Prussia and Russia were hesitating on the brink of war, far away to the West Soult had been driven out of Portugal, and a British expedition had landed in Walcheren. Even Wagram, though an Austrian defeat, was not a rout, and was only worth an armistice. But when it became clear that Russian aid was not coming, and that Vienna itself was exposed to attack, the Austrian Emperor gave up the struggle and bought peace with more territorial concessions – a large part of Galicia to the Duchy of Warsaw, Salzburg and the Tyrol to Bavaria, the Illyrian provinces, in accordance with the requirements of the Continental System, to direct French rule.

Victory still followed the imperial eagles but one thing was lacking to Napoleon's ambitions. The intrigues of Talleyrand and Fouché had made the insecurity of his position clear. His clan evidently depended entirely on himself: there was no hope in it for the establishment of a Bonapartist dynasty. Josephine would now never give him a child, but he knew through a mistress, in 1807, that he was capable of getting one. For some time schemes for a divorce and re-marriage had been mooted, and after a few unsuccessful approaches to the old dynasties, the Habsburgs, unlucky in battle, remembered their tradition – *Bella gerant alii; tu, felix Austria, nube*. They had an available princess, Marie-Louise, ready for the sacrifice, and as the young Austrian minister Metternich wrote, the Austrian Emperor 'will shrink from nothing that may contribute to the welfare and peace of the state'. He would however have shrunk from a civil marriage, which in any case would not have been adequate for Napoleon's purpose. Josephine therefore had to be got rid of, not by a divorce, but by a declaration of the nullity of her marriage. This involved proving the invalidity of the religious ceremony which she and Napoleon had gone through on the eve of the coronation in 1804. Though performed by a cardinal – Napoleon's uncle, Fesch – this marriage had been clandestine, it was argued, and without adequate witnesses. To complete the conviction of the religious court that tried the case, it was established that Napoleon had acted under compulsion from Josephine. The religious requirements of the Church were thus met, and it was disappointing – seeing that everything was in order – that thirteen cardinals out of twenty-seven should have stayed away from the marriage ceremony with Marie-Louise in 1810. Napoleon in revenge assigned to them compulsory residences and forbade them to wear their robes of office. Hence they became known as the black cardinals. In 1811 was born the little boy who was proclaimed King of Rome but never to inherit an Empire in which the cracks were already visible.

Now that Austria had been once more defeated, and by the dynastic alliance had apparently accepted defeat, Russia remained the only continental power that was not subordinate to France. The nominal ties of Tilsit could not prevent the growth of mutual suspicion and conflict of interests. Alexander and Napoleon suspected each other – and rightly – of preparing an attack when the opportunity came. They had more concrete grievances. Napoleon strengthened his position in the Baltic by the annexation of Oldenburg in December 1810, although Alexander's sister was married to the heir to the Duchy, and despite the guarantees of Tilsit. He began to move his troops eastwards, garrisoning Danzig, turning the Grand Duchy of Warsaw into a great military base and gathering huge magazines of supplies there. Meanwhile Russia, like the rest of Europe, was suffering from the economic crisis. To cope with the consequent discontent Alexander imposed heavy duties on French imports and opened his ports to neutral shipping. In effect he was withdrawing Russia from the Continental System, and although British trade with Russia was insignificant, this may have influenced Napoleon. More alarming was the fact that in May 1812 Russia concluded peace with the Turks. This was perhaps the decisive event, for Napoleon knew that it freed Alexander's hands in a way that nothing else could have done. Alexander had also concluded an agreement with Bernadotte of Sweden, received promises from Austria that her support for Napoleon would be only formal, and was negotiating secretly with Great Britain. Of all this Napoleon was not unaware. A defensive reaction would have been against the nature of the man and his system. War it had to be.

On 24 June 1812 the Grand Army began to cross the Niemen. Napoleon had gathered in the Grand Duchy of Warsaw 675,000 men and 1,350 cannon. Poles, Prussians, Austrians, Dutch, Swiss, Italians, all the nations of Europe had sent their conscripts tramping across Europe. Russia was to be overwhelmed by sheer weight of numbers. Instead it was Napoleon's own military machine that, in the long barren distances of Russia, was to collapse under its own weight. As the Russian armies avoided battle and withdrew, Napoleon moved forward, his armies struggling on through the heat of summer. At last, in front of Moscow, the Russians stood and Napoleon could fight the battle for which he had been longing. But it was not the *coup de grâce* he needed to deliver. At Borodino some 30,000 of his troops were killed, and though the Russians lost more they retreated in order. The occupation of an empty Moscow, the burning of the city, the retreat after five weeks waiting for peace emissaries who never came, with an army already reduced to about 100,000, with officers and men, baggage-trains, horses, carriages loaded down with the spoils of Russia's conquered and looted capital, across a region that it had already desolated, in the rain and mud of autumn, turning to the snows of winter – all this is a many times told tale of greed and cruelty, heroism and despair. After the tragic crossing of the Beresina on 27 November, famine and frost and the pursuing Russians completed the annihilation of the army of the Empire. It was not beaten in battle; under the stress of a long, starving retreat, the great cosmopolitan military machine collapsed and disintegrated, leaving behind it a legend in history. Some 1,000 of the Guards, out of the great host that had set out, held together when Ney re-crossed the Niemen on 14 December.

Napoleon had already, on 6 December, deserted an army that no longer existed and was hastening back to Paris, where the essentially ephemeral nature of his *régime* had just been demonstrated by the Malet conspiracy. In this extraordinary episode a republican general, Malet, and a royalist priest, Lafon, both in custody as political prisoners, came near to overthrowing the Empire in its capital by the simple device of forging a document announcing the death of Napoleon and the constitution of a provisional government under the banished general Moreau. In his name Malet assumed command of Paris, and arrested the Minister of Police, the War Minister, and the Prefect of Police – all in the space of a single morning. Only when the commander of the Paris garrison challenged the news, and the little band of conspirators failed to keep up the pretence of Napoleon's death successfully, were they resisted. Then, of course, they were easily seized and after a rapid trial executed. It was a gallant adventure and deserved a better sequel. It was also clear evidence that the whole government of Napoleon rested on the cohesion of the military and administrative machine he had created and that this in turn depended exclusively on his person.

Back in Paris, Napoleon set the administration to the task of raising conscripts from France, for the first time really ruthlessly. Europe was now rising everywhere against his domination, but there were still Napoleonic armies and garrisons far and wide. Indecisive battles against Russians and Prussians, at Lützen and Bautzen, in May 1813, were followed by an armistice. If Napoleon had been capable of concessions, he might now have kept the Austrians out of the war and disintegrated the alliance; but such moderation had long since ceased to be possible for him and the struggle was resumed. He had some half a million men in the field, the allies rather more. Moreau was advising them and Bernadotte bringing an army down from Sweden. A French victory at Dresden in August was followed, in October, by the battle of the nations at Leipzig. After this, with its soldiers dead in battle or by disease, deserters or prisoners, or uselessly shut up in fortresses scattered about Germany, the Army of 1813 followed that of 1812 into the void. Only a fragment retired across the Rhine.

More conscripts were called up from France: there were no foreign allies or dependents left to exploit. Still, in December 1813, Napoleon refused to negotiate in time for a recognition of the 'natural frontiers' of France. By now the armies of the coalition were in Switzerland and on the Rhine, and Wellington had crossed the Pyrenees. In January 1814 Murat deserted Napoleon and Italy was lost. In France itself his régime was patently breaking down. It had entered the winter of its discontent. Under the frozen surface of dictatorship resentment brooded. Conscription had reached the point at which it was meeting open resistance even from the inert peasantry. They were touched more closely when Napoleon's armies, fighting for the first time on French soil, supplied themselves by the normal method of requisitioning which had carried them all over Europe. The *droits réunis*, the hated taxes on alcoholic drinks, tobacco, and salt, were a long-standing grievance of the peasantry. Industry had lost its markets with the collapse of the Empire and unemployment was widespread in the towns. Commerce was languishing and the finances in disorder. The clergy, who had never quite forgotten their loyalty to the Bourbons, were a centre of opposition everywhere. All those who had acquired wealth and jobs saw the need to insure against the future. An underground royalist movement, a kind of royalist and catholic free-masonry, which had been created in 1810, was reviving the memory of the Bourbons in a country that had begun to forget them. But though the royalists were active and beginning to emerge above ground, the nation as a whole remained passive.

When the allies invaded France, it accepted the foreign invaders as passively as it had borne the rule of Napoleon. Épinal surrendered to fifty cossacks, Rheims to a platoon, Chaumont to a single horseman. The one demand of the country was peace. The Senate, called together by Napoleon in December 1813, performed its last act of homage towards the man to whom so many of its members owed fame and fortune. But the Legislative Body, that collection of insignificant yes-men, voted by 223 to 51 an address of unprecedented independence: 'Our ills are at their height. The *patrie* is threatened at all points of the frontier; we are suffering from a destitution unexampled in the whole history of the state. Commerce is destroyed, industry dying ... What are the causes of these unutterable miseries? A vexatious administration, excessive taxes, the deplorable methods adopted for their collection, and the even crueller excesses practised for the recruitment of the armies ... A barbarous and endless war swallows up periodically the youth torn from education, agriculture, commerce, and the arts.' This was strong language, and the Legislative Body ended with an appeal for abandoning the ambitious schemes which had been for twenty years 'so fatal to all the peoples of Europe'. No wonder that Napoleon banished the authors of the address, forbade its publication, and prorogued the Legislative Body.

If he had been willing to buy peace by renouncing the Empire he might still have got it and remained the ruler of France. In February and March 1814 negotiations with the allies at Châtillon proved that he could not bring himself to do this. Instead, with a small army of some 60,000 men, largely untrained conscripts, he manoeuvred brilliantly between the invading armies in the East of France and inflicted reverses on them. The requisitions and brutalities of the invaders aroused patriotic feeling in the occupied areas, but this did not spread to the rest of France. The allies, realizing the scarcity of Napoleon's troops, ceased to

play his game, by-passed his forces, and advanced on Paris.
On 29 March, in accordance with orders from Napoleon,
Marie-Louise and the King of Rome left the capital. All the
higher officers of state were commanded to leave with them
but many found means of remaining. On 31 March Paris
capitulated and the troops garrisoning it moved to Fontaine-
bleau, where Napoleon established his headquarters. The
same day the allied forces entered through the porte Saint-
Denis, marched across Paris amidst curious crowds and
bivouacked in the Champs Élysées.

A provisional government, of which Talleyrand was the
leading member, was set up. The Senate and the Legislative
Body voted the deposition of Napoleon. But what was to
take his place? Talleyrand, who had established close
relations with the Czar, had largely won him over to a
restoration of the Bourbons. The Paris press, now under
royalist control, agitated for a restoration. But the allies
were still hesitant. Europe had been conditioned to fear the
French nation and was still alarmed at what it might do if
an unpopular régime were forced on it. At this stage what
was happening in the South-west was perhaps decisive. The
army of Wellington, having crossed the Pyrenees, was
advancing towards Toulouse in pursuit of Soult. A small
British force, detached from the main army, was sent off to
occupy Bordeaux. The imperial authorities fled across the
Gironde, and on 22 March the British advance-guard, to
which a squadron of young royalists had attached themselves, entered the city, to be welcomed by the Mayor of
Bordeaux, a member of the royalist secret society of the
Chevaliers de la Foi, with a white cockade and the cry of
'*Vive le Roi*'. In the afternoon arrived the duc d'Angoulême,
greeted with wild demonstrations of joy. The influence of
this spontaneous French rejection of Napoleon and proclamation of the Bourbons, on both the allies and the French
leaders in Paris, was considerable. Napoleon himself, faced
with the refusal of the marshals to engage in another battle,
had abdicated in favour of the King of Rome and sent
plenipotentiaries to Alexander. It was already too late to

save even this from the wreck. Marshal Marmont, despite a short-lived mutiny among his troops, marched them to the enemy lines and surrendered. On 6 April Napoleon abdicated unconditionally. Four days later, so slow did news travel, the last battle of the allied invasion was to be fought, a bloody assault in which Wellington overcame Soult's entrenchments before Toulouse.

On 12 April the comte d'Artois, as lieutenant-general for his brother, Louis XVIII, entered Paris in triumph. Through decorated streets and applauding crowds, he went to Notre Dame where the *Te Deum* was sung. Louis XVIII himself landed at Boulogne on 24 April and, received everywhere with enthusiasm, moved slowly to Saint-Omer where he met a delegation from the Senate and issued a royal proclamation. 'Louis, by the grace of God, King of France and Navarre', recalled by the love of his people to the throne of his fathers, promised France representative government in a Senate and Chamber of Deputies, taxation only with consent, public and individual liberty, freedom of the press, freedom of religion, responsible government, judicial independence, a career open to talent, and – not least – that no one should be punished for opinions or votes during the fallen régime, the recognition of the national debt, of pensions, grades, and military honours, of titles of both the old and new nobility, and of the sales of national property. It was a compromise between divine right and the Revolution, rather to the advantage of the latter. On 3 May Louis XVIII and the royal family made their ceremonial entry into the capital.

Napoleon, largely by the mediation of Alexander, was meanwhile journeying to a smaller kingdom in Elba. While he travelled through country that had experienced the allied occupation his reception was favourable, but as he moved south, according to the Prussian commissioner who accompanied him, it became increasingly hostile. He got through Lyon at night. At Orange there were shouts of '*Vive Louis XVIII*', and at Avignon '*À bas le tyran*'; he saw himself hanged in effigy and after this disguised himself in an old blue coat, put up a white cockade, and preceded his carriage in the guise of a courrier. Later he dressed himself as an Austrian officer. He embarked from Fréjus, where he had landed fifteen years earlier on his way home from Egypt, leaving then also a defeated army behind, but with the triumphs of *brumaire* and the Empire before him. Fearing assassination he refused to embark on the French ship provided for him and sailed to Elba in a British frigate. He left a France which, it has been estimated, had lost in his wars 860,000 men between the ages of 23 and 44, half of them under 28.

The Restoration did not begin well. Talleyrand confined himself to foreign affairs. The old system of government by a *conseil d'en haut*, with no chief minister, no unity, and therefore no policy, was revived. The two most important ministers were baron Louis for Finance, and Dupont, remembered only for his defeat at Baylen and perhaps unmerited disgrace, at the Ministry of War. By an austere financial policy Louis put the budget into better shape, but at the price of maintaining the unpopular *droits réunis* and of economies which cut down pensions and salaries. Dupont's policy demoralized the army. He retired many officers and put many more on half-pay, brought into it, over the heads of Napoleonic veterans, a host of *émigrés* who had never seen a battlefield or commanded a man, recreated the Household Guard – the Light Horse, Grey and Black Musketeers, the Cent Suisses, and the rest, crammed with dissatisfied royalists, expensive, intriguing, and useless – 6,000 men, all with the rank and pay of officers, costing twenty million francs a year. 'The indignation and exasperation of the army', wrote Philippe de Ségur, himself a noble of the *ancien régime* but one who had acquired other ideas and other loyalties in the Imperial Army, and a veteran of the Moscow campaign, 'had become so violent that at the Tuileries, among the officers of the Old Guard on half-pay, spectators like myself of the reviews which were held, I had difficulty in preventing an outburst.' The flag also was already a burning issue. 'They imposed on us', wrote de Ségur, 'the flag under which they had fought us.' At the same time, the old court ceremonies and the King's household were recreated as though nothing had happened since 1789.

Napoleon at Elba was not uninformed of the dissatisfaction in France, and at the end of ten months was sufficiently dissatisfied himself with ruling a tiny island in place of half Europe to be ready to set out on his last and most reckless venture. On 1 March 1815 he landed with 1,050 troops, once again at Fréjus, and avoiding this time royalist Provence, took the mountain road from Cannes to Grenoble. Opposition melted away wherever he appeared. By itself the march from Fréjus to Paris is sufficient evidence of his magnetic personality. It is clear, however, that what he could appeal to now was primarily the loyalty of the old soldiers to a great leader, and their habit of obedience. The survival of revolutionary sentiments, and the possibility of their re-awakening, was shown at Lyon, where enthusiastic crowds added to cries of '*Vive l'Empereur*' those of '*À bas les prêtres*', '*À bas les nobles*', '*Mort aux royalistes*'.

The news of Napoleon's landing reached Paris on 5 March. Before anything could be done, on the next day he was at Grenoble, and in the capital complacency was rapidly being succeeded by frantic and futile orders and counter-orders, and something approaching panic. The defection of Ney, in command of the royal troops in Franche-Comté, was decisive. At midnight on 19 March, Louis XVIII, accompanied by a few horsemen only, took the road for Lille. Finding the garrison there hostile, he crossed the frontier to Ghent.

Napoleon was once again master of France, but what use would he make of his revived authority? He announced that he had given up the Grand Empire, but was alarmingly ambiguous as to the scope he envisaged for the French Empire to which he now promised to limit himself. No promises could have disarmed the enmity of the other Great Powers. They declared Napoleon outside the pale of civilized society and had 7–800,000 men under arms to back up their ban.

To give the new régime a more liberal cloak, Napoleon issued, with the advice of Benjamin Constant, an *Acte additionel*, proposing a constitution not so very dissimilar from that adumbrated in Louis XVIII's *Charte*. Either believing in Napoleon's professions of liberalism, or thinking him a lesser evil than the Bourbons, Carnot emerged from retirement to become Minister of the Interior. But even if Napoleon had been sincere, and there is little reason to suppose that he was, he could not give France what its people still wanted more than anything else – peace, or its ruling classes what they wanted – stability, and security for their property and jobs. The chief reason for his successful return, after the loyalty of the old army, was the passivity, the political inertia of the nation. Of course, protestations of loyalty flowed in from the same officials who a year earlier had hastened to offer their allegiance to Louis XVIII and were to repeat the performance once the Emperor had been defeated. The weakness of the royalists was shown by their inability to offer serious resistance, except in the Vendée, where a rising pinned down 30,000 men whom Napoleon could well have used in Belgium.

The thought of an appeal to the masses, if it ever entered Napoleon's head, was rejected. There is no evidence, of course, that the masses would have risen, or what they could have done if they had. Instead, the governmental machine was put into operation in the orthodox way to raise a new conscript army. 600,000 men were called up, but when Napoleon invaded Belgium he could only assemble an army of 125,000, though these included many veterans, gathered back in France from the scattered remnants of his former armies. He marched off, leaving treachery behind him in the person of Fouché, once again Minister of Police, working with the liberals, protecting royalists, in secret correspondence with Metternich and Talleyrand at Vienna and Artois at Ghent, and revealing half of what he was doing to Napoleon, with a foot in every camp. He calculated on Napoleon's survival for some three months, in the course of which the duc d'Otranto reckoned to make himself – as for a short while he was to be – indispensable to all parties.

In Belgium, the only forces ready to oppose Napoleon were 120,000 Prussians under Blucher, and a mixed force of Belgians, Dutch, Hanoverians, and English under Wellington. The Prussians were driven back at Ligny and Wellington's forces, held by Ney at Quatre Bras, retreated on the hill of Mont-Saint-Jean near the village of Waterloo. There, on 18 June, Napoleon flung his massed columns at them with little attempt at manoeuvre, in increasingly desperate attacks as the threat of the Prussian army, coming up on his flank, became greater. In the later stages of the battle only a retreat could have saved the French army, but Napoleon knew that farther off were the Austrians and Russians, and that if he did not win his first battle his chance was gone for ever. The retreat therefore became a rout and his last army vanished.

> *Comme s'envole au vent une paille enflammée*
> *S'évanouit ce bruit qui fut la grande armée.*

Back in Paris, on 21 June, Napoleon still talked of fighting on, draining the country of men, but there were none now to follow his frantic egoism. He signed his second abdication. If he had not done so the Chambers would have done it for him.

The liberals in Paris, being rid of the Emperor, did not want to replace him with a king, least of all a Bourbon. The man of the moment, however, was Fouché, who had turned to the royalists. He secured the withdrawal of the French army covering Paris and by a series of masterly manoeuvres was able to present to Louis XVIII, returning as rapidly from the frontier as he had fled there, a peaceful and unopposed restoration, and himself as his Minister of Police.

Meanwhile, Napoleon was *en route*, by way of Rochefort, though he did not suspect this as yet, to St Helena. From the *Bellerophon*, on which he had taken refuge, he wrote to the Prince Regent in a last fine gesture, 'I come, like Themistocles to seat myself at the hearth of the British people.' The hearth of the British people was a very cold one but we need not waste too much sympathy on Napoleon. The last fling of his ambition had to be paid for, like the earlier ones, by France; not only in the loss of life and the expense of war, but in a severer treaty of peace. France was reduced to the frontiers of 1789, with the additional loss of one or two small areas for strategic reasons, the most important being the Saar, its future economic importance not yet suspected. An indemnity of 700 million francs was extorted. The works of art looted from Europe were to be returned. The fortresses of the North and the East were to be occupied by 150,000 allied troops for a period of from three to five years. The price of the Hundred Days in the terms of a treaty can easily be stated: its price in terms of the subsequent history of France remains undefinable.

II

THE CONSTITUTIONAL MONARCHY

1. THE RESTORATION

THE Second Restoration was to take place under very different auspices from those that had presided over the First. Fouché prepared the way for it in Paris. Talleyrand, hurrying back from Vienna, met the King at Saint Denis – where the kings of France had been buried for centuries, until the revolutionaries dug them up – and presented Fouché, vice leaning on the arm of crime Chateaubriand said, to Louis XVIII, who accepted the regicide as his Minister of Police. It was a very different homecoming from the first. Even if Wellington and the King's advisers, who urged on him the necessity of accepting Fouché and Talleyrand as his ministers, were mistaken in believing that this was the only way to a peaceful second restoration, the fact that they believed it, and that the King yielded to their opinion, is in itself significant of the latent weakness and even contradiction in his position; for despite his ministers Louis XVIII did not intend to return the second time, any more than he had come back the first, as the king of a crowned Revolution. When, on the news of the abdication of Napoleon in 1814, a courtier announced to him, 'Sire, you are King of France,' he had replied, 'Have I ever ceased to be?' His sense of indefeasible, hereditary, divine right, which supported him in the years of exile, had become second nature. It gave him a dignity which his physical appearance might otherwise have prohibited. Immensely fat and walking only with difficulty, he occupied the throne like an old idol, self-sufficient in divinely sanctioned egoism. If he compromised with new conditions it was without faith and with very little hope.

Louis XVIII's English exile had not taught him the virtues of parliamentary government. At bottom he shared the views of his younger brother, who once declared that he would sooner earn his living as a wood-cutter than be King of England. This did not mean that the restored Bourbons intended, even if they had had the power, to bring back the absolute monarchy. The question is often discussed as though there were no other choice, at least in ideology, than that between the absolutism of a Louis XIV and the principles of the Revolution. This is to forget that it was not the ministers of Louis XVI but the *émigrés* who returned in 1814, and that the kings of the Restoration had formerly been, when they were Provence and Artois, the leaders of the Counter-revolution. Their programme had been that of the aristocratic revolt, of the Assembly of Notables and the Royal Session of 1789. These were the political ideas that Louis XVIII and his advisers embodied in the Charter of 1814.

The concessions it offered should not be underestimated. The recognition of the principles of liberty and equality, with which it commenced, perhaps meant less, but not in practice so much less, than it had in 1789. More important was the assurance that a curtain of forgetfulness was to be dropped over opinions and votes expressed before the Restoration: this was necessary if the political, administrative, military, and religious personnel which had served the Empire was to continue to serve the restored monarchy. The Civil Code and all existing laws which were not contrary to the *Charte* were maintained in force: this was to retain the administrative and social structure given to France by Napoleon, and here the fundamental contradictions of the Restoration begin. To superimpose the pseudo-Gothic of an aristocratic reaction on the pseudo-classical pillars of the Napoleonic system was to create a piece of wedding-cake architecture, essentially ephemeral.

A second problem was that of land ownership. It was met by a recognition of the inviolable right of all existing property, including specifically all the lands of the Church and the *émigrés* which had been confiscated by the Revolution and had passed to new possessors. Legal recognition of the changes in land ownership was doubtless inevitable, but could those who had been despoiled reconcile themselves to the fact that even if the King was enjoying his own again, they were not?

Thirdly, religious toleration was proclaimed. This was an achievement of the eighteenth-century Enlightenment, consolidated by the Revolution; but Roman Catholicism, a declining, emasculated force in the eighteenth century, was now moving towards a new militancy on the crest of a wave of religious revival. The immediate question was whether it would continue passively to tolerate its enemies. A more fundamental issue was whether the anti-clerical spirit, now deeply rooted among the educated classes, would ever be prepared to accept willingly the recognition in the *Charte* of the Catholic, apostolic, and Roman religion as the official religion of France, and the close alliance between Church and State that was the natural corollary. A minor problem, but one which was to give the Restoration much trouble, was slurred over in the clause which recognized both the liberty of the press and the right of the government to repress its abuse.

When we turn to purely political issues, contradictions are equally apparent in the *Charte*, though here there was more scope for a compromise to be worked out in practice. The aim was to establish a constitutional but not a parliamentary monarchy. The King embodied the executive power and had the initiative in legislation; but a parliament composed of two chambers was to discuss and vote the laws and the taxes, and the Chamber of Deputies had the right of impeaching the King's ministers before the upper chamber. These provisions were illogical but reasonable. They were to prove quite workable and to give France a valuable apprenticeship in parliamentary government. The issue that had divided the *noblesse* in 1789, the creation of a house of peers, was settled without any dispute, and here perhaps the example of Great Britain and of the institutions of the Empire were not without influence. An assembly of the highest dignitaries, lay, ecclesiastical, and military, of both the old régime and the Empire, nominated by the King, formed a decorative, impressive, and workable upper chamber.

The fundamental problems of the Restoration were, however, essentially extra-political in the narrower meaning of politics. Louis XVIII recognized clearly what they were when he wrote to his brother, in 1817, that he did not intend to be the King of a divided people. 'All the efforts of my government', he said, 'are directed to the effort to fuse the two peoples, who exist only too much in fact, into a single one.'

Unhappily the Hundred Days had broken the spell of general reconciliation which seemed for a moment to be operating in 1814. A White Terror raged in the South before the central government was able to regain control. La Bourdonnaye, in the Chamber at Paris, demanded chains, executioners, tortures. 'Defenders of humanity', he cried, 'learn how to shed a few drops of blood to spare a torrent of it.' Doubtless to the disappointment of such real enthusiasts, the legal proceedings resulted only in a few thousand imprisonments. Fouché connived at the escape of many of those who had compromised themselves during the Hundred Days. Ney, bravest of the brave, whose execution was undoubtedly a political blunder, was given every opportunity of escaping before his trial, even though his desertion to Napoleon had been flagrant.

The first step out of the provisional for the Second Restoration was the election of a Chamber of Deputies. The government of Talleyrand and Fouché appointed the prefects and the presidents of the electoral colleges, and perhaps assumed that having chosen the makers of elections, the election was as good as made. But, not for the last time in the nineteenth century, it was shown that there were limits to what the administration could achieve by electoral management. Local notabilities dominated an election which took place in two stages, the primary electors having the task of choosing the actual electoral colleges. Out of a total electorate of 72,000, those who voted numbered 48,000. The result, which has never received a fully satisfactory explanation, was an overwhelmingly reactionary and royalist assembly, the famous *Chambre introuvable*. In the face of this striking repudiation by the electorate even the cleverness of Talleyrand and Fouché could do nothing and they faded from the scene. In their place Louis XVIII called on the duc de Richelieu, whose disinterested loyalty was well known, who had proved his capacity as an administrator in the service of Russia, where he had been governor of the newly conquered territory on the Black Sea, and who because of his long absence was uninvolved in any of the factions of the Emigration. Wellington said of him that his word was equal to a treaty. His colleagues, however, were weak, and the *Chambre introuvable* ungovernable. Louis XVIII has been praised for breaking with the reactionary elements which dominated it and at the same time blamed for rejecting, at the outset of his reign, the principle of parliamentary government; but the former was probably inevitable and the latter he had never accepted. The Chamber was dissolved in September 1816 and in the new elections the government of Richelieu obtained a working majority. Under him, by one of those remarkable financial recoveries which are a feature of French history, the indemnity imposed after the Hundred Days was paid off and the occupying armies withdrew in November 1818. Richelieu resigned in December 1818 but he had brought France back into the comity of nations.

The resignation of Richelieu, much more than the dissolution of 1816, was the proof that the régime was still a monarchical and not a parliamentary one, and that a minister could not hold office without the favour of the king. Louis XVIII was not ill disposed to the minister, but behind the scenes he was taking the advice of a personal favourite. This was Decazes, son of a notary of the Gironde. Decazes had become prefect of police for Paris after the Hundred Days, as such obtained access to the King, and completely won his devotion. 'Come to receive the tenderest embraces of thy friend, thy father, thy Louis', the King would write to him. Decazes has perhaps been unduly written down because of the way in which his political fortune was built up. If he had not an elevated character and was no great statesman, he was successful in reconciling the rôle of royal favourite with moderate concessions to the left. In the new government, of which he was virtual though not nominal head, he combined the offices of Police and the Interior. Where Richelieu's administration had rested on the centre but looked for support towards the right, Decazes, equally with a centre government, relied on the support of the left.

The difficulty for any such government was that the one strongly organized and coherent party in Parliament belonged to the right. This was the party of the Ultras or pure royalists. It looked towards the King's brother, Artois, and represented the purest ideas of the Counter-revolution. Its strength in the country came from the support of the secret society of the Chevaliers de la Foi. Its leader in the Chamber of Deputies was the able parliamentarian, Villèle, and in the Chamber of Peers it had Polignac, Montmorency, and Chateaubriand to speak for it. The paradox was that the pure royalists from the beginning found themselves in opposition to the King; the less pure royalists who supported him formed the political centre, with a right wing represented by Richelieu and a left wing by Decazes. The left proper, only gradually returning to the political arena after the fiasco of the Hundred Days, took cover under the title of Independents.

With the revival of political life had come also that of political thought. The chief theorist of the left was Benjamin Constant, who saw the safeguard of the liberal principles to which he was devoted in a parliamentary monarchy after the English fashion, and whose political thinking, possibly for that reason, has lacked in France the recognition it deserves. The centre-left found its theorists in the doctrinaires Royer-Collard, Barante, Guizot, de Broglie,

Charles de Rémusat, who saw political life as a careful balancing of interests, and recognized no authority but that of law, or impartial reason, which however they tended to identify in practice with the interests of the socially dominant classes. The Ultras obtained doctrinal support from the writings of the theocrats, Joseph de Maistre, de Bonald, and Lamennais, for whom politics was the handmaid of religion and kings were the servants of the Pope, in whom was embodied the divine will on earth.

Political realities were far below this realm of high theory. They have to be discussed in terms of the membership of parliaments and cabinets, of party manoeuvres, franchise adjustments, and electoral wangling. The *pays légal,* those who had the vote, was restricted to some 90,000 electors in a nation of well over twenty-six millions, the qualification being the payment of 300 francs in direct taxation. Since by far the greater proportion of the wealth of France was in the form of land, and it was in land that those who had made money chiefly tended to invest it, this was primarily a landowners' franchise. To be eligible to stand as a candidate it was necessary in addition to be subject to a tax of 1,000 francs and to be over forty years of age. The number of possible candidates in the whole of France was some 15,000 of the wealthiest men. Nothing very revolutionary, it might be thought, could emerge from such an electorate. An analysis of the last Chamber of Deputies of the Restoration gives 38·5 per cent higher officials, 14·8 per cent engaged in trade, finance, or industry, 5·2 per cent belonging to the liberal professions, and 41·5 per cent large landowners, apart from such members of the previous categories as were also landowners, as probably most were.

The large proportion of the deputies who had played a part in public life under the Revolution and the Empire is an indication that the Restoration assemblies were not likely to be wholly swayed by ultra views; nor was there much chance for the left in the elections. But to obtain a reliable body of supporters the government had to resort to methods of electoral management such as had been used experimentally under the Directory and were to become classic in nineteenth-century France. Reducing the taxes of known opponents for the purpose of robbing them of the franchise was a common device. To prevent appeals against exclusions, the lists of electors might be posted up only at the last moment, at night, not in alphabetical order, and at a height which made them unreadable without a ladder. The prefects who managed the elections for the government saw to it that all government servants voted for the right candidate. Electoral meetings were prohibited. The electoral colleges were presided over by officials, and although the ballot was in theory secret, supporters of the government took care not to conceal their votes.

Once in the Chamber, the functions of the deputies were limited. The choice of ministers rested in the hands of the King, and the cabinet system was as yet only imperfectly evolved. Under Talleyrand, Richelieu, and Decazes there was an effective President of the Council, who co-ordinated the policy of the ministers. Villèle, on the other hand, when he became head of the government, adopted the practice of working alone with the King, and Charles X aspired to be himself the real leader of the ministers. The identification of the last of the Bourbons with the policy of his government was so close that it was impossible to prevent the fall of the government from bringing with it the abdication of the monarch.

In spite of the narrowness of the franchise and the control exercised by the government over elections, the multiplicity of parties stood in the way of stable administration during the Restoration. Decazes tried to conciliate the opposition, but when he went to the country in 1819 the result was merely an electoral victory for the left, in which even the former constitutional bishop and regicide, Grégoire, was returned, it is true with the aid of ultra-royalist votes. This was a blow to Decazes, but the fatal event for him was the assassination, in February 1820, of the duc de Berry, as he was leaving the Opera. It was an isolated crime but it gave an opening to all the enemies of the minister, and enabled them to force Louis XVIII reluctantly to abandon his favourite and recall Richelieu to office. To bring under control the reviving political activity, laws permitting the arrest of suspected persons, extending the censorship of the press, and conferring a double vote on the wealthier members of the electorate were passed. In September 1820 the birth of the posthumous son of the duc de Berry guaranteed the continuance of the Bourbon line.

The left now began to flirt with revolutionary movements. Representatives of small secret societies met under the chairmanship of La Fayette to discuss insurrectionary plans; but Richelieu, who was as well informed of these plans as the left-wing leaders themselves, took steps to make them aware of this fact and the embryo revolution was still-born. The international secret society of the Carbonari, which had perhaps as many as 40,000 members in France, was stirred into activity by the revolutions in Spain and Naples, but achieved nothing beyond a few petty local disturbances. The best known was the attempt of the four sergeants of La Rochelle to subvert their regiment. Denounced, they were arrested, tried, and executed. The left, however ineffectively, was thus abandoning the policy of compromise; the right was preparing to take over power; and the centre, on which Richelieu based his government, was fast disappearing.

France under the Restoration was not yet a parliamentary monarchy, and when the second Richelieu ministry fell, in 1822, it was again not because of a change in the balance of power in the Chamber but because the King had acquired a new favourite. Some years earlier a young woman named Zoë, Countess of Cayla, had sought the royal protection in a lawsuit against an 'unworthy spouse'. Beautiful, witty, and aged twenty-seven, Mme du Cayla won her suit and the royal affections at the same time. Given the age and infirmity of the King she could hardly become a royal mistress in the full sense of the term; but every Wednesday she visited the Tuileries for a private game of chess with the King, during which the doors of the royal apartment were guarded; and every day she wrote the King a letter, in composing which she was assisted by Villèle. Not surprisingly, Villèle, who had entered the government in 1820, in September 1822 became President of the Council.

Villèle, a minor noble from Toulouse, short, ugly, intriguing, and ambitious, was the leader of the ultra-royalist party in the Chamber of Deputies, so that even without Mme du Cayla he would have been the appropriate minister for the royalist reaction. He was inexhaustible in his capacity for work, a master of detail, and unwilling to share his authority with anyone. Louis XVIII, now completely preoccupied with his health and Mme du Cayla, left the control of affairs almost entirely to his brother and successor, Artois, along with Villèle, whose great achievement was in the field of finance. Between 1822 and 1827 he put public finances in France on foundations which kept them sound and stable until the crisis of the twentieth century. The task of establishing a budgetary system and strict control of governmental expenditure, which had proved beyond the powers of the Controllers General of the *ancien régime*, but to which the Finance Ministers of Napoleon had made an important contribution, was now completed. This was perhaps the most important service of the Restoration to France. It was the return to peaceful international relations which made financial stability possible, of course. It is no accident that while the eighteenth and twentieth centuries, which were centuries of large-scale wars for France, were marked by instability in the national finances; the nineteenth century, with no really great and prolonged war between 1815 and 1914, was one of balanced budgets.

Peace after 1815 also brought with it a marked improvement in trade. According to one set of statistics French foreign trade more than doubled between 1814 and 1825. It is true that according to another set it remained stationary, but the former seems on the face of it the more likely. Altogether the Restoration gave France efficient and honest government, and, so long as Louis XVIII lived, moderation and a reasonable degree of stability, which endured long enough to prove that there was no inherent reason why it should have broken down.

2. CLERICALISM AND ANTI-CLERICALISM

THE failure of the Restoration was not primarily in the field of government, where it was weak, but in that of religion, where it was strong. Although the succession of Charles X may have precipitated the crisis, its beginnings can already be seen under Louis XVIII. Europe, in the early years of the nineteenth century, witnessed a widespread religious revival. This strongly affected the French church, in which there was now a zealous episcopate and a lower clergy gradually growing in number and unexceptionable in devoutness. Religious houses for women increased from 1,829 in 1815 to 2,875 in 1830. Orders for men were tolerated, though only in the case of three missionary orders were they authorized by law, but these also were increasing in number. The Jesuit-inspired Congregation engaged in energetic religious propaganda throughout France. An attempt was even made to annul the Napoleonic Concordat and return to the relations between Church and State that had prevailed under the *ancien régime*; but the terms of the Concordat – and this is perhaps the ultimate judgement on it – were too favourable for the Papacy to abandon and the negotiation for its revision proved abortive.

The Gallicanism of the Restoration was an anachronism, as became quite evident after 1830, when there was no longer a king with the sanctity of hereditary divine right on the throne. With Bonald, de Maistre, Lamennais, force of argument and literary talent were both on the side of the Ultramontanes. The religious revival naturally worked to the benefit of Rome. Gallicanism now stood for the authority of the French bishops, authoritarian and often aristocratic, with all the enhanced power conferred on them by the Concordat over the lower clergy, who could be transferred from parish to parish, or deprived of their office, at the bishop's arbitrary will. No wonder that a habit of looking, or even appealing, to Rome grew up among the clergy: they had no one else to appeal to.

Napoleon had attempted to use the Concordat to reduce the Church to the rôle of an instrument of the State: under the Restoration there seemed a danger that the State might be made the instrument of the Church. In the interests of religion the episcopate did not hesitate to call on the support of the administration. With the Ultras in power this tendency was intensified. The Panthéon, purged of the infidel remains of Voltaire and Rousseau, was given over to religious uses. Secondary education was placed, in 1821, under the supervision of the bishops. A high ecclesiastic, Mgr Frayssinous, was appointed Grand Master of the University. In 1824 the appointment of all teachers in primary schools was given to the episcopate. In 1822 two new press offences were created – criticism of the divine right of kings and outrage on religion. A law against sacrilege made the profanation of sacred vessels punishable with imprisonment for life, and, in the case of profanation of the consecrated host, with death, though in fact the law was never applied.

When Charles X, who succeeded to the throne in 1824, was crowned in the cathedral at Reims, it was with all the apparatus of the religious revival. The assembled multitude cried *Vivat Rex in aeternum*; but it was noted when the King returned after the ceremony to Paris that his reception in the capital was distinctly lukewarm. Eternity was to last for five years.

While the depth and seriousness of the religious revival in France must not be underestimated, its limitations also should not be forgotten. Rationalism and anti-clericalism had driven too deeply into French soil to be easily uprooted. The intellectual life which had flourished under the *ancien régime* had been blighted but not killed by the frosts of the Revolution and the Empire. Now, in a milder, if still somewhat austere, climate, it reburgeoned as in a new spring. Science continued its progress, uninfluenced by, and uninfluencing, the changing political scene. Lamarck, who had studied under Buffon, links the zoology of the encyclo-pedists with the evolutionary theories of the nineteenth century. Cuvier practically created palaeontology, and Ampère has been called the Newton of electricity. The son of the great Carnot, Sadi Carnot, founded thermo-dynamics and Fresnel produced the wave theory of light.

History experienced a remarkable revival, amounting almost to a rebirth, under the Restoration. The famous École des Chartes was founded and the publication of the great collections of memoirs relating to the history of France was begun. Barante's *History of the Dukes of Burgundy* (1824–6) was as successful as a novel, and Augustin Thierry wrote a notable history of the Norman Conquest of England (1825). Guizot's *Essais sur l'histoire de France* (1823) was followed by the six volumes of his lectures on modern history at the Sorbonne in 1828–30. As opposition became bolder, historians turned to more recent times with the histories of the French Revolution by Thiers in 1823–7 and Mignet in 1824.

Above all this was a period of rebirth in literature. The new romantic spirit which crossed the Channel with Walter Scott and the Rhine with Mme de Staël's *De l'Allemagne* (1810) was in the beginning religious, monarchical, hierarchic, its eyes turned backwards to the Middle Ages. Lamartine, Victor Hugo, Mérimée, Alfred de Vigny, Stendhal, Chateaubriand raised the flag of romanticism. The paintings of Géricault and Delacroix might have been conceived as illustrations of their writings. The new trend appeared in music with Weber, Rossini, Berlioz.

Literature was not at first hostile to the Restoration, which represented emancipation from the strait-jacket of the Empire and an age of poetry after prose. Louis XVIII, a patron of poetry, impressed by the merit of a young begin-ner in the art who had determined to do what few dared to attempt – make literature a career – gave him a pension of 1,000 francs, and so eased the first steps of Victor Hugo, whose writings were to be a changing illustration of his age.

He was the son of a general of Napoleon, who had somehow picked up the title of count in the service of Joseph in Spain. After 1815 General Hugo, like so many others, transferred himself to the service of Louis XVIII, and by discovering a noble family of Lorraine with the same name, which had conveniently died out, annexed a more distinguished ancestry for himself. Victor Hugo was not only a poet but a vicomte; and in both capacities Catholic and royalist, writing poems on the death of the duc de Berry, the funeral of Louis XVIII, the war in Spain, attending the *Sacre* of Charles X at Reims.

But despite its initial affiliations the new wine of romanticism was too heady to be confined in the old bottles of Restoration politics or Vatican religion. Literature has during the last two centuries traditionally migrated to the opposition in France. In the years that preceded the revolution of 1830 romanticism deserted Catholicism and monarchism and formed an alliance with liberalism, carrying into the camp of its new partner some of that passionate vigour and anti-rationalist spirit which it had perhaps in part acquired from its former ally. Victor Hugo's *Préface de Cromwell*, a more notable piece of writing than the unplayable drama it introduced, is an invocation to liberty; and in 1830, in the preface to *Hernani*, Hugo denounced the Ultras of all brands.

The clerical reaction continued without the support of many of its former adherents in the literary world. Charles X, who presided over a régime which was now throwing off the hesitations and compromises which had marked the reign of Louis XVIII, had forgotten little; in intellectual goods his mind was so sparsely furnished that there was little for him to forget. At sixty-seven still youthful in manner and child-like in mind, he was determined to be king. However, he continued to support Villèle, whose government had added foreign victory to its financial successes.

The civil war, which had begun in Spain in 1820, could not leave the sister Bourbon monarchy in France unconcerned. Villèle, who was anxious to avoid military intervention, managed to drive the extremer Montmorency out of the ministry on this issue; but his place was taken by Chateaubriand who adopted the same policy. Despite Villèle's reluctance, in 1823 a French army was despatched to restore the Bourbon King of Spain, an ill-omened venture which unexpectedly achieved rapid and complete success. The invasion was little more than a military promenade. By lavish expenditure the financier Ouvrard, in charge of supplies, bought both provisions and an almost unopposed passage through Spain. French intervention re-established the king on his throne without difficulty. Comparisons were drawn, naturally, between this speedy success and the disasters that had encompassed Napoleon's armies in Spain. Villèle was not the better disposed to Chateaubriand because his policy had proved successful, and when the Foreign Minister refused to support a governmental finance measure took the opportunity to secure his dismissal. This was a great mistake, for Chateaubriand flung himself into opposition with vigour, taking the influential *Journal des débats* with him. The Spanish war, thus, though successful, crystallized an incipient split in the ranks of the right, and promoted the growth of a royalist counter-opposition. This is in part attributable to the narrowness and inflexibility of Villèle; but it is difficult not to believe also that the royalists were so unaccustomed to the compromises necessary in government, and the nobility so deeply imbued with the Frondeur spirit, that opposition came naturally to them.

They had a material reason for dissatisfaction. Disappointed under Louis XVIII, with Charles X the *émigrés* expected at last to receive the fruit of their sacrifices in the form of the undoing of the revolutionary land settlement. Villèle gave them the laws on sacrilege, the press, and education, but they wanted something of greater substance. The solution Villèle found was to create 30 million francs in annual new *rentes*, representing the interest at 3 per cent on a capital nominally of a thousand million francs, at which the value of the confiscated property was calculated, in fact of about 630 millions. The former *émigrés*, or their heirs, now numbered some 70,000 and the indemnity to be divided between them came to an average of some 1,377 francs a year each. It did not satisfy their wishes, while it exacerbated the feelings of the great majority of persons of property who felt that in one way or another they were paying for it.

The propertied men who were aggrieved by the indemnity to the former *émigrés* included also those who were most suspicious of the clerical influences at work in the new reign. The outburst of anti-clerical propaganda which occurred in 1825 has been attributed to the subtle tactics of the liberal opposition, hoping to achieve by this means the electoral success which it had not been able to gain by more legitimate methods. All the measures in favour of the Church and religion were attributed to the influence of the Jesuit Congregation; the existence of the secret Chevaliers de la Foi was unknown to the general public. In fact, while the extent of the clerical reaction was exaggerated, the strength of anti-clerical feeling in France had also been under-estimated. If the liberals were able to use the fear of clericalism to achieve political results that could not have been achieved by more direct methods in a country that was not very interested in politics, this is in itself proof of the strength of anti-clerical sentiment. It was the major current in a rising tide of hostility against Charles X and his government. What two and a half years of ultra rule had done was shown in March 1827, when the King, reviewing the National Guard of Paris composed largely of the well-to-do middle class, was greeted with cries of 'Down with the Jesuits!', 'Down with the Ministers!', '*Vive la liberté de la presse!*' It was hardly possible to impose any sanction in reply except to dissolve the National Guard.

Meanwhile the extreme Ultras had been becoming increasingly discontented with what they regarded as the excessive moderation of Villèle. A naval intervention in the Greek struggle for independence, which resulted in the successful engagement of Navarino in 1827, had little repercussion in France. If Villèle was to remain in office, he would have to try to secure a change in the composition of the Chamber of Deputies, but after elections held in November 1827 the government found itself with some 160 to 180 supporters in the new house, against an approximately equal liberal opposition, and with a group of 60 to 80 extremists forming a royalist counter-opposition on its right flank. Villèle had now no choice but to resign. The King appointed a ministry of technical experts, without any President of the Council, though the new Minister of the Interior, Martignac, was its spokesman in the Chambers and is often referred to as its head. This government offered some minor concessions, especially in matters of education, to the left; but it was clear that it would not be more than a stop-gap. Charles X was determined not to compromise with the liberal opposition, and if the Villèlists and the royalist counter-opposition could be brought to work together a majority of the right seemed still possible.

The fall of the last Bourbon king of France was so little determined by the nature of things, that in spite of the acute struggle over clericalism it took almost inconceivable imbecility on the part of Charles X and his minister to bring it about. For the new king also had his favourite. This was Polignac, his 'dear Jules'. In secret correspondence with Polignac by the back-stairs of the palace, a new ministry was arranged. Jules de Polignac, a prisoner of Napoleon from 1802 to 1814, was an *exalté* with no grasp of political realities. To him was added La Bourdonnaye, who had been identified with the White Terror of 1815, as Minister of the Interior, and Bourmont, who had deserted Napoleon on the eve of Waterloo, as Minister of War. At the Ministry of Justice was Courvoisier, a recent convert from infidelity to Catholicism, whose chief political guide was the Apocalypse. The government thus oddly constituted took office in August 1829. For six months it proceeded to do nothing, while the opposition prepared itself for resistance. Under the patronage of La Fayette, the society

Aide-toi, le ciel t'aidera organized electoral committees. The students of Paris formed a republican society called *Jeune France*. Inspired by Talleyrand and organized and financed by the banker Lafitte, the Orleanists made their preparations and founded a new paper, the *National*, edited by the liberal historians, Thiers and Mignet.

While the forces of the left were gaining coherence, the ministry was becoming increasingly incoherent. Except for Polignac it was completely renewed, with ministers whose names are not worth recording. The Chamber was dissolved and elections were held in June and July 1830. The customary methods of administrative pressure were employed, and the king issued a personal appeal to the electors to support the official candidates. All was in vain: the opposition won 274 seats against 143 for the government, and 11 of doubtful allegiance. The Polignac ministry had been decisively rejected by the *pays légal*. Everything would now depend on whether the king was prepared to accept the verdict of the electorate and appoint a President of the Council who could work with the new Chamber.

Charles X and Polignac had no such intention. Divine right could not make compromises. Moreover they wore fresh laurels of victory, won in the colonial field, on their brows. After Napoleon the French overseas empire was an attenuated one. In 1815 France possessed five trading stations in India, the isle Bourbon (formerly La Réunion), Saint-Louis and Gorée in Senegal, the small West Indian islands of Guadeloupe and Martinique, Guiana in South America, and the rocky islets of Saint-Pierre and Miquelon off Newfoundland, chiefly valuable because of the fishing rights that went with them. It was not much. The Restoration picked up the scanty and broken threads of French colonial policy, resuming rather the traditions of power politics of the *ancien régime* than the more liberal if muddled policies of the Revolution; there was nothing to inherit from Napoleon. Expansion began in Senegal and a foothold was won in Madagascar; but the major achievement of the restored Bourbons was the result of the Polignac ministry's need for prestige: the expeditions to Spain and Greece were followed, in 1830, by one against Algiers. Efficiently organized and well led by Bourmont, anxious to retrieve his reputation, in three weeks it achieved complete success; the foundation stone of the French North African Empire had been laid under the last and least considered of the legitimate sovereigns.

News of the victory at Algiers reached Paris on 9 July. Charles X and Polignac, encouraged by this success abroad, proceeded to take the steps necessary to reverse their electoral defeat at home. On 10 July Polignac produced the first draft of proposals which, after discussion in the King's Council, were issued on 25 July as the Four Ordinances. These prohibited the publication of any journal or pamphlet of less than twenty-five pages without official authorization; dissolved the Chamber which had just been elected; restricted the effective use of the franchise to the wealthiest 25 per cent of the existing electors; and convoked the electoral colleges to choose a new Chamber.

The first step in opposition was taken by the journalists, led by Thiers and the *National*. They issued a manifesto calling on France to resist. Shops and workshops in Paris were closed on 26 July: the King, as though to model himself on Louis XVI, spent the day hunting. Polignac, who in his blind infatuation did not for a moment expect the opposition to pick up the gage of battle which he did not even realize that he had thrown down, had taken no military precautions. Indeed the best troops, to the number of 40,000, were in Algiers. On 27 July, when it began to dawn even on Polignac that the situation was not quite normal, Marmont was put in charge of the garrison of Paris. On 28 July rioting began in the streets. A number of deputies met and sent a deputation to Polignac which he refused to see. By 29 July, Marmont having found it necessary to concentrate his troops, Paris was in the hands of the rioters, who had lost some 1,800 killed against 200 among the soldiers, in the course of the fighting. The deputies now decided to accept the leadership of the revolution to prevent it from falling into the hands of extremists, and the Orleanist Lafitte joined other deputies in a self-elected municipal council, the next day to promote itself to the rank of provisional government. Three days of street fighting – *les trois glorieuses* – had been sufficient to overthrow the restored monarchy.

On 30 July Charles X at last recognized that something had happened and that concessions were necessary; but already on the walls of Paris was the placard, drawn up by Thiers and Mignet, calling on the people to place the Duke of Orleans on the throne. The self-chosen provisional government invited him to become lieutenant-general of the kingdom. Orleans, who had been hesitating at a safe distance from Paris, accepted and on 1 August appointed provisional ministers. Meanwhile Charles X, threatened by the populace of Versailles, had taken flight to Rambouillet. There he himself appointed Orleans lieutenant-general and abdicated in favour of his own grandson, *l'enfant du miracle*. Orleans himself still had some legitimist scruples, and if he had accepted this solution it might have been better for France and better perhaps in the long run for himself. The monarchical principle would have been preserved, the fatal cleavage between legitimists and Orleanists averted, and a parliamentary government set up in the name of the legitimate line. But the Orleanists had waited and intrigued too long for this moment to give up the prize at last within their grasp. Orleans convoked the Chambers and announced the abdication of Charles X, without any reference to his grandson. The fallen king slowly made his way with the royal family to Cherbourg, where he dismissed his bodyguard and took ship for England.

The Restoration had failed: this does not prove that it was from the beginning inexorably doomed to failure. On the contrary, the Revolution of 1830 seems at first impression rather the result of a series of accidents, and above all of the obstinacy of Charles X, who went from blunder to blunder as though driven by a blind fate, or as though the little sense there had ever been in that addled pate had entirely vanished with age. He was such a nonentity as to be hardly worth a revolution, and indeed, looking behind the passing events of 1830, one can see that it was not really directed against him; it was against the anachronistic reappearance of a *noblesse* which believed that the eighteenth century had never ended and a clergy which, since the eighteenth century was, so far as the church was concerned, a rather unfortunate episode, looked back to the century of the Compagnie du Saint Sacrement, Bossuet, and the Revocation of the Edict of Nantes. On the other hand, an important section of the educated classes in France, even if they thought that religion might be good for the masses, did not intend that priests should rule, or that their own sons should be educated by them. They turned against a régime in which the influence of the Church seemed to be increasingly dominant.

They also found that the Restoration was robbing them of one of the chief perquisites resulting from the Revolution. The new aristocracy of office created by the Revolution and Napoleon found its ranks swollen after 1815 by an unwelcome accession of strength from *ancien régime* families, who joined in the competition for even the humblest official appointments, and who, because of their ancestry and loyalty to the crown, had what seemed an unfair advantage in the game. The unemployed educated proletariat, searching for a career and especially concentrated in the student population of Paris, which has been wrongly seen as a factor in 1789, was perhaps a reality by 1830. At a higher social level the bankers and businessmen of the chaussée d'Antin looked with jealousy on the aristocratic exclusiveness of the faubourg Saint-Germain. The monarchy, which might have bridged the gulf between ancient names and new fortunes, in the person of Charles X allowed its policies to be dictated and its councils to be monopolized by clergy and *noblesse*. At the same time, inconsistently, it attributed the franchise exclusively to men of wealth. It is true that this was mainly wealth in the form of land, but the extent to which land had passed into the possession of new men was perhaps not realized. Only this can explain the fact that the Restoration lost the support of even such a restricted electorate.

One thing more was needed to make a revolution possible: a mob to riot in the streets of Paris. Economic conditions supplied the material to fill this gap. The population of France had increased by nearly two and a half million between 1815 and 1830, without any marked increase in agricultural or industrial productivity in these years. After a short economic recession in 1817, a new and severer crisis began in 1826 and was to last until 1832. In 1828, out of 224,000 workers in the department of the Nord 163,000 were receiving some form of charitable assistance. That misery alone does not make revolutions is suggested by the significant fact that the populace provided insurrectionary mobs only in Paris, where the political agitation was concentrated.

Having won Paris with the aid of the mob, the journalists and politicians speedily brought the disturbances under control. The *noblesse* as a whole had perhaps not put up much of a fight in the first Revolution, outside Brittany and the Vendée. In 1830 they offered no resistance at all. In 1789 and the subsequent years at least they fled abroad to start a Counter-revolution; in 1830 they merely gave up their jobs and took refuge in that abstention from public life which has been called *l'émigration intérieure*, which robbed France of the services of a host of families whose position and traditions called on them to contribute to the ruling *élite*, but who had learnt under the bureaucracy of an absolute monarchy to disassociate rights from duties and who had ceased to be a governing class while remaining an aristocracy.

3. THE FOUNDATION OF THE
JULY MONARCHY

IN 1830 a political movement which had begun as an attempt to force Charles X to dismiss an unpopular minister turned into a revolution. The republican leaders, who now re-entered the political arena with the Paris mob behind them, were determined that the monarchy should disappear with the monarch. They had a ready-made candidate for President of the republic they believed they were about to establish in the person of the Commander of the National Guard, Lafayette, that distinguished relic of 1789, who was far too ingenuous and well-intentioned, and convinced of other people's good intentions, ever to succeed in politics. If a republic had been possible in 1830 he would have made an admirable president, but to the politicians, financiers, and men of property who had led the campaign against clericalism, the *émigrés*, Polignac, and Charles X, the Republic was still a name of terror. Lafayette was to be, in 1830 as in 1789, a mere cathartic agent, who precipitated events without really sharing in them.

The only practical alternative to a republic seems to us so obvious that there is a temptation to believe that the revolution must have been encompassed for the purpose of bringing it about. For the third time the shadow of an Orleanist conspiracy appears on the stage of history, and undoubtedly the Orleanist alternative to the Bourbons had been envisaged by some during the Restoration. There is no evidence, however, of the existence of any real conspiracy. The change in the dynasty was not a consciously calculated result of the 1830 Revolution: it was a pragmatic response to largely fortuitous circumstances.

The incoherence of the July Revolution was demonstrated in its first government. Lafayette and the conventionnel Dupont de l'Eure represented the Revolution, Sébastiani and Gérard, Napoleonic generals, the Empire; Guizot and baron Louis had served Louis XVIII, the banker Lafitte and the journalist Thiers were active in the Orleanist interest, Casimir-Périer and the duc de Broglie had been less committed opponents of the Bourbons.

There is little significance in this *olla podrida* of a government. More important in the long run than those who were included was the fact of those who were excluded, or excluded themselves. Each of the successive revolutions in modern France has eliminated a section of the political personnel. In the 1830 Chamber of Deputies, 52 members refused to take the oath to the new king and 68 others lost their seats. There was a holocaust in the administration – 20 of the 38 members of the Conseil d'État, 76 prefects, 196 sub-prefects, 393 mayors or deputies, were dismissed. Of 75 generals, 65 were removed from the active list. Practically the whole diplomatic corps was changed.

This was not enough for the more violent revolutionaries, who were determined on revenge for the bloodshed of the streets and called for blood in return. The government would have been very glad to forget all about revenge, but under pressure from public opinion it had to bring the last ministers of Charles X to trial before the peers. While the National Guard, or at least its more advanced members, surrounded the Chamber and threatened lynch law, the accused ministers were got away by a trick to Vincennes. In their absence they were sentenced to life imprisonment and released a few years later.

To the new king and the more conservative among his supporters, the great danger seemed indeed to be the National Guard and its commander Lafayette. Aged as he was, he remained the symbol of revolution, but not for long. When his proposals, including a generous extension of the suffrage and a ministry of the left, were rejected, he resigned. The National Guard was reorganized by a law of March 1831 which confined effective membership to those who paid direct taxation; and although its officers were elected, its administration and finance were put under the control of government officials. It was to be the bulwark of the régime – or so they thought.

The hopes of a great international revolution, which have always accompanied domestic revolution in France, were also to be frustrated. The July revolution had sparked off a Belgian revolt against the Dutch. But if the left saw this as the opportunity to reverse the decisions of 1815 and renew the conquests of the First Republic, Louis-Philippe knew that the other powers would never tolerate a French annexation of Belgium. He believed that Great Britain might be persuaded to accept an independent Belgium, and appointed Talleyrand ambassador in London to implement this policy. He accepted the perpetual neutrality of the new state – envisaged as a safeguard against France – to win British support, and he resisted manfully the temptation presented by the offer of the new throne of Belgium to his son, the duc de Nemours. The success of his policy was demonstrated when, in August 1831, the Dutch king, rejecting the decisions of an international conference, launched his army against Belgium. Louis-Philippe was able, with British approval, to despatch an expeditionary force which preserved Belgian independence.

The conservative nature of the July revolution was marked from the start and embodied in the terms of the new constitutional Charter. It could hardly have been otherwise when the Chamber which drew up the Charter of 1830 was the last elected, on the narrow Restoration franchise, under Charles X, minus the ultra-royalists. There was inevitably a breach with the divine-right monarchy, and if the constitutional changes were more marked in symbols than in positive institutional arrangements, those who made them knew that men are governed by symbols. The new king would have been Philip VII or Louis XIX if he had succeeded legitimately to the throne; instead he became king as Louis-Philippe. In recognition of the fact that he was one of the new national sovereigns of the nineteenth century he took the designation – already given to Louis XVI in 1789 – of *roi des Français* instead of *roi de France*. And that he was the heir of the Revolution and not of the Bourbons was shown by the return to the *tricolore*, in place of the white flag and the fleur-de-lys, the personal emblems of the dis-possessed dynasty. Louis-Philippe had fought under the flag of the Revolution at Jemappes. According to a story, when he first appeared in revolutionary Paris and was greeted with cries of '*À bas les Bourbons!*', Thiers and Mignet rapidly produced a placard announcing, '*Ce n'est pas un Bourbon, c'est un Valois*'. This was nonsense: his ancestry was nothing to the point. His *raison d'être* was to stand between France and a republic.

Yet the principle of popular sovereignty was tacitly admitted. The Charter was not a concession granted (*octroyé*) by the King, as in 1814, but a declaration of the rights of the nation. Apart from this, the changes made in it were significant, but hardly revolutionary. Catholicism was no longer to be 'the religion of the State', but the religion 'professed by the majority'. The power of suspending or dispensing with laws was specifically taken away from the king, who also had to share the initiative in legislation with parliament. Censorship was to be abolished for ever: which meant that journalists in future were, with certain qualifications, to be allowed to publish before they were damned.

The sessions of the upper chamber were to be public, though when the Charter was drawn up views on its future composition were too contradictory to allow more to be said than that the question of the peerage would be re-examined later. The interests of the king in this matter coincided with left-wing opinion, and a law of December 1831 suppressed the hereditary peerage and made the upper chamber in effect a house of royal nominees. This was a more important decision than might be thought: aristocratic France was doubtless already dead of the kind of pernicious anaemia which had been sapping it for centuries, but this was the last nail in its coffin. The 'Corinthian capitals of polished society' had been finally knocked away, and their removal left the bare structure of power exposed in all its rather unlovely nakedness. Perhaps those, like Guizot and Broglie, who opposed the measure, were not wrong in fearing its social and political implications. The government of France could now be seen to be a combination of bureaucracy and plutocracy. The legitimist gentry and aristocracy withdrew into their manor-houses, or the salons and inner courts of the faubourg St Germain, and abandoned public service of all kinds, though they returned to the Army later in the century. Political power was shared by the king and the Chamber of Deputies. What this meant in practice can be seen from an examination of the electoral laws. The age of eligibility as a deputy was lowered from forty to thirty, and the *cens*, or electoral qualification, to the payment of 200 francs annually in direct taxation. In this respect it seemed that a revolution had been made to raise the total electorate of France to a number estimated in 1846 as 241,000, some 2·8 per cent of the male population over the age of twenty-one. Moreover, since even the great Revolution had never ventured to introduce such a frightful socialistic measure as an income tax in France, direct taxation fell mainly on real estate. Therefore about 90 per cent of the tiny electorate of Orleanist France, it has been calculated, obtained their qualification from taxes on property, the remaining 10 per cent representing commerce, industry, and the professions. The so-called 'bourgeois monarchy' was in fact an oligarchy of landowners. In the absence of a more detailed analysis of Orleanist society, we must not read too much into this statement; but at least it suggests that the landed wealth of the country was no longer mainly in the hands of old legitimist families, but partly in those of a class of new men, who had doubtless made their wealth in many ways in the course of the *ancien régime* and the Revolution. Their figures, like that of père Grandet, dominate the novels of Balzac. Their new wealth had largely been invested in land, and they were now a well-established propertied class, with a sufficiently strong sense of its own interests to use the revolution of 1830 to oust the legitimist-clericalist régime of the restored Bourbons, and at the same time prevent the republicans from acceding to power.

The narrow oligarchical pattern extended from central

to local institutions. The Municipal Law of 1831 established
elected councils, but on such a narrow basis that a town of
5,000 inhabitants might have only 300 electors, one of
15,000 could have 700; and towns of 100,000 might reach
the figure of 3,000 electors. Even these petty municipal
oligarchies were kept under strict government control. The
maires continued to be chosen by the central government for
the larger towns, and by the prefect for the rest.

It was not to be expected that France would at once
settle down peacefully after the disorders of 1830. The
economic depression continued into 1832, and while in
Paris political interests called the tune, in Lyon, always
more influenced by economic considerations, industrial
disturbances continued. Although the silk weavers of Lyon
had not suffered from unemployment, the prices paid by the
merchants for their handwork had been greatly reduced and
the tariff to which they were accustomed was abandoned.
In October 1831 a mass demonstration won the restoration
of a minimum tariff of payments, but it was soon repudiated
by the merchants. In November, at a review of the National
Guard of Lyon, ill-feeling developed between the wealthier
members with an elaborate uniform and the artisans in
their ordinary clothes. The next day a crowd of several
hundred weavers started to go round the town proclaiming,
and enforcing, a strike. They were fired on and eight were
killed. This was the normal pattern for a revolutionary outbreak in nineteenth-century France. It set fire to Lyon.
The weavers rose as a man, barricaded the streets, descended from their quarter on the hillside of the Croix-Rousse.
They were joined by companies of the National Guard and
in pitched battle with the royal troops captured Lyon.
Having won their victory, they policed the city, set guards
on the Monnaie and the Recette Générale, and repressed
all looting, for these were Lyonnais, sober and serious
workers, master craftsmen, men of order. But of course not
quite of the prevailing order, as the government realized.
A large body of troops was despatched to Lyon, its National
Guard was dissolved, the prefect – who had been too reason-

able – was dismissed, and the tariff of prices revoked. The workers of Lyon were crushed, but not for good.

In Paris, at the same time, the effervescence assumed a different form. As always, political and ideological motivation was more evident than economic in the capital. There it had not been forgotten that the threat which had stimulated the July Revolution had been clericalism, and the struggle of clericalism and anti-clericalism took a little while after 1830 to settle down. At the outset a group of ardent Catholics had been stirred up by the July Revolution to envisage the possibility of a reconciliation of religion with liberty and to found a journal to advocate this. The leaders – it is not certain if there were any followers – were Lamennais, by now a republican, Lacordaire, a liberal, and Montalembert, a romantic medievalist. Their paper, *L'Avenir*, founded in October 1830, was abandoned in November 1831. While it lasted it had advocated, among other proposals, the abolition of censorship, freedom of education, universal suffrage, and the separation of Church and State. In 1832 the Encyclical *Mirari vos* pronounced the wickedness of all these ideas and the editors submitted to the verdict of the Pope.

Anti-clericalism was less easily brought under control, and it is not certain that all those in positions of power wanted it to be controlled. Whatever its deeper roots, anti-clericalism naturally appears above ground wherever the aspiration of priests to political power and the exercise of control over the life of society brings them into conflict with secular interests. The Church in France had overbid its hand in the twenties, so naturally it lost some tricks in the thirties.

Anti-clerical sentiments formed the excuse for a violent outbreak on 14 February 1831, when a Mass for the duc de Berry, assassinated ten years earlier, was held at the Church of Saint-Germain-l'Auxerrois, with white flags and fleurs-de-lys, a congregation of devout legitimists, and rows of aristocratic carriages with armorials waiting outside. It is difficult to believe that a crowd of rioters also found themselves there by accident, or that they unintentionally allowed the legitimists to depart without more than an ugly scene, before beginning the real attack. A detachment of National Guard which now arrived escorted the priests away through the mob, which was left to pull down and destroy images, crucifixes, and all the destructible furnishings of the church. Some of the rioters then made their way to the Archbishop's palace, next to Notre Dame, where a fine thirteenth-century building and a great library offered the prospect of even more enjoyable destruction. Books are always a temptation: they burn so well. The task was broken off when night fell, but was resumed the next day till the whole building had been demolished. In true revolutionary tradition mock religious rites were performed in the ruins. Similar scenes were witnessed in other towns, the authorities remaining neutral. Then, as rapidly as it had flared up, the agitation died down. The episode is a curious one. It is difficult to believe in the spontaneity of the outburst, but who organized it, and how did it spread through France? How far was there a deep-rooted and extensive anti-clericalism among the urban population, and how far was it artificially incited, the work of a mere handful stirred up by bourgeois anti-clericals? If we knew more about the provincial movements it might be possible at least to attempt to answer these questions.

Even the legitimists contributed to the prevailing disorder after 1830, with one feeble attempt to reverse the decision of July. The duchesse de Berry, mother of the legitimist heir, the young comte de Chambord, was the heroine of this romantic adventure. She travelled in disguise across France from Marseille, finding, like Bonnie Prince Charlie in similar circumstances, much profession of loyalty but little willingness to take up arms, until she reached the old centre of royalist resistance, the Vendée. There, a small rising was easily crushed. The duchess escaped and went into hiding but was captured later in the year. It then gradually became impossible for her to hide the fact that she was pregnant. Obviously this could not be a second *enfant du miracle*, and she had in the end to confess to the awful truth, that she was re-married to a minor Italian count. This ended the political significance of the romantic duchess. As a royalist supporter said, a mistake might have been forgiven the duchesse de Berry, a marriage excluded her from the royal family. This pathetic episode was the sum total of the Counter-revolution after 1830: things had certainly changed since 1789.

The last outbreak of violence linked with the July Revolution came in 1832, when the funeral of General Lamarque, a former Napoleonic general and a popular member of the Chamber of Deputies, was used by republicans and bonapartists – to whom legitimists joined themselves – as the excuse for an attempted insurrection in Paris. The army and the National Guard, both now well under government control, suppressed it at the cost of some 800 killed and wounded. After this it was clear that the revolutionary movement was over; indeed this miserable affair looks forward to the street affrays of the Third Republic rather than back to the great *journées* of 1789 and 1792.

The new régime might not have survived its growing pains if it had had to rely on its first government. Its leading figure, in so far as there was one, was the banker Lafitte, but his conduct of affairs was so notoriously incompetent that he had to resign. Since France could not yet afford the weak government that Louis-Philippe really preferred, power fell into the hands of the most forceful of the existing ministers. This was Casimir-Périer, who declared that his policy was to combine order with liberty; but there is no doubt that the emphasis was on the former. France, he said, must be governed. In the elections of July 1831, Casimir-Périer made it clear that his government had no intention of being neutral. The prefects were instructed to use all their influence to secure the return of suitable candidates, though everyone was so new and untried that they found it difficult to know who was suitable. However, the great majority in the new chamber was conservative and prepared to accept a strong hand so long as there seemed any danger of reaction or further revolution.

Of the two bankers who had been patrons, and perhaps financiers, of the liberal movement under Charles X, Lafitte inclined to the left, whereas Périer, who regarded 1830 as not a change of system but only of person, was a leader of the 'resistance' to any liberal concessions. Naturally, whereas Lafitte has left the reputation of a weak minister, Périer was able to justify his reputation as a strong man. The new President of the Council also found his task of pacifying France facilitated by the ending of the economic slump. Louis-Philippe, however, whose position was now becoming securer, was not altogether happy with a strong minister who kept him out of cabinet discussions, and it was perhaps rather a relief to him when the cholera epidemic, failing to observe the strict class discrimination of the Périer régime, carried off his prime minister in May 1832.

Although the struggle to put curbs on the revolution had now in effect been won, the republican secret societies were still agitating and there was a good deal of repressed popular discontent. The government determined to take the offensive. The popular associations were attacked by direct prohibitions, by extending penalties from the organizers to all members, and by transferring trials arising out of breaches of the laws against political associations to courts without juries. The debate on these proposals suggested that the prime motive behind the new law was the fear of political revolution. The insecurity of the régime was still such that all opposition seemed dangerous. Resistance, declared Guizot, is turned by the opposition leaders into revolution. Thiers described the opposition as an illegal government, prepared to use the associations to overthrow the legal government. And in fact the Society of the Rights of Man was planning an armed rising, and a secret committee was formed to organize it. But in the event the government itself was responsible for provoking the armed outbreak.

Lyon was once again the scene of the major disturbances. In February 1834 the silk merchants again reduced their rate of payment to the weavers. A ten-day strike failed and the silk weavers returned to work. The city was peaceful when the government arrested six leaders of the strike, and anticipating the opposition that this action was bound to arouse, sent 10,000 troops to occupy the strategic positions and chief buildings of Lyon. Sporadic rioting broke out, and as so often, the authorities only offered a weak resistance until the insurrection had thoroughly developed. This is often attributed to callous calculation; it seems more likely to have been due to a natural slowness to react, and perhaps to mere stupidity. The rising, having been allowed to develop, was then ruthlessly crushed. A merciless struggle went on for four days. The royal troops gradually forced their way back into the town, while the forts on the outskirts bombarded the rebel-held quarters.

At the news of the revolt of Lyon troubles also broke out in many other towns, but only in Paris was there an attempt at actual insurrection. There, in the quarter of the Marais, some desperate republicans and their followers erected barricades. But Paris had a large garrison, and a National Guard which feared social revolution and the revolt of the workers more than anything else. They descended on the tiny nucleus of revolution, crushed it without difficulty, and proceeded to engage in a little private massacre in the rue Transnonain. Daumier made one of his most pathetically effective cartoons of it. The government might defend the actions of its supporters on the plea that it was just that those who had appealed to force should perish by force. Another view might be that what had happened in Paris was an attempt to exploit the genuine economic grievances of the workers by a small faction of political republicans. And yet a third view is that the republicans had played into the hands of the authorities, who were not sorry to have the chance of damning the workers of Lyon as revolutionary republicans for their attempt to defend their standard of living, and the republicans of Paris as social revolutionaries because of their connexions with the workers' movement.

After the failure of this pathetic attempt at a revolution,

out of 3,000 prisoners rather over 100 were selected for trial – a moderate measure of repression compared with the sequel to social struggles later in the century, when class hatred had become much more intense. And after the danger, or supposed danger, was over, public sympathies began to veer on to the side of the accused, whose trial was thoroughly mismanaged. Twenty-eight of them escaped from prison; and apart from a number of sentences to deportation or imprisonment, most of the prisoners were only condemned to periods of police supervision. On the whole, in spite of the massacre of the rue Transnonain, the republicans had discredited themselves by the events of 1834 and the government had behaved with comparative moderation.

An attempted assassination of Louis-Philippe in July 1835, by a bomb explosion which killed several National Guards, other persons round the king, and spectators, strengthened the hand of the government further, for the assassin, a Corsican named Fieschi, had been assisted by two members of the Society for the Rights of Man. Steps were taken after this to check the incitements to violence in the republican press. The Charter of 1830 had abolished censorship, but this did not mean that the government was powerless in its relations with journalists. Political journals had still to deposit a substantial sum as caution money. Conviction on such charges as offering an affront to the king or holding the government up to contempt might bring a fine of 1,000 francs, accompanied by a term of imprisonment for the editor. On the other hand, though juries were chosen only from the wealthy class which possessed the right of franchise, they had a regrettable tendency to acquit journalists charged with press offences. Louis-Philippe and his government continued to be showered with insults, and portrayed in venomous caricature by Daumier, Grandville, and other less brilliant but equally bitter cartoonists.

Casimir-Périer, from whom Louis-Philippe had been relieved by the hand of fate, was succeeded by a 'doctrinaire' ministry, including the able conservative peer

Broglie, Thiers, and Guizot, with a 'non-political' general, Marshal Soult, as nominal head. This was still much too strong a government for a king who wanted to hold the reins himself. A palace intrigue eliminated Broglie in April 1834, but after nearly a year of confusion he returned in March 1835, making the condition, like Casimir-Périer, that the cabinet should not meet in the presence of the King. But Broglie's authoritarian style was as little to the liking of the Parliament as of the king, and in February 1836 he lost his majority again. Louis-Philippe had now to split Thiers and Guizot, which he did by inviting Thiers to form a ministry. It lasted only six months; the king broke with Thiers over foreign policy, and then called on Molé, a peer who had served Bonaparte and the Bourbons in turn, and was equally willing to serve the house of Orleans. He was an official and a capable one, not a statesman; but it was an official that Louis-Philippe wanted, for, as he put it in rather unkingly language, '*c'est moi qui mène le fiacre.*' The series of events that began in July 1830 may be said to have been completed now, with all political or social opposition to the new monarchy driven underground, and Louis-Philippe himself the real head of his own government.

4. LOUIS-PHILIPPE

THE one and only Orleanist king came to the throne at the age of fifty-seven. He was already sixteen in 1789 and had been educated in the sentimental philanthropy of the *ancien régime* by Mme de Genlis. His presence in the armies of the Revolution provided Orleanist propagandists with the material for a military reputation, which somehow never stuck. An *émigré* in 1793, as the son of Philippe Égalité and an officer of the revolutionary army, he could hardly seek refuge among the allies. Wanderings in neutral countries, such as Switzerland, Scandinavia, the United States, and disagreements with Great Britain, occupied the next twenty years, leaving him a man of neither Revolution nor

Counter-revolution, a suitable king for a régime of the *juste milieu*; leaving him also with a love of wealth and power which were concealed beneath habits of bourgeois modesty. What he lacked was style. Louis-Philippe had neither the decadent grace of the eighteenth century nor the romantic panache of the nineteenth. He was gossiping, fussy, undignified, and with his pear-shaped face a gift to caricaturists. Above all, he was already ageing when he came to the throne. The skill and determination he showed in 1830–1 too soon turned into smug complacency and self-satisfied intrigue.

Yet Louis-Philippe had a good deal over which he might well feel self-satisfied. He had a model queen in Marie-Amélie of the Sicilian Bourbons, and five sons – Joinville, Orléans, Nemours, Aumale, Montpensier – handsome, distinguished, able in their different fields, and damned for ever by the wit who called them a family of brilliant second lieutenants. Within ten years he had established himself so firmly on the throne that his dynasty seemed secure. Legitimism had ceased to be a political force; republicanism was discredited among all proper-minded people and reduced to an underground intrigue; and that Bonapartism was not to be taken seriously had been shown when it could not even make a bid for power in 1830, as well as by the Strasbourg fiasco of Louis Napoleon in 1836, of which more later.

Hopes of a Napoleonic restoration apparently ended with the death of the young duc de Reichstadt, son and heir of the Emperor, *l'Aiglon* of romantic legend, in 1832. So innocuous did the Bonapartist legend seem, that the régime even tried to exploit it. Thiers filled in the gaps in his political activity with the composition of his *History of the Consulate and the Empire*. In 1833 Napoleon I was put back on the Vendôme column, though in civil attire. And in 1840 Joinville was sent to fetch the Emperor's remains from St Helena for reburial in the Invalides. The second fiasco of Louis Napoleon, this time in the form of a day excursion to Boulogne in 1840, showed once more that Bonapartism was not a force in France. Orleanist politics could pursue their placid if erratic course undisturbed by any fear of rapids ahead.

The absence of any effective nucleus of opposition was perhaps one reason for the weakness of Louis-Philippe's governments. The other was his own aversion from ministers with policies of their own. Molé was obviously no more than a stop-gap. With all the great figures in parliament ranged against him, his tenure of office was uncertain. In 1839 he appealed to the electorate, and in spite of all that official pressure could do, lost some thirty seats. The king had to look for a successor. He was in the dilemma of George III: weak ministers could not control parliament, and strong ministers pursued their own policies. Soult reappeared transiently, then Thiers, but once again foreign policy was the apple of discord. Since 1832 Louis-Philippe had been the effective manager of French foreign policy. He prided himself on his knowledge of Europe and his success in coping with its problems, not without some justification. He had kept the peace, brought about a *rapprochement* between France and the other great powers, played his part in solving the Belgian problem satisfactorily, and maintained French prestige.

Unfortunately he had given one hostage to fortune by encouraging Mehemet Ali's revolt against the authority of the Sultan. French opinion, tending to divide the world between friends of France and others, enthusiastically supported the Pasha of Egypt. But the success of Mehemet Ali, when war with Turkey broke out again in 1839, alarmed the other great powers, which in July 1840 issued an ultimatum calling on him to cease hostilities or face military intervention. French opinion was indignant. Thiers was all for war in defence of the French protégé, though it would be without an ally and against the four other great powers. France had a good deal at stake. With officers, teachers, business men, and loans, she was the dominating influence in the Egypt of Mehemet Ali, and stood to gain or lose a major position in the Near East according as Mehemet

Ali succeeded or failed. Thiers was the minister for a foreign policy that recalled the ambitions of Napoleon. On the other hand, the British government saw French influence in the Ottoman Empire as a menace to vital British interests. To British representatives Thiers replied that France would never tolerate the use of force by the other European powers against Mehemet Ali. This has been regarded as a policy of bluff, though it was one that might have led to war. But when British and Turkish troops intervened in Syria, and the local population turned against the occupying Egyptian forces, Thiers realized that he had over-estimated the strength of Mehemet Ali and accepted the situation. Having done so, he still wanted to save his face by making the threatening and now meaningless gesture of inserting a bellicose statement in the speech from the throne in October. This was too much for Louis-Philippe, who had been watching with increasing alarm Thiers' policy of going to the brink of war before he withdrew. He now exercised his influence in the Chamber to overthrow Thiers.

The game of general post that the king had been playing with his governments since 1832 was resumed with the appointment of Guizot as Minister of Foreign Affairs and Soult as nominal President of the Council. Contrary to all expectation, however, the new ministry was to last, with minor changes, to the final catastrophe. Guizot was perhaps the most intelligent and high-minded minister ever to preside over the ruin of a political system. A Protestant, with all the austerity of a French Huguenot, he accepted the politics of wealth and influence; a distinguished historian with profound critical powers, who envisaged behind changing circumstances the movement of great historical forces and the evolution and conflict of classes, he behaved as if he thought his own régime could somehow escape from historical fatality; a doctrinaire who had asserted mildly liberal principles under the Restoration, he never moved beyond the narrowest interpretation of them when he was in power.

Distain for all opposition, and a certain noble serenity,

insulated him from the effects of the attacks that were continually made on him, but he gave the impression of rather more deviousness than seems compatible with his elevated character. He was undoubtedly a man of remarkable intellectual calibre, but one must not exaggerate the political skill that was shown by his long tenure of power; Guizot was free from the weakness which had undermined previous ministers – the intrigues of the king – for Louis-Philippe had found a minister who was indispensable to him. As for the support of parliament and the country, that was guaranteed by the electoral system. Each constituency had its college, many as small as 150 voters, and easily managed by the administration. The whole conduct of the elections was in the hands of the prefects, subprefects, and *maires*, one of whose chief functions was to secure the return of the official candidate. They practised every form of chicanery that was possible before the Second Empire turned the system of official candidatures into a fine art, though perhaps only fully in the election of 1846. Not that it mattered much: the propertied class was satisfied so long as its own wealth and social position were safeguarded. It was entirely content with a profoundly conservative régime that proposed no changes at home, and only such adventures abroad as were likely to involve no new taxes.

True, a new French Empire was founded under the constitutional monarchy, but this was the result more of the force of inertia than of considered policy. The Orleanist monarchy saw no profit or prestige in colonies, and if the forward movement begun under the Bourbon Restoration did not cease, this was due rather to the officials than to the ministers. After the first step had been taken with the attack on Algiers more determination was needed to stop the slow forward movement than to continue it. From the three initial conquests of Algiers, Oran, and Bône, French occupation was gradually extended until, in 1839, the Arab chief Abd-el-Kader abandoned his treaty and took to arms in the endeavour to check its progress. Bugeaud, promoted corporal on the battle-field of Austerlitz, who had already had much experience of fighting in Algiers, was put in charge by Guizot. He dealt with the scattered threat of Arab warfare by lightening the equipment of his troops and organizing them in mobile columns. He had under his command Cavaignac, Changarnier, Lamoricière, and the king's son Aumale, a group of able subordinates, but it took an army of some 88,000 men and several years campaigning before Abd-el-Kader was finally defeated and captured in 1847. The war was bloody and barbarous on both sides. The Algerians massacred their prisoners; the French destroyed crops, orchards, villages, and asphyxiated 600 men, women, and children, who had taken refuge in a cave. Behind the fighting, colonization was slowly but steadily proceeding. By 1847 Algeria had 109,000 Europeans, about half of them French, and the new French Empire, with its promises and problems, was solidly founded. It was the achievement of the constitutional monarchy, even though Louis-Philippe had taken no particular interest in it himself.

Foreign policy was what Louis-Philippe regarded as his special expertise, for he knew Europe well, though he knew it as an exile. Yet he had no luck in international affairs after the initial and well-deserved success over Belgium. The trouble was that, while he was wisely determined not to get involved in war, he hoped to collect some useful trophies at a cheaper price. As the failure of the gamble on Mehemet Ali showed, this was not possible. Louis-Philippe always felt something of an outsider among the sovereigns of Europe. If Victor Hugo's account of a conversation of 1844 is to be believed, the king confessed to a belief that both France and its ruler were hated by the kings of Europe, and he himself even more than France. 'I tell you frankly, they hate me because I am an Orleans, and they hate me for myself.'

This was perhaps the reason for the *rapprochement* with Great Britain, though to call it an entente is to stretch the meaning of the term. Superficially friendly relations were patched up after the failure of Mehemet Ali and the dismissal of Thiers. Queen Victoria paid a state visit to Louis-Philippe in 1843, when she seems to have been mostly impressed with the muddle and lack of dignity of the French Court. The French king repaid the visit the following year.

Essentially the so-called Franco-British entente was no more than an expression of the personal liking and mutual trust of the French and English ministers, Guizot and Aberdeen. It was not even proof against a trivial dispute in a Pacific island, which arose out of the rivalry of French and English missionaries in Tahiti, and the not altogether incomprehensible habit of the local ruler of accepting the protectorate of whichever power had last sent a gun-boat there. An ambitious English missionary named Pritchard, who believed that the flag followed the Bible, attempted to interfere with this amicable arrangement and got himself expelled by the French in 1844. This produced much British indignation, for these were the days of *civis Britannus sum*. Under pressure from the Foreign Office, the French government expressed its regret, which aroused corresponding French wrath. In 1847, the French protectorate was recognized, which restored the situation as it had been before the Pritchard affair, but rumblings of discontent continued. As for the shadowy entente, that vanished when Palmerston returned to the Foreign Office in 1846.

Anglo-French rivalry had been particularly evident in the affairs of Spain, where marriage with the young queen Isabella was a political triumph which either the house of Coburg or that of Orleans might aspire to. Since either could have been happy with her, it was decided, in September 1843, that by a mutual renunciation neither should enjoy the prize. But Guizot, who was being out-manoeuvred by Palmerston, had to take counter-measures. He arranged a double marriage of the duc de Montpensier, son of Louis-Philippe, with the sister of Isabella, while the queen of Spain herself was to marry her cousin. Thus it was assumed that in due course there would be an Orleanist heir to the

Spanish throne. However, there must have been a mis-calculation somewhere, for Isabella had a son and the whole intrigue came to nothing.

The lack of a glorious foreign policy, along with a supposed revival of Bonapartist sentiment, have been accounted main factors in the failure of the Orleanist monarchy. It will be more convenient to discuss the part played, or not played, by the 'Napoleonic legend', and the attempts of Louis Napoleon Bonaparte, at Strasbourg in 1836 and Boulogne in 1840, to exploit it, at a later stage. As for the lack of a glorious foreign policy, the belief that this was a cause of the revolution in 1848 may go back to a phrase of Lamartine, in 1839, which has had only too much success, – '*La France est une nation qui s'ennuie*'; but there is no reason to suppose that the poet was complaining of the absence of military glory. Like so many young literary men a royalist under the Restoration, Lamartine had become a liberal by 1830, and under the Orleanist monarchy was converted to the principle of universal suffrage, in reaction against the narrow and selfish plutocracy that ruled France. There was a cleavage growing up in France, not so much between the two nations of Disraeli's *Sybil*, for, unlike Great Britain, France had not yet come anywhere near that stage of industrial development, but between the mind and heart and ideals of France and its political and social structure. Genius was bored, as it normally is, with the rule of vested interests. Louis-Philippe had nothing to offer to a romantic generation.

5. AN AGE OF IDEALISM

THE politics and economics of the July Monarchy were perhaps no more sordid than such things usually are: if they seemed so it was because this was a generation of unex-ampled idealism, of romantic and not always rational hopes or despairs, and of a widely diffused religiosity which was now spilling over the bounds of the Catholic revival, producing a crop of new cults in England and America, and in France becoming closely linked with schemes for social regeneration.

In the history of art and literature there is no dividing line at 1830. Theocracy, of course, became a memory then; the romantic writers who had been royalists, like Hugo and Lamartine, now moved over to liberalism; and the humanitarian themes of the Enlightenment were resumed, though with a more emotional tone infused into them by the revival of religious feeling, the new sense of history, and the cult of the people. Politically, romanticism may be said to have migrated to the opposition in 1830, though a simple formula like this can hardly do justice to such a complex movement, with such diverse sources.

The strongest influence over the nascent romantic movement had been that of Rousseau, who set the tradition of romantic melancholy, self-enquiry, reverie, which was continued by Bernardin de Saint-Pierre and Chateaubriand. Lamartine, in the *Méditations* of 1820, brought the Rousseauist spirit of soul-searching, sorrow for lost love, search for religious consolation, into poetry. There was something deeper and more classic in the pessimism of Alfred de Vigny; and the lyrical spirit was to be carried on in the sentimental, easy, and attractive poems of Alfred de Musset, in the prose of Théophile Gautier, who inspired the ballet *Giselle* (1841), which remains the perfect expression of a certain romantic feeling, and in the charm of the rustic Berrichon romances of George Sand.

But this muted note was not the characteristic or the dominant one in French romanticism. More exotic influences were also at work. Normally, in the history of art and literature, inspiration has come from France and spread to the rest of Europe; but the French spirit has been too self-contained and insular, and the French too unwilling to read foreign languages, for much to be accepted back in return. The Emigration and the Empire temporarily changed this situation. Mme de Staël's *De l'Allemagne* in 1810 introduced France to *Sturm und Drang*. Shakespeare was adapted for the

French stage in the late twenties by Alfred de Vigny. Gérard de Nerval translated Faust in 1828. One cannot pretend that the romantic drama which flowered in France under these influences was quite up to the level of Shakespeare or Goethe. It was closer to, and more directly influenced by, the historical novels of Sir Walter Scott, which had a great vogue in France under the Restoration, and inspired in 1826 the austere *Cinq-Mars* of de Vigny, in 1829 the *Chronique de Charles IX* of Mérimée, and, going back to the Middle Ages, that astonishing, ridiculous, and wonderful source-book of romantic clichés, *Notre-Dame de Paris* by Victor Hugo, in 1831.

The historical movement was also evident in painting. Delacroix painted scenes from recent and ancient history – the *Massacre of Scio* (1824) or the *Death of Sardanapalus* (1829) – with brilliant colour and drama. Géricault, as in his most famous painting, the *Raft of the Medusa* (1819), drew scenes of violent action and death. With Daumier romantic art became the expression of the social conscience and abandoned the Middle Ages.

Romantic medievalism had its most disastrous effects in architecture. The destruction of famous medieval buildings, including Cluny, mother house of the Benedictine Order and greatest abbey of medieval France, aroused the indignation of both romantic and religious medievalists. Led by Montalembert and Victor Hugo, a press campaign produced a Commission on National Monuments, with Prosper Mérimée as its secretary. The chief living authority on medieval architecture, Viollet-le-Duc, was put in charge of the work of preservation. Alas, the most complete neglect would have been more salutary. A new Vandal invasion could not have done worse, for that would merely have pulled down whereas Viollet-le-Duc also rebuilt. Moreover he did not work alone but had his emulators. Abadie raged through the West, restoring: at Angoulême he dealt with the deficiencies of the cathedral by taking down everything that was not text-book thirteenth-century style – this was most of the cathedral – and rebuilding it as he thought it ought to have been built if the medieval architects had read the right text-books.

In literature and art the more ridiculous aspects of romantic medievalism, which was never married very happily to French traditions, can easily be overstressed. In contemporary life it was linked with an awakening of the social conscience. For all its enlightenment and humanitarianism, the eighteenth century never really faced the problem of poverty; perhaps it believed, with the Church, that the poor we shall always have with us. Particularly after the July Revolution, however, the humanitarian tradition of the Enlightenment combined with a new, and largely Rousseauist, religious influence, to make the amelioration of the condition of the poor the central object of social thought. 'Religion', wrote Saint-Simon in his *Nouveau Christianisme*, 'should direct society towards the great end of the most rapid amelioration possible of the lot of the poorest class.' The goodness of the people became a romantic doctrine, and the people was now no longer the idealized peasantry and honest craftsmen of the Rousseauist illusion, still surviving in the rustic idylls of George Sand, but the ragged and starving populace of Paris. They appeared in medieval guise in Hugo's *Notre-Dame*, and in a more contemporary costume in Eugène Sue's serial, *Les Mystères de Paris*. The fellowship of poet and pauper was exemplified by de Vigny, himself from a family of lesser nobility ruined by the Revolution, in his play *Chatterton* (1835), in which also can be detected the first shots in the war that was now beginning between the artist or man of letters and bourgeois society.

Though there was much idealistic republicanism, the battle was against a social order based almost exclusively upon distinctions of wealth, rather than against the monarchy as such. True, Louis-Philippe was for many the symbol of this social order, but the prosaic nature of the Orleanist monarchy has been exaggerated. The sons of Louis-Philippe were, in their various ways, a surprisingly intelligent and cultured group of men. The heir to the throne, the duc d'Orléans, had genuine literary interests;

his duchess, the adorable Hélène, was an admirer and patron of Victor Hugo. It was through her influence that Hugo became one of the exceptional men of literary genius in France to be admitted to the Académie Française before he was moribund, if at all, and it was through the duchess that he became a peer of France. He never forgot his debt to the house of Orleans or wrote ill of Louis-Philippe.

The cartoonists were less sparing of the king. The editor of *Charivari* fought a running battle with the censorship, and if a great cartoonist like Daumier experienced short prison sentences, it did not prevent him from creating a gallery of sub-human figures out of the Orleanist officials, judges, lawyers, and financiers. The character who symbolized the whole régime was taken from an inferior play about an amoral adventurer named Robert Macaire, who was built up by the great actor of the period, Frédéric Lemaître, into a monster of cynical rascality, and portrayed by Daumier as an out-at-elbows ruffian. He became the type of a society on the make, with no conscience, no pity, no standards of conduct. On a higher literary level we have the long series of novels that make up Balzac's *Comédie humaine*, which exhibits a society dominated by money, a world of men of property like the Forsytes without their principles. Oddly enough, Balzac himself, with his grandiose ideas, frantic struggle for fortune, financial adventures, bankruptcies, passionate love affairs, and craving for luxury, was a man of his age almost to exaggeration, and like so many of his own characters, and for the same reason, he was a believer in authority and the social function of religion.

The wealth of the rich might have seemed less blatant if it had not been for the equally unconcealed misery of the masses, particularly in Paris. The population of France grew from some 29 millions in 1815 to nearly 36 millions in 1851, and since the countryside already supported as many as it could under existing conditions, the bulk of the increase took refuge in the towns, particularly Paris. There was as yet no industrial development in France equal to providing them with work. Paris in 1848 had nearly 65,000 industrial undertakings, of which only 7,000 employed more than 10 workers. It is probable that the standard of living of the urban populace had deteriorated drastically since the eighteenth century. The government, dominated by laissez-faire ideas, as well as by class interests, made no attempt to improve conditions.

In the third and fourth decades of the century many writers, a class in which the social conscience seems to have been more lively than in others, were acutely aware of the conjunction of extreme wealth with dire poverty. They were passing over from humanitarian sympathy to aggressive criticism of the social order and positive proposals for a new and better one. Thus Lamennais, under the Restoration a leading Catholic apologist and offered a Cardinal's hat which he wisely declined, found after 1830 that there was no room for his liberal ideas inside the Church. His *Paroles d'un croyant* marked the breach with Rome and he then moved on from religious heterodoxy to political liberalism. The people was the new Messiah, and Lamennais wrote passionately of its sufferings in *Le Livre du peuple* of 1841: 'They have said you were a flock and that they were your shepherds; you, the beasts; they, the men. Theirs, therefore, your fleece, your milk, your flesh. Pasture under their crook and multiply, to warm their limbs, quench their thirst, and satisfy their hunger.'

Lamennais himself did not offer any remedy for social injustice other than liberal democracy, though he was one of the founders of Catholic social reform. But this was a period of intense and original social speculation, in which socialist ideals first burgeoned. The greatest name to be mentioned in this connexion is that of the comte de Saint-Simon, of *ancien régime* nobility, who had fought in the war of American Independence and became an ardent revolutionary in 1789. His enthusiasm was not lessened when he made a fortune by speculating in nationalized property. An extravagant way of life under the Directory ruined him and he turned to plans for social regeneration. Among his collaborators were the young historian Augustin Thierry and the founder of positive philosophy, Auguste Comte. These fell away, but when Saint-Simon died in 1825, he left behind him a small band of disciples, including Hippolyte Carnot, future minister of the Second Republic, Michel Chevalier, the economist and later adviser of Napoleon III, and the Péreire brothers, the financiers of the Second Empire. The leadership of the group, which was rapidly developing into a Saint-Simonian Church, was taken over by the 'père' Enfantin, who turned it into one of the many nineteenth-century religions of love, and whose practical exercises in that direction brought him into conflict with the law. The real importance of the ideas of Saint-Simon was only to appear under the Second Empire.

Another social theorist whose writings pre-date 1830 was Fourier, in whom, as in the whole movement of which he is not the least eccentric representative, the influence of Rousseau is marked. The evils of civilization and the inability of government to remedy them are traced to property; the emphasis has now shifted from politics to economics. The social compact is seen as guaranteeing the rich the enjoyment of their wealth and impunity for their crimes. Fourier's solution was based – and this again indicated a new century – on new psychological principles, in which the passions were more important than the reason. He saw human nature as based on the *papillonne* or principle of variety, and to cater for this each man should take many jobs, not merely in his life but in each day. Fourier's new society was to be organized in Phalanges – self-contained communities which were to produce, on a principle of co-property, all that they consumed. The practical significance of these ideas was slight. Fourier, like nearly all the socialist or utopian writers of the period, was not as mad as he sounds, but he was planning for a pre-industrial world.

Among others, Buchez, the co-editor of the forty-volume *Histoire parlementaire de la révolution française*, combined Christianity and cooperation in the name of science. Pierre Leroux, a former Saint-Simonian, developed the idea of a religion of humanity. Cabet, who was influenced by

Owenite ideas from England as well as by a Rousseauist faith in the goodness of human nature, described a Utopian community in his *Voyage en Icarie*, and subsequently tried to realize it in America. Louis Blanc, a journalist, produced the idea with the most immediate appeal. His *Organisation du travail*, in 1839, was a simple but effective assertion of the 'right to work', and proposed to put it into practice by state intervention on the labour market. The most influential of all these socialist writers in the long run, as well as the most striking personality, was the working printer Proudhon, who became the *bête-noire* of the bourgeois by his work *Qu'est-ce que la propriété?* (1840), in which he gave the answer to his own question – '*C'est le vol*'. But his great influence on the French labour and socialist movements came later in the century.

The social thought of the period is a remarkable mixture of sense and nonsense, of a realistic appreciation of social evils combined with the proposal of sometimes fantastically utopian solutions. The element of escapism that is to be detected in this literature is also to be seen in the novels of adventure that proliferated at the time, exploiting the new medium of newspaper serials. Alexandre Dumas ransacked history for picturesque periods; Eugène Sue found mysteries in Paris; Mérimée and Balzac combined romanesque themes with realistic detail. Béranger played a part, by his popular lyrics, in turning the propaganda of the First Empire into a Napoleonic legend.

Yet even in the hey-day of the Romantic movement there were signs that it would not last. Stendhal's *Le Rouge et le Noir* and *La Chartreuse de Parme* are packed with romantic detail, but the spirit of their author was closer to that of the eighteenth century. Gautier's *Mademoiselle de Maupin* belongs to the same perverse genre as *Les Liaisons dangereuses*. In 1838 a young actress, Rachel, played Racine in a way that swept the trivialities of romantic drama off the boards. And already, while the romantic wave seemed to be engulfing everything, signs of a new attitude were appearing. Théophile Gautier whom Lanson has described as the pivot of French literature in the nineteenth century, proclaimed the new gospel of 'art for art's sake' as early as a preface of 1832. Gérard de Nerval looked back to the *illuminés* of the eighteenth century and forward to the symbolists. That literature was not unaffected by the current preoccupation with the social problem can be seen in the novels of Hugo, Balzac, Sue, George Sand; and the first attempt at a scientific treatment of it brought the beginning of sociological thought, particularly in the work of Auguste Comte. He began as a teacher of mathematics and a disciple of Saint-Simon, but soon broke away and devoted the remainder of his life to developing the school of Positivism, which by an equal misconception of the nature of science and of religion, offered a new secular religion of science to those who had lost their traditional faith but could not manage without an inspired teacher and at least one form of certainty. More distinguished thinkers, like Renan and Taine, experienced strongly the influence of Comte's positivism, which has continued to exercise a spell over the French mind.

However wild or *a priori* much of the social thinking of the first half of the nineteenth century in France was, at least men were speculating about the problems of society. But between this thought and the policies of government there was an almost impassable gulf. The men who ruled France were not economically minded, and their electorate, as has been said, was largely one of landed proprietors. Hence the ruling élite was not likely to be interested in industrial development; and the comparative backwardness of French social conditions and economic development, for which the social structure of the *ancien régime* and the diversions of the Revolution and the Empire were in part responsible, continued under the so-called bourgeois monarchy.

A glance at some figures will easily substantiate this statement. The horse power at the service of French industry in 1832 was under 1,000; by 1848 it had multiplied by nearly seven times, but in Great Britain six times as much horse power had already been employed in the twenties. In 1790 French production of coal was about one-twentieth of that of Great Britain. Its production increased by about three times under the July Monarchy, but it was still not sufficient to satisfy even the modest needs of France. The amount of iron ore mined more than doubled; but behind a high protective tariff the price of iron was far higher than in Great Britain and production far lower. Modern methods were only gradually introduced in smelting. The last charcoal furnace in France ceased production in the course of the First World War.

More progress was made in transport but adequate capital for its development was lacking. There was a historical reason for this. The provision of highways and bridges in France had always been the prerogative of the public service of the Ponts et Chaussées, and it was traditional for the state to finance them. Under the July Monarchy the nation demanded improved means of transport and the government was in fact prepared to go a long way towards meeting this demand. It could only do so, however, by government expenditure; and as fast as the announcement of a programme of public works aroused support, the finance necessary to pay for them aroused opposition. Moreover, since the wealthy class which formed the narrow electorate also included those who contracted for the works, suspicions of corruption, which were often too well founded, were naturally aroused. Some progress, of course, was made. A law of 1836 on the construction and upkeep of local roads was of considerable benefit to the rural population; and the length of canals in use doubled under the July Monarchy.

Railways were developed very slowly and with a good deal of discouragement from above. When a line was projected from Paris to Saint-Germain, Thiers declared it might be worth constructing as an amusement for the Parisians; and the scientist Arago warned against the menace to human health involved in travelling by rail. Private capital was unwilling to risk itself in the construction of railways; while the Charter blocked the spending of public money on them. In 1842 a compromise was reached by which the state should buy the land, and plan and lay out the lines, while private capital supplied the actual rails and rolling-stock. There followed, from 1844 to 1846, the first French railway mania. It was of short duration and was followed by a collapse of railway shares and a financial crisis. Too many of the new lines, indeed, had been constructed to serve the interests of local politicians rather than economic demand. In 1848 many of the little local lines were bankrupt, and France had 1,921 kilometres of railways, compared with 3,424 in Prussia and 6,349 in Great Britain.

The first half of the nineteenth century in Great Britain has been described as the period of the race between population and industrialization. In France, while population was increasing only slowly, the level of production was rising even more slowly. Inevitably the standard of living fell and the material for a social revolution piled up, at least in the large towns. A bad harvest or a slump in business would produce a critical situation. Economic factors do not make revolutions by themselves, however, and to understand how the Orleanist régime met its fate we must turn back to politics.

For all the apparent strength of the Guizot administration, it was attacked with increasing vehemence from both left and right – this should not have surprised a régime which claimed to represent the *juste milieu*. The attack from the right took the form of a challenge to its educational policy. The quarrel was bound to become acute with the progress of both religious and state systems of schools. The achievement of the Restoration in education has seldom been adequately appreciated. A decree of 1816 laid it down that there should be a school in every commune and that education should be free for the children of parents who could not afford to pay. This represented an ideal rather than a fact, but by 1820 out of 44,000 communes there were schools in 24,000, a great advance on the previous situation.

The last government of Charles X issued an abortive law reorganizing the teaching service. Guizot, in 1833, repeated the effort in a law which has been called the first charter of primary education in France. Each commune, or group of neighbouring communes, was to have a primary school, and each department, or group of departments, a training college for elementary school-teachers, the *école normale primaire*. Between 1830 and 1848 the number of *écoles normales* grew from 12 to 47. Secondary schools were obligatory in the chief towns of each department, and in all towns with more than 6,000 inhabitants. These schools were either conducted by lay *instituteurs*, teachers who had to have a certificate from a training college, or by brothers of a religious order who were exempted from the requirement. This privilege of the religious schools of course ensured that the state schools would gradually come to be educationally superior. At the same time, by putting the teachers under rigid local and central control, the law of Guizot ensured that they could only escape from the control of the Church by falling under that of the state.

The importance of the rôle of the teachers in inculcating law and order and a proper respect for the powers that be was recognized from the beginning, recognized that is in principle, but not in material recompense. Guizot's circular to the teachers in 1833 was engagingly frank on this point. 'A profound sentiment of the importance of his work must sustain and animate the teacher,' he wrote; 'the austere pleasure of having served mankind and contributed to the public weal must be the worthy payment which his conscience alone gives him. It is his glory to use himself up in sacrifices and to expect his reward only from God.' This was true to the facts, if tactless; but a class of underpaid teachers, with at least more instruction than the petty local tyrants of Church and State who rendered them fully conscious of their social and financial inferiority, was not in fact likely to provide a cement of society.

Of course the more schools there were, the more intense became the competition between Church and State for the control of them. The July Monarchy had started off, as we have seen, to the accompaniment of a violent anti-clerical reaction against the clericalism of the Restoration. The affiliations of the Church, moreover, were naturally with the divine-right monarchy and therefore with the legitimists. By 1841, when the new Archbishop of Paris, Mgr Affre, paid an official visit to the king, relations between Church and State seemed much ameliorated; but a strong faction in the Church, led by the clerical journalist Louis Veuillot and the *Univers*, persistently agitated against what was called the 'University monopoly' of education. The parties of the left retaliated by reviving the Jesuit bogey. In 1843 Michelet and Edgar Quinet published jointly the courses they had given at the Collège de France under the title *Des jésuites*; but the clerical campaign, organized by the Catholic writer Montalembert, was the more effective.

The government offered a new law on education in 1844, making various concessions. Quinet's lectures were suppressed. Guizot brought himself to declare, in 1846, that children belonged to the family before the State, and that the State did not claim the exclusive right of education: religion also had its rights. Unfortunately clerical ambitions had grown with the success of the clerical propaganda, and it turned out that the new educational law proposed by the government, because it provided definitions where there had previously been laxity, threatened to make the situation of clerical education worse instead of better. Moreover the anti-Jesuit campaign had unexpected success. Montalembert and the party of 'liberty of education' were dissatisfied. Legitimism, which was also practically invariably ardently Catholic, remained unreconciled to the rule of Louis-Philippe. Religious opinion was in no state of mind to support the régime in an emergency, if one occurred.

On the other side, the left, so badly defeated in the early thirties, had been continuing its apparently hopeless opposition in the press and at the polls. The *National*, edited by Armand Marrast, denounced the corruption of the political system unceasingly, though it only called for moderate and peaceful reforms. Those for whom it was too moderate, inspired by the eloquent young lawyer, Ledru-Rollin, the rising hope of the more advanced reformers, founded, in 1843, the *Réforme*, as an organ of more democratic opinion. The radicals were now rallying their forces for the first time since the disaster of 1834, and in the demand for universal suffrage they had found a principle on which to unite.

Though Ledru-Rollin, surprisingly, given such a narrow franchise, secured election to the Chamber of Deputies, the parliamentary opposition as a whole had really more quarrel with the personnel than with the system of government. In 1845 Odilon Barrot and Thiers, tired of seeing another minister instead of themselves in office for the unexampled space of nearly five years, joined forces on a programme of electoral and parliamentary reform. It seemed the only way to shift Guizot, and it gave them the opportunity to join in the cry, always popular in France, of corruption.

In 1846 Guizot appealed confidently to a satisfied electorate, which hardly needed the nips and nudgings of the prefects to be gathered safely into the fold. The governmental machine could congratulate itself on a notable triumph when, after the elections, the address from the throne was accepted by a vote of 248 to 84. The majority was indeed almost too large for its own good. There were too many 'progressive conservatives', like de Tocqueville, in its ranks – enough in fact to elect an opposition candidate as vice-president of the chamber. The awkward subject of parliamentary reform and the extension of the franchise reappeared, though the government produced the – to it – decisive argument that if the country – that is the existing privileged class of electors – had wanted the franchise to be extended, it would have shown this in the election. Guizot revealed behind the demand for the extension of the franchise the terrifying shadow of universal suffrage, and made the classic pronouncement, '*Il n'y aura pas de jour pour le suffrage universel.*'

The cry of corruption was still the most effective weapon that the opposition had, and though there is no reason to suppose that the Guizot régime was any more corrupt than those which preceded or followed it, circumstances enabled this cry to be exploited effectively at what was to be a critical time. A criminal trial in 1847 brought out in evidence the correspondence of a former Minister of War, which revealed large payments, for the purpose of securing industrial concessions, to the then Minister of Public Works, Teste, now President of the Appeal Court and a peer of France. Teste was prosecuted and attempted suicide. Both of the former ministers were condemned to civic degradation and three years in prison.

This was followed by the affair of the duc de Praslin, who battered his wife to death for love of an English governess. Brought to trial before the peers, he succeeded in committing suicide with arsenic. Together these cases were taken as a revelation of the manner of life of the governing class, which itself had its confidence sapped by such apparent justification for the continual denunciations of corruption to which it was subjected.

Meanwhile the parliamentary opposition, seeing how hopeless the situation was in the Chamber, determined to carry the campaign to the country. In July 1847 it organized the first of a series of political banquets, at which leading orators denounced the government, made much play with corruption, and called for parliamentary reform. Thiers, who abstained from the banquets, was himself conducting an unrestrained campaign of speeches in the Chamber against the foreign policy of Guizot. The minister and the king, confident in their parliamentary majority and forgetting how little it really represented in the country, did not weaken before the verbal attacks from all sides. In January 1848 they prohibited further banquets, and the opposition, now becoming a little alarmed at its own boldness, but unwilling to lose face by yielding too obviously, made a private arrangement with the authorities. Its supporters were to assemble for the banquet, but to accept a police order to disperse peaceably, and the case would then be tried in the courts. This was very reasonable for it was really only a squabble between different factions in the small governing class. Banqueteers do not come from the ranks of the disinherited, and the opposition only wished to exert sufficient pressure to put themselves and their friends in, and Guizot and his friends out.

But while the parliamentary leaders were preparing to retreat, their followers were pressing forward. The two journals, the *National* and the *Réforme*, were the centres of a more determined agitation. They called on the people of Paris to take up the struggle that the deputies had abandoned. This was to introduce a factor into the situation which on all sides had been curiously ignored. It is a striking comment on the class structure of France that the governing class, engaged in its political rivalries, does not appear to have thought that the condition of the people was anything that needed to be taken into consideration.

A bad harvest in 1846 and potato blight had affected most of Western Europe. An industrial crisis also brought widespread unemployment. The slump had perhaps touched bottom in 1847 and the curve of economic activity was beginning to rise again, but those who were suffering from it, with little attempt at relief from public or private charity, could hardly be expected to appreciate this fact. Again, as in 1787–9, and to a lesser extent in 1830, a political agitation coincided with an economic crisis, and those who had started the agitation, found that it led them much farther than they ever intended or expected. As in 1830, the basic fact was the refusal of the king to be parted from his minister until it was too late, and in his fall the minister dragged the king down with him.

In place of the abandoned banquet of 22 February 1848 there was a popular procession of protest through the streets. The government felt the need for a counter-demonstration, and though the king had not reviewed the National Guard since 1840, it was summoned to his defence. Unwillingly it assembled on the morrow at the *mairies* of the different *arrondissements*, but as its members made their way to their appointed places they called out '*Vive la Réforme!*', presented a petition at the Palais Bourbon, where the Chamber of Deputies sat, sang the Marseillaise, prevented the troops of the line from controlling the crowds, and shouted '*À bas Guizot!*' Unwillingly Louis-Philippe, after a fatal delay, through the veils of aged self-satisfaction and obstinacy appreciated that something unusual was happening, and asked for the resignation of his minister.

Now it was seen that there had in fact been some point in his clinging to office, for the whole system disintegrated when the man who had been the key-stone of the arch fell. Indignation among those who had staked their whole political future on the survival of the régime, was followed by a *sauve-qui-peut*. The politicians began to look for an alternative, and in the streets the crowds were getting out of hand. The king appointed Molé to succeed Guizot, and Bugeaud, who had mastered Paris in 1831 and 1834, to the command of the army. The dismissal of Guizot took some of the edge off the crowds ranging up and down the boulevards, and it still seemed that the situation might be saved. But then, late on the evening of 23 February, occurred the incident which turned a riot into a revolution. Victor Hugo gives a vivid description of the episode. He writes, 'The crowds which I had seen start cheerfully singing down the boulevards, at first went on their way peacefully and without resistance. The regiment, the artillery, the cuirassiers opened their ranks everywhere for their passage. But on the boulevard des Capucines a body of troops, both infantry and cavalry, was massed on the two pavements and across the road, guarding the Ministry of Foreign Affairs and its unpopular minister, M. Guizot. Before this impassable obstacle, the head of the popular column tried to stop and turn aside; but the irresistible pressure of the huge crowd weighed on the front ranks. At this moment a shot rang out, from which side is not known. Panic followed and then a volley. Eighty dead or wounded remained on the spot. A universal cry of horror and fury arose: Vengeance! The bodies of the victims were loaded on a cart lit with torches. The cortège moved back amidst curses at a funeral pace. And in a few hours Paris was covered with barricades.'

On 24 February the king replaced Molé with Thiers, ordered Bugeaud to withdraw his troops, and spent the day in political negotiations. Paris was now in the hands of the mob, which had captured the Hôtel de Ville and advanced on the Tuileries. After the disaster of the previous day there seems to have been no serious thought of an appeal to the army, though it was still loyal and had its links with the dynasty. The sons of Louis-Philippe were closely associated with the army. The duc d'Aumale had fought in Algeria, where he was now governor-general; the duc d'Orléans was popular in military circles because of the interest he had always taken in the army. Nevertheless, outside Paris, and once the riots had triumphed there, not a shot was fired in defence of the dynasty.

On the afternoon of 24 February, collapsing in senile despair, Louis-Philippe abdicated in favour of his grandson, the little comte de Paris. It was the end of a régime that had been so lacking in principle that it could only be known by the name of the month of its founding, as the July Monarchy.

III

THE SECOND REPUBLIC AND
THE SECOND EMPIRE

———

1. 1848: FROM THE FEBRUARY
DAYS TO THE JUNE DAYS

1848 IN FRANCE was a revolution by accident. If the revolution had not happened then, it may be said, as of other revolutions, that it would have happened at some other time, whenever the 'conjuncture' – the term in current French historical jargon that has replaced the 'psychological moment' – was appropriate. But of course, if it had occurred later or earlier it would have occurred in different circumstances and would have been a different revolution. The revolution was not the fore-ordained result of the emergence of new social forces that could not be contained in the old institutions, for none of adequate importance had yet arisen; it was rather the accidental though highly probable result of the inherent weakness of government in France. Since 1789 no régime had possessed the conditions necessary for stability. A series of political upheavals had fragmented conservative forces, the unity of which was the prerequisite of political stability, by introducing ideological cleavages which cut across economic ties and destroyed the cohesion of the forces of property and order. Simplifying the situation, we may say that in 1848 the propertied classes were split between the old *noblesse*, legitimists, and clericals, for whom an Orleanist king was worse than no king at all; those men of property and officials who liked to think themselves liberal, who were inclined towards anti-clericalism and reasonably satisfied with Louis-Philippe; and a rising class of educated and professional men, of varied economic standing, with republican sympathies. As for the mass of rural small proprietors, because of the memory of 1789 the peasants were still labelled in the public mind as potential revolutionaries: the events of June 1848 were to show how mistaken was this opinion, but in February there was no way in which their weight could be cast into the scales against change.

Indeed, hardly any element in French society outside Paris could materially influence events in the crisis of February. This was a second inheritance from the Revolution and Napoleon: authority had been concentrated so thoroughly in the ministries at Paris that whoever held Paris held France. And Paris, of course, was the most difficult part of France to hold. Under the Orleanist monarchy it was a witch's cauldron fermenting with dangerous ideological ingredients.

The collapse of divine right left a void, which the revolutionaries of 1789 attempted unsuccessfully to fill. Their principles were too self-contradictory, and too difficult to reconcile with hard political and social facts, to provide the ideological basis for a new society. The new ruling classes that emerged from Revolution and Empire had used democratic and egalitarian ideas to justify their attack on the older privileged classes, but with no intention of allowing the same principles to be turned against themselves. France, throughout the nineteenth century, was an oligarchy of wealth, especially landed wealth, and office; but unlike the British governing classes in the same period, the French *élite* was insecure, not only because its internal divisions went much deeper, but also because it did not believe in itself. It had no reason to: it had neither inherited an old tradition of government nor had it evolved any Burkian or Benthamite philosophy to provide a moral basis for its new powers and privileges. Too often its self-justification took the form of a cynical assertion of material interests. At the same time it lacked the crude virtues of a get-rich-quick society. Sunk in a stubborn and unimaginative defence of its vested interests, it lacked the enterprise necessary even for its own economic progress. With only a little harshness, we might say that the French ruling class, heir of the great Revolution, was devoid of social conscience, devoted – inevitably – to its own property rights, and indifferent – not quite so inevitably – to the conditions of life, or death, of the populace beneath it. Because the ruling classes were weak they feared to make concessions in advance, but were quick to appeal to force when a threat had materialized. The Orleanist monarchy has been unfairly blamed for its failure to alleviate the misery caused by the economic crisis of the forties: this is to be attributed to the forces of society rather than to the fault of the government.

There was no reason to fear any threat to the social order from conditions in the countryside or in the provincial towns, apart from Lyon. Paris was another matter. The population of the capital was both growing and changing in character. The centralization of the life of France in Paris played its part in promoting the drift of population there, even from comparatively distant provinces and before the railway era. Beginning as a seasonal immigration, it turned into a permanent transfer. Under the Orleanist monarchy the population of Paris, within what were to be the increased limits of 1860, grew from roughly 860,000 to 1,250,000. There had been little industrial development to give work to these extra arms, and little increased agricultural production to provide food for the mouths. There is no coincidence in the fact that two countries which escaped serious trouble in 1848 were the only two in which industrialization had made substantial progress – Great Britain (but not Ireland) and Belgium. In France the population, already before 1789 rather more than the country could support without a declining standard of living, had continued to grow, though at a slower rate, with no substantial industrialization to assist in its absorption.

How a political quarrel between the Ins and the Outs unintentionally set fire to this inflammable social situation has already been indicated. Perhaps it would not have done so if there had not already been 1789 to provide such a model. So de Tocqueville thought. In the presence of the revolutionary mob which invaded the Assembly, he could not persuade himself, he said, that there was a real danger of bloodshed, despite the muskets and bayonets and sabres. '*Nos Français,*' he wrote, '*surtout à Paris, mêlent volontiers les souvenirs de la littérature et du théâtre à leurs manifestations les plus sérieuses.*' It seemed to him, he added, that they were playing at the French Revolution rather than continuing it. The revolution of 1848, Marx said, could find nothing better to do than to parody that of 1789–95. Nevertheless the fighting in February was real enough to destroy a monarchy; the days of June 1848 were to see a bitterer social war than ever the first Revolution knew; and an empire was to emerge from the republic in four years instead of fourteen.

Once the régime of Louis-Philippe and Guizot had collapsed in Paris, its hollowness was shown by the rapidity with which its adherents joined in a general *sauve qui peut* and proclaimed their allegiance, along with legitimists, republicans, clericals, anti-clericals, liberals, socialists, and all, to the revolutionary government. In its opening days this was a revolution of fraternity and universal love. The hero of Flaubert's *L'Éducation sentimentale,* after the February Days revisiting the fair friend whom he had left on his previous visit in a somewhat disgruntled frame of mind, found that the revolution had restored harmony. 'Now that all was peaceful and there was no cause for fear, she kissed him and declared herself for the Republic – as Monseigneur the Archbishop of Paris had already done, and as, with a marvellous alacrity, the Magistrature, the Council of State, the Institute, the Marshals of France, Changarnier, M. de Falloux, all the Bonapartists, all the Legitimists, and a considerable number of Orleanists, were to do.'

The government to which France entrusted its fate, of course provisionally, on the morrow of the February revolution, was as accidental a product as the revolution itself. The Chamber of Deputies, which was an

Orleanist chamber, was watching with hearts full of sentiment the lovely Duchess of Orleans, mother of Louis-Philippe's grandson in favour of whom he had abdicated, and listening to emotional appeals on their behalf – 'The crown of July', declared Odilon Barrot, 'rests on the head of a child and a woman' – when the *blouses* and the National Guards burst into the hall with shouts of '*À bas la Chambre*', '*Plus de députés*'. The courage of the members and the hopes of the dynasty vanished together: only a republican government would pacify the mob. Out of the tumult the names of seven leading republican figures – Lamartine, Ledru-Rollin, Marrast, Arago, Crémieux, Marie, Garnier-Pagès – emerged. At the Hôtel de Ville a left-wing demonstration had put forward the socialists Flocon and Louis Blanc, and a solitary, symbolic (of nothing in particular) worker, Albert. These names were added, and thus did France receive its new government.

The first act of the Provisional Government was to proclaim the right of universal suffrage, swelling the electorate overnight from a quarter of a million to nine millions, and laying the foundations for the subsequent Bonapartist dictatorship. Next, it abolished slavery on all French territory, thus freeing about half a million slaves, a belated reform, introduced without any preparation or precautions, which brought immediate economic disaster to the slave colonies.

A more pressing problem was that of unemployment in France, and principally Paris. The general European slump had reached bottom in 1847 and conditions were slowly improving; but in France the uncertainty produced in the business world by the Revolution prohibited any recovery and in 1848 the economic crisis was intensified. Shops were closed, craftsmen without work, men dismissed from the few factories; credit was lacking, private charity quite inadequate, and government assistance totally absent. To the starving horde of unemployed, or to those who were vocal amongst them, one idea had filtered down. How the economic position had changed in the past half century is shown by the shape of this idea. They no longer, as between 1789 and 1794, called for a maximum on prices; the demand now was for work, embodied in Louis Blanc's formula, *le droit au travail*. It is evidence that the labouring masses in the towns now thought of themselves primarily as producers rather than as consumers.

In a revolutionary situation something had to be done to satisfy their demands or those of their spokesmen. It was not too difficult to find an innocuous solution. Louis Blanc and Albert, political innocents compared with the politicians, were put at the head of a Parliament of Industry which met at the Luxembourg and was allowed to talk its way through the crisis. Louis Blanc's plan for National Workshops, which involved the state in providing credits for industry, was rejected. To the Minister of Public Works, Marie, and many others, it seemed a revolutionary proposal, alien to the spirit of brotherhood that had prevailed in February. If the name National Workshops was adopted, it was only as a sop to the followers of Louis Blanc; in fact all the Workshops, or Ateliers, ever amounted to was a system of registering the Paris unemployed for the payment of a wretched dole. By June 1848 some 120,000 were in receipt of this pittance and the lists had been closed to exclude perhaps 50,000 more. To give the impression that something was being done, a young engineer named Thomas was entrusted with the task of organizing the so-called Workshops. In spite of opposition, he managed to set about 12,000 men to work levelling a small hill on the site of what was later the boulevard Montparnasse. The prevailing attitude of mind among the wealthy classes, though intensely protectionist in relation to foreign trade, was sternly non-interventionist in respect of internal economic activity. When the government of Louis-Philippe had proposed to meet the economic crisis of 1847 by a programme of public works, a legislative body of proprietors naturally rejected the proposal. The Provisional Government, in so far as it ever even contemplated the same programme, met with the same resistance.

Orthodox economics also insisted, and more successfully than in 1789, that the National Debt was sacred. To maintain public credit, interest continued to be paid scrupulously on state loans, the budgetary gap being filled by imposing an extra tax of 45 centimes, which fell mainly on the peasantry. This was the most misconceived of all the Provisional Government's measures. Whereas the National Assembly of 1789 had, intentionally or unintentionally, lightened the burdens of the peasantry, the revolution of 1848 actually increased them. Here is at least one factor which helps to explain the changed attitude of the peasants to revolution.

The mutual fear and suspicion of the middle classes and the populace in Paris, which had been violently intensified, though not created, by the economic crisis, came into the open very early in the Revolution. On 16 March the better-off members of the National Guard, distinguished by their uniform and fur caps, staged a rather futile demonstration which is known as the manifestation of the *bonnets à poil*. There followed on the next day an imposing and far larger counter-demonstration by masses of Paris workers. The situation was tense but Ledru-Rollin, known as the most sympathetic to the people among the middle-class republican leaders, acquired considerable, though not lasting, prestige by pacifying the demonstrators. Though the great body of conservative republicans did not trust him and detested his ideas of moderate social reform, it was evident that he could not be dispensed with while the danger from below existed; so he had to be tolerated.

In the key position of Minister of the Interior, Ledru-Rollin had the responsibility for organizing the election of a Constituent Assembly. Universal suffrage represented a leap in the dark, and the more they thought about the implications of this sudden and unprepared granting of their democratic demands, the darker the outlook seemed to the democratic factions; for the great mass of the new electors were illiterate peasants, likely to follow the lead of their clergy, local landowners, and notables. The only hope the left-wing politicians could see lay in a postponement of the elections, to give them time to indoctrinate the peasants and teach them who their real friends were. Hence a series of petitions flowed in from the clubs of Paris in favour of postponing the elections, which was also one of the demands of the demonstrators of 17 March. In more general terms it may be said that the democrats of 1848 were faced with the constant dilemma of democracy: can the sovereign people, if it so wishes, be allowed to abdicate, has it the right to repudiate democracy? Suppose it chooses to follow a conservative, or even a reactionary policy, instead of a progressive and reforming one, is this permissible? The members of the great Committee of Public Safety had been faced with the same question and their answer was the Terror. Ledru-Rollin and the republicans of 1848 did not contemplate this solution. They would doubtless have been less despised by historians if they had been more bloody-minded. Unfortunately they were idealists who believed in their own principles.

Within the limits which seemed legitimate to him, Ledru-Rollin did what he could towards the winning of the elections. The essential first step was the replacement of the Orleanist administrative machine. All the prefects, and all but twelve of the sub-prefects, were dismissed, and revolutionary commissaires appointed in their place. By mid-April tried republicans were at the head of practically every department. The Provisional Government instructed them not to imitate the usurping governments of the past in corrupting the electors. Ledru-Rollin, rather more frankly, addressed them with the rhetorical question 'What are your powers?' and replied, 'They are unlimited. ... The elections are your great task.' By this he meant that the duty of the commissaires was to enlighten the electors and purge the administration of non-republican officials who might exercise a dangerous influence.

The discredited and disorganized Orleanist machine could not resist Ledru-Rollin. On the other hand the clerical party, with an anti-Orleanist record behind it, was not afraid to engage in open political agitation under the leadership of Montalembert's central Committee for Electoral Liberty. It was supported energetically by most of the bishops. Few leaders of the Church were as far-seeing as the bishop of Viviers, later Cardinal Guibert, who wrote, 'I am convinced that we are doing an imprudent thing, and that the few votes in favour of religious liberty we may be able to send to the Chamber are not worth the sacrifice of the fine position we have won by our isolation from political power since 1830.'

Faced with the clerical threat, the Minister of Education, Hippolyte Carnot, called on the village school-teachers to counteract the clergy by spreading the republican faith. This was the beginning of the ideological struggle between the *curé* and the *instituteur*, but the struggle was as yet a very uneven one. The Church was still far stronger than the State in the rural communes, and the republicans were not unaware of this fact. Possibly they fixed on Easter Sunday for the elections in the hope of keeping the faithful away from the elections. If so, it was a gross miscalculation. Mass was celebrated at an early hour in the morning, and the villagers marched to vote with the priest at the head of the procession, sometimes in harmony, sometimes in undignified rivalry, with a republican *maire*.

Apart from propaganda, a game at which the local notabilities and priest could usually defeat Ledru-Rollin's commissaires, the elections were notably free. The failure of the more advanced republicans supported by Ledru-Rollin is evidence of that: Ministers of the Interior did not normally lose elections in nineteenth-century France. There was a poll of 84 per cent and the vote of the peasantry ensured that the Constituent Assembly should be in a majority conservative and traditionalist in its complexion. Four-fifths of the deputies were men of the district which elected them; four-fifths were also over 40; nearly 700 out of nearly 900 were men of substance paying a tax of over 500 francs a year. Half the deputies were monarchists, divided into some 300 Orleanists and 150 Legitimists.

About 350 were committed to support the clerical campaign for freedom of education. There was a mere sprinkling of red republicans, and still fewer socialists. The conservative nature of the Assembly was demonstrated by the voting on two proposals. Only 82 members supported a motion recognizing the right to work; and only 110 out of 900 were in favour of that most revolutionary of all measures, a graduated income tax. Of course, even a vote of one in eight for such a measure would have been inconceivable in the great French Revolution. Ledru-Rollin's attempt to secure an advanced republican Assembly had thus decisively failed. His influence in the government naturally declined, and he would probably have been pushed out of it by the new Assembly if it had not been for the support of Lamartine, who thereby sacrificed much of his own prestige.

It was an Assembly interested in political, but opposed to all economic change. From the beginning it exhibited the besetting sin of the Second Republic, an obsession with political dogma. This appeared in the Assembly's insistence on turning the Provisional Government into an Executive Commission, appointed by the Assembly, which had the duty of deliberating on policy, while a separate body of Ministers had the duty of carrying it out. This division was introduced for the purpose of maintaining the sacred principle of the separation of powers.

The left-wing leaders of Paris, frustrated by the elections, carried on an increasingly bitter agitation in the press and the popular clubs. Their violent speeches, invocations to social revolution, songs like

> *Chapeau bas devant ma casquette,*
> *À genoux devant l'ouvrier,*

did not lessen the alarm of the middle and upper classes. Since one thing that all France definitely wanted was not to be involved in a revolutionary war, with characteristic ineptitude the club leaders decided to use a petition for assistance to the Polish revolution as the excuse for an attempt to overthrow the National Assembly by a mob demonstration after the established model. This attempted 'push' on 15 May, under the revolutionary leaders, Barbès and Blanqui, who hated one another even more than they hated their opponents, was easily put down by the regular troops and the National Guard. Its only result was that practically all the left-wing agitators disappeared from the political scene, either in flight abroad or into prison. Hence they cannot be held responsible for the great popular rising of June.

The revolt of the June Days is one of the most mysterious episodes of its kind. It is not easy to find another popular movement, especially of such magnitude, in which not a single leader, even of the second or third rank, can be identified. The psychological preparation for the June Days is not difficult to see, and it can be granted that there was plenty of inflammable material in Paris. The hope of salvation, with which the unemployed and starving masses had poured out of their garrets and cellars in February, had given place to disillusionment when under a republic economic conditions became worse instead of better. Class hatred in Paris reached perhaps its highest point, before the Commune, in 1848. De Tocqueville, returning to the capital after the elections, found the aspect of Paris terrible and sinister. 'I saw society split in two: those who possessed nothing united in a common greed; those who possessed something in a common fear. No bonds, no sympathies existed between these two great classes, everywhere was the idea of an inevitable and approaching struggle.'

It is a classic fact of revolutions in a predominantly agrarian economy that the late spring or early summer is the point of greatest danger, when the previous year's harvest is exhausted and the new one has not yet come in. Semi-starvation was the lot of the masses of unemployed in Paris. The dole handed out by the so-called National Workshops was only a slight alleviation of their misery, and even so, many of the unemployed were excluded from it and the National Assembly was determined to get rid of it as rapidly as possible. For the chairman of the Labour Committee of the Assembly, the comte de Falloux – a devoted son of the Church and proud aristocrat, whose grandfather, a cattle-merchant, had been ennobled by Louis XVIII in 1823 – the National Workshops were 'a permanent and organized strike', 'an active centre of dangerous agitation'. To the suggestion that if they were dissolved there might be resistance, he replied, 'Have you not the National Guard? ... Take what measures you choose, we guarantee they will not meet with serious resistance; and if we do encounter it, let us not be afraid to use force, force without the shedding of blood but that moral force which belongs to the law.'

As a result partly of de Falloux's pressure, on 22 June it was decreed that all unmarried workers in the National Workshops should join the army, and the remainder go to the provinces, under penalty of losing their payments. This seems to have been the spark which set off the rising in Paris, though how or why is far from clear. It is alleged that those who were enrolled in the National Workshops did not in fact participate in the June Days to any great extent, but there is no doubt that it was, as it seemed to contemporaries like de Tocqueville, a workers' movement, a revolt of the helots, a servile war. The numbers involved in the actual fighting must not be exaggerated; they were probably not more than 20,000, one in ten or less of the workers of Paris. Their first step was to erect barricades, which cut off the poorer quarters of Paris. These were necessary because with the black powder then used it was difficult to fire from other than a standing position. Held by desperate men, with flanking fire from windows, in the narrow, winding streets of old Paris, the barricades could only be taken when cannon had been set up against them, which was a slow and dangerous process. Then, when a barricade had been rendered untenable, its defenders could move back, breaking through the party walls of the houses, to another line of defence prepared in advance.

The unresisted opening stages of the revolt were possible

because of the absence of troops, which was due not to calculation but to the difficulty of provisioning them in Paris and to the lack of barracks; but once the regular troops were brought into action the result was a foregone conclusion. The general entrusted with putting down the revolt, Cavaignac, a staunch republican but also intensely conservative, moved in infantry and artillery steadily for the kill. The army was reinforced by detachments of National Guard, volunteers from the provinces, where the hatred of Paris had reached fever pitch. Even at the time of the election of the Constituent Assembly de Tocqueville had been struck with the spirit of fraternity which sprang up between all owners of property, rich or poor, in his rural department of the Manche, and the universal hatred and terror which they experienced at the thought of the 'anarchists' of Paris.

In six days of bitter street fighting the rebel quarters were conquered street by street. How many of the insurgents were killed in the struggle or shot out of hand when captured cannot be estimated. The prisoners, thousands of whom were to be sent as forced immigrants to Algeria, were piled into improvised dungeons such as Flaubert describes: 'Nine hundred men were there, crowded together in filth, pell-mell, black with powder and clotted blood, shivering in fever and shouting in frenzy. Those who died were left to lie with the others. Now and then, at the sudden noise of a gun, they thought they were all on the point of being shot, and then flung themselves against the walls, afterwards falling back into their former places. They were so stupefied with suffering that they seemed to be living in a nightmare, a funeral hallucination. The lamp hanging from the arch looked like a patch of blood; and little green and yellow flames flew about, produced by the effluvium of the vaults. Because of a fear of epidemics a commission of enquiry had been appointed. On the first steps its president flung himself back, appalled by the odour of excrement and corpses. When the prisoners approached a ventilator, the National Guards on sentry duty stuck their bayonets, haphazard, into the crowd, to prevent them from loosening the bars.

'The National Guards were in general pitiless. Those who had not been in the fighting wanted to distinguish themselves now, but all was really the reaction of fear. They were avenging themselves at once for the journals, the clubs, the mobs, the doctrines, for everything that had provoked them beyond measure in the last three months; and despite their victory, equality (as if for the punishment of its defenders and mockery of its enemies) was triumphantly revealed – an equality of brute beasts on the same level of blood-stained depravity; for the fanaticism of vested interests was on a level with the madness of the needy, the aristocracy exhibited the fury of the basest mob, and the cotton night-cap was no less hideous than the *bonnet rouge*. The public mind became disordered as after a great natural catastrophe, and men of intelligence were idiots for the rest of their lives.'

Victor Hugo said that in the June Days civilization defended itself with the methods of barbarism. They were a turning-point in many respects. The army, like the peasants of which its ranks were so largely composed, passed from one side of the barricades to the other in June 1848. The Grande Peur of 1789, Valmy and Jemappes, the four sergeants of La Rochelle, and a host of other memories identified the peasant with social disorder and the army with revolution. Almost at a blow the myth – for it had become a myth by 1848 – was ended: the peasant became the embodiment of social conservatism and the army the bulwark of order.

2. THE TRIUMPH OF LOUIS NAPOLEON

AFTER the June Days the Army held power in France and the Assembly survived under its protection. 'This poor Assembly', wrote Victor Hugo, 'is a true soldier's girl, in love with a trooper.' The trooper was Cavaignac, whose principles excluded military dictatorship. He took the place of the discredited Executive Commission and appointed a moderate republican ministry to hold office while the Assembly completed its constitutional proposals. It did this by November. The Constitution it made was much more influenced by theory than any of the preceding Constitutions since 1789. The change in social ideals in the course of sixty years can be seen in its preamble, which – significantly enough – took the place of the former declaration of rights. The individualism of 1789, with its emphasis on rights, now had to share its claims with a recognition of duties and a new emphasis on fraternity. This may not have meant much in the France of the June Days, but even lip-service was a sign of a changing climate of opinion. Politically there had been rather less change in republican ideals. There was still the old attempt to reconcile the principles of separation of powers and sovereignty of the people. All power comes from the people, but this power must be divided: the conclusion was the election of a single chamber and a unique head of the government, both by universal suffrage and both directly responsible to the people, the one entrusted with total legislative authority and the other with all executive power.

The crucial decision as it turned out later, and indeed as it appeared at the time, was the embodiment of the executive power in the person of a President elected directly by the whole nation. The election of the President by direct universal suffrage was supported by the right and the moderates, and opposed by Ledru-Rollin and the red republicans. The fear of the tyranny of a Convention still haunted moderate opinion: de Tocqueville warned against the danger of turning the President into a mere agent of the Legislative Body. Grévy, the author of a famous amendment, admitted the danger, but saw a more dangerous precedent in the career of Napoleon I. 'Are you sure', he asked the Assembly, 'that there will never be found an ambitious man, anxious to perpetuate his power, and if he is a man who had been able to make himself popular, if he is a victorious general, surrounded with the prestige of that military glory which the French cannot resist, if he is the offspring of one of the families which have reigned over France, and if he has never expressly renounced what he calls his rights [there could hardly have been a more obvious reference to Louis Napoleon], if commerce is languishing, if the people are in misery . . . will you guarantee that this ambitious man will not succeed in overthrowing the republic?' The answer was given by Lamartine: If you want to do so, he said, confuse the legislative and executive powers, add the judicial and call your system by its true title – the Terror. He admitted that there were names which attracted the crowd as a mirage draws the flocks to it; but concluded, in a phrase from which his reputation has never recovered, '*Il faut laisser quelque chose à la Providence.*' The Grévy amendment was defeated by 643 to 158 votes and the Second Republic had committed a delayed suicide.

The Presidential election followed in December 1848. Among the candidates Cavaignac was the standard-bearer of the conservative republic and Ledru-Rollin of the red republicans; Raspail and a sprinkling of other candidates represented the left-wing; and there was a name of destiny – Louis Napoleon Bonaparte.

It is time to say something of Bonapartism as a political movement in France, now that at last it was on the point of becoming one. It may seem paradoxical, yet it is probably true, that the Napoleonic Legend, while essential to the existence of the Second Empire, played only a secondary part in its creation. About the origin of the Legend there need be little dispute; it was the deliberate creation of Napoleon I, by his official propaganda while he was Emperor, and in the imaginative picture he tried to draw while he was in exile of himself and his aims. To the legend of the pacifier who suppressed the internecine strife that had been tearing France apart, the protector of religion who had brought persecution to an end, the saviour who rescued society from the Jacobins and the Terror, the administrator who gave France efficient government and restored its financial and economic prosperity, the great general and military hero who had made Europe into a French Empire, was added an even more mendacious picture of the great champion of liberal ideals, of freedom for the oppressed nationalities of Europe, and of peace. In 1815 the facts were a little too close for all this to have very much effect, and by 1830 the Napoleonic legend was no more than a romantic survival of no political significance. It seemed so little dangerous that the Orleanist régime did not hesitate to exploit Bonapartist sentiment for the purpose of acquiring a little badly needed popularity.

The two adventures of Louis Bonaparte, at Strasbourg in 1836 and Boulogne in 1840, confirmed the belief that Bonapartism, if it was not a spent fire, was one that was too damp ever to burst into flames again. The Emperor's nephew, it is true, had shown rather more skill with the pen than with the sword. He had produced, in 1832, a volume of *Rêveries politiques* – possibly not the best title to advertise its author as a man of action. More effective for the creation of a public image of the pretender – even if only an *image d'Épinal* like the popular cut-outs of Napoleon and his soldiers – were an artillery manual and a booklet on the extinction of pauperism. Louis Napoleon Bonaparte's most important production was *Des idées napoléoniennes* in 1839. This should have been taken more seriously than it was. As with later dictators, if it had been possible to believe that Louis Napoleon meant what he said, the subsequent history of France would have come as less of a surprise to contemporaries.

After the Boulogne adventure, Louis Bonaparte's light was extinguished for the next six years by not very rigorous imprisonment in the fortress at Ham, where he was provided with the modest amenities of life including a mistress, and from which he walked out disguised as a builder's labourer in 1846. In February 1848, therefore, he was again a potential saviour at the disposal of France, only hardly anyone as yet seemed to think of him in that capacity. He made a fleeting appearance in Paris soon after the revolution but found the political climate uncongenial and returned to London, where by enrolling as a special constable against the Chartists he did something to bury the memory of the carbonarist and conspirator and build up a picture of himself as the defender of law and order. So slight was the Bonapartist sentiment in France on the morrow of the revolution, that a Bonapartist paper could only survive from 25 February to 3 March, and the tiny group of devotees of Louis Napoleon could make no impression on public opinion.

By June there was evidently a change in this respect. Possibly the apparently imminent collapse of the social order had already started the swing to a potential saviour of society. Supplementary elections then returned Louis Napoleon for Paris and four other departments, with practically no organization or propaganda to support his candidature. This should have been an omen, but a miscalculated letter that he sent from London to the President of the Assembly aroused feeling in the Assembly against him. Wisely he appreciated that the time was not yet ripe and resigned. Further elections, in September, saw him returned in five constituencies and at the head of the Paris list. Despite this, the republicans of the Assembly for the most part remained unimpressed by the Bonapartist danger. When he rose in the Assembly, the insignificant appearance of the bearer of such a great name, and a halting speech in a German accent, convinced them that they were right. But though it would still be an exaggeration to speak of a Bonapartist party, supporters were gathering and conducting a more active propaganda, by journals and by the production of prints, medals, brooches, and knicknacks of various kinds with Napoleonic inscriptions or associations.

As the presidential election came nearer the obscure Bonapartists who had been backing what had seemed for so long a forlorn hope found themselves joined by more prominent figures. Ambitious Orleanist politicians like Thiers and Odilon Barrot, disappointed in their expectation of office by the revolution they had done so much to provoke, hoped to use Louis Napoleon to return to power.

Barrot called him 'our excellent young man', and Thiers, who advised him to shave his moustache, said he was 'a cretin whom we will manage'. De Tocqueville, with a mixture of shrewdness and misjudgement, described him as 'an enigmatic, sombre, insignificant numskull'. Whatever their views of him personally, many former Orleanists, unfettered by attachment to political principles but with a keen eye on the main chance, prepared to jump on the Bonapartist band-wagon. More idealistic motives inspired Victor Hugo, who also kept a sentimental attachment to the memory of the Emperor his father had served. From the time of the *Ode à la colonne* his poems had done as much as any writings, except those of Béranger, to keep the Napoleonic memory alive. In 1848 he saw himself as the prophet and adviser of a liberal Bonaparte; and Louis Napoleon was not indifferent to the prestige that the support of France's greatest poet could give. After the election the poet was a guest at the first dinner given by the new President at the Élysée. The offer of the Madrid embassy tempted Hugo, with his memories of imperial Spain, but it was not what he had hoped for. In youth he had declared, '*Je veux être Chateaubriand ou rien*', and Chateaubriand had been Foreign Minister. Though disappointed, he continued to support the President until the 2 December added political to personal disillusionment.

The beautiful Miss Howard, with whom Louis Bonaparte had lived since 1846, came over in the autumn of 1848 to add her fortune to the others that were being invested in his future, and after the election to be for a time official mistress in the Prince President's little court. Spiritual support was added to secular. The clerical party, headed by Montalembert and Falloux, was legitimist in principle but prepared to do a deal with Louis Bonaparte in the interest of clerical control of education. Because Louis Napoleon had the support of the great banker Fould, it has been supposed that the financiers and also the industrialists were among his backers; but in fact they were more firmly Orleanist than the politicians, and suspicious of both the ideas and the associates of Louis Bonaparte. On the other hand his connexion with the Saint-Simonians brought him the support of that sect and its adherents, such as the Péreire brothers. While the republicans remained aloof, some socialists saw hope in Bonapartism.

The two great journals of the February revolution opposed the Bonapartist candidature, the *Réforme* supporting Ledru-Rollin and the *National* Cavaignac. Louis Bonaparte had on his side Girardin's *Presse*, because of its editor's enmity to Cavaignac, the *Constitutionnel* under the influence of Thiers, Victor Hugo's *Événement*, and a number of provincial journals. But though the Bonapartists spent as much as they could on propaganda in the press, they only had the support of a minority of papers.

It is possible to believe that even if he had had none of this support Louis Bonaparte might still have been elected President. The populace in the large towns had no reason to vote for the victor of the June Days and the repressive and reactionary régime with which he was identified. The peasants of the countryside, who formed the great mass of the voters, were under the influence of a panic fear of red terror and confiscation of property spread by the men of order; they needed a saviour of society and who could fill that rôle better than a Napoleon. 'The idea of authority is attached to that name', wrote Barante, 'and it is authority that they want.' The idealism behind Ledru-Rollin, the social conservatism and official influence behind Cavaignac, were powerless against this wave of emotion. Ledru-Rollin secured 370,119 votes, Cavaignac 1,448,107, and Louis Napoleon 5,434,226; on the extreme left Raspail had a pitiable 36,920. Lamartine's star had long since set: in all France he could only gather 17,910 votes.

The first act of the new President was to take the oath of loyalty to the Republic and swear to defend the Constitution. If he had any mental reservations he kept them to himself; he was always good at keeping his own counsel. He appointed a conservative Orleanist ministry under Odilon Barrot, which reflected the political complexion of the

Assembly, left the government to them, and devoted his time to tours through France. This enabled him to exhibit his real brilliance as a propagandist, and at the same time to leave the onus of repressing the forces of the left on the Assembly. The red republicans had reacted to their defeat by drawing closer together in a nation-wide organization under the name of the Solidarité Républicaine, with central and local committees and a staunch Jacobin, Delescluze, as its secretary. The task of repression was begun with the outlawing of this society in January 1849.

The Constituent Assembly had no real justification for its continued existence now that the Constitution had been made and put into effect, but it hung on as long as it could, in a moribund condition. Finally it had to dissolve and in May 1849 elections were held for a Legislative Assembly. The conservative forces of all kinds, sometimes called the 'party of order' though they were too divided to constitute a real party, organized themselves for the election through a committee in the rue de Poitiers. It included legitimists, Orleanists, Bonapartists, Catholics, and even moderate republicans. The prefects, who had replaced Ledru Rollin's commissaires, now returned to their customary rôle and played a large part in the elections. Of course, the supporters of order obtained a large majority of 500 out of 750 members. The conservative republicans of the *National*-Cavaignac school were reduced to a small group of 70; the men of February – Lamartine, Dupont de l'Eure, Garnier-Pagès, Marie, Marrast, Carnot, and others – were rejected by the country. What was unexpected and alarming to the forces of order was the comparative success of the red republicans, with 180 seats. Ledru-Rollin came second on the Paris list. The explanation, of course, lay in abstentions from voting, especially of many of the peasantry. The total vote in the country had sunk to 40 per cent of those entitled to vote, and of these one-third had voted for the reds. Evidently the left was still far from defeated. But what the conservative forces could not achieve in the elections, the left-wing politicians in Paris managed to do in a single day.

Undeterred by the lessons of 1848 they staged a futile attempt at revolution on 13 June 1849. Whereas in 1848 the cry had been Poland, now it was Rome. There was at least this justification for the demonstration: that a French force under Oudinot was about to overthrow the Roman Republic and reinstate the authority of Pius IX, which it did shortly after. The attempted insurrection in Paris and a number of provincial towns obtained no popular support. Ledru-Rollin and most of the left-wing deputies fled abroad, others were imprisoned; and the government and the Assembly had a fair excuse for passing more severe repressive legislation.

As well as an energetic suppression of the reds by police measures, the conservatives now began to feel that a more positive inculcation of the principles of social order was needed. The 'panic of property' which followed the June Days had weakened the anti-clericalism of many of the propertied classes and of their leaders such as Thiers. The merit of clerical education as a means of instilling the principles of social discipline and the sacredness of property into the minds of the lower orders was now more adequately appreciated. It found expression in an educational law proposed by Falloux in June 1849 and finally voted in March 1850. Meanwhile, in January 1850, had been voted the so-called 'little law' on education. This attributed the appointment and dismissal of primary teachers to the prefects, a right which they kept until 1944. The *loi Falloux* itself gave members of religious orders the right of opening schools without requiring any further qualification, and introduced councils with strong clerical elements to control the University.

On a general policy of weakening the left, the President and the Assembly were able to co-operate. But Louis Napoleon soon showed the Barrots and the Thiers that he was not the puppet President they thought they had elected. In October 1849, though it still had a majority in the Assembly, he dismissed the Odilon Barrot ministry and issued a message justifying his action to the country. 'To strengthen the Republic menaced on all sides by anarchy,' he began, turning against themselves the chief weapon of the parliamentary factions, 'to maintain externally the name of France at the height of her renown, men are needed animated by a patriotic devotion, proof against everything, who understand the need for an undivided and strong rule and for a clearly formulated policy, who will not compromise authority by irresolution, and who will be as deeply conscious of my responsibility as of their own.' For his new ministry, therefore, he chose new men from outside parliament; and to show that it was to be a presidential and not a parliamentary government, he appointed no president of the council. He himself was to be its head.

President and Assembly, however, were still capable of receiving a shock from the country. In March 1850 by-elections were held to replace the 30 deputies condemned after the events of 13 June 1849. In the face of intense repression the democratic republicans rallied their forces once again. Despite all the efforts of the administration the left won 20 seats out of the 30, and in Paris the three left-wing candidates were returned with large majorities. In a subsequent election to fill a vacancy at Paris, the novelist Eugène Sue, now a name of terror to the respectable classes who had read his newspaper serials with avidity, was returned.

The panic of the Assembly revived: in spite of all the measures of repression, universal suffrage was still, it appeared, dangerous. In May 1850, therefore, a law was introduced to deprive of the franchise all who had suffered any condemnation by the courts – given the repressive legislation this would eliminate most of the militants of the left – and all who had not three years residential qualification in the same canton. The effect was to exclude about 3 million out of $9\frac{1}{2}$ million voters. Supported by Thiers with an unmeasured denunciation of the 'vile multitude', the law was passed in May 1850 by a majority of 433 to 241. It gave the President the opportunity to present himself once more as the defender of the rights of the people, and his demand for the abrogation of the law, in November 1850, was only rejected by 355 to 348.

Louis Napoleon had by now attracted to himself the support of a substantial group in the Assembly. By his propaganda tours, and the fact that his star was obviously still rising, he obtained an increasing backing in the country. He particularly worked on the army, and in January 1851 felt strong enough to dismiss the republican general Changarnier, who commanded the forces, both regular and National Guard, in Paris. Despite its earlier suspicions, the world of business, fearing a renewal of disorder when the President's mandate came to an end in 1852, and dissatisfied at the rather slow recovery from the slump, was now beginning to see its best hope in the continuance of Louis Napoleon at the head of the state.

Unfortunately this was not possible, or so it seemed. The constitution did not permit the re-election of the President. To overcome this obstacle the administration organized a campaign of petitions for its revision. So energetic and so successful were the prefects, that nearly all the *conseils généraux* in France supported the plea for revision. The Assembly yielded to this pressure by appointing a commission to examine the question, which concluded against the proposal. A vote in July 1851 was by 446 to 278 in favour of revision, but this was not the constitutionally necessary two-thirds majority. There was a renewed flood of petitions, but now Louis Napoleon and his little group of intimates had decided to settle the matter in an extra-parliamentary way.

The support of the army was ensured by bringing over from Algeria Saint-Arnaud and other colonial generals, with no civilian prejudices in favour of republics or parliamentary methods. The Bonapartist inner circle was now fairly complete. Louis Napoleon's half-brother Morny, a gambler of genius, was the chief organizer of the *coup d'état*. De Maupas, a *préfet à poigne*, was brought from Toulouse to become prefect of Police. Persigny, who had shared Louis Bonaparte's defeats before 1848, rightly joined in his coming triumph. After several postponements the *coup* was finally fixed for 2 December, the anniversary of Austerlitz.

On the night of 1-2 December the conspirators moved into action. Troops under an Algerian general occupied the Imprimerie Nationale, the Palais Bourbon, newspaper offices, printing works, and the main strategic points in Paris. In the *mairies* of the *arrondissements* the drums were broken, the bell-towers of the churches were guarded. The Parisians woke in the morning to find placards announcing the dissolution of the Assembly, the restoration of universal suffrage, new elections, and a state of siege in Paris and the neighbouring departments. In an *Appel au peuple* the President accused the Assembly of conspiracy – a nice touch – and fomenting disorder. A proclamation to the army declared, 'Soldiers! it is your mission to save the country.' Sixteen members of the Assembly and some 80 other known opponents were seized by troops in their homes. Some 300 deputies, excluded from their chamber, met in the *mairie* of the X^e *arrondissement* to protest, and were duly arrested in their turn.

On the morning of 2 December the saviour of society, accompanied by his generals, rode out from the Élysée. In a city occupied by 50,000 troops there was little danger, but also, to his disappointment, little enthusiasm. There were even some slight hostile demonstrations, but the day passed with no sign of resistance. On 3 December, however, Victor Hugo and a few republicans formed a Committee to organize opposition. A barricade was erected in the faubourg Saint-Antoine and on it a deputy, Dr Baudin, was killed. His name was not forgotten. The danger was slight for the masses were on the side of the dictator. When Flaubert's hero asked a worker if they were not going to fight, he received the answer, 'We're not fools enough to get ourselves killed for the bourgeois! Let them settle it themselves!' They did in their way. On 4 December more barricades appeared, manned by a few hundred republicans who had not forgotten 1848. The generals were determined to have done with this nonsense: 30,000 troops, with artillery, musket, and bayonet, were let loose against the resistance, which was crushed in a few hours. Only a few hundred were killed, either in the fighting or shot when taken prisoner. The most dramatic episode occurred on the boulevard Poissonière, where the soldiers, in a state of natural excitement, fired several volleys into a large crowd of passive onlookers. It was not a very glorious beginning for the Second Empire.

3. A BOURGEOIS EMPIRE

IT was difficult to make a *coup d'état* without breaking some heads as well as an oath, and so Louis Napoleon had found, doubtless to his regret for he was a humane man. If he could have obtained the power and glory by honourable and peaceful methods he would certainly have preferred them. In addition he had to begin with repression, not so much because the feeble resistance in Paris and a few minor movements in the provinces needed repressing, as because unless there were some repression there would hardly have seemed any reason for a *coup d'état*. Altogether 26,884 arrests were effected throughout France. Of those arrested, 9,000 were transported to Algeria and 239 to Cayenne, 1,500 expelled from France, and 3,000 given forced residence away from their homes. Soon after, a commission of revision freed 3,500 of those sentenced, and by 1859, when an amnesty was offered to all the remainder except Ledru-Rollin, the number still penalized was only 1,800. The Second Empire might have been astonished at its own moderation and one would have expected it easily to live down the slight splashes of blood that accompanied its birth-pangs. Somehow it did not, and even the Emperor never quite put them out of his mind.

One of the first steps of Louis Napoleon was to confiscate the extensive property which Louis-Philippe, with almost excessive paternal affection, had collected for his large family as well as for himself. It was used to make grants to societies for mutual aid, for constructing workers' dwellings, and so on; but it looked a little too much like bribery with stolen property, even for a number of Louis' supporters. His enemies called it, '*le premier vol de l'aigle*'.

Such comments showed a bad spirit. It was desirable that the country should envisage recent events in the proper light; so by a decree of 17 February 1852, largely the work of Rouher, the press was brought under a more severe control than it had known since the First Empire. No journal dealing with political or social questions was to be issued without the permission of the government; the caution money was heavily increased; the list of press offences was enlarged and penalties strengthened; those accused of press offences were to be tried without a jury; after three warnings by the Minister of the Interior to Paris journals, or by a prefect to provincial ones, a journal could be suspended by administrative action and in the last resort suppressed.

The general clauses of a new constitution did not need long discussion, for Louis Napoleon regarded himself as invested with the constituent power by the plebiscite that had confirmed his seizure of power. The President was to have, as before, the nomination of all officials, from top to bottom, as well as of the Senate, the Conseil d'État, the High Court of Justice, and the Ministers. There was to be a Legislative Body, elected by universal suffrage in single-member constituencies, in which the prefects and sub-prefects, experts at electoral management, the majority of whom had passed over from the service of Louis-Philippe to that of Louis Napoleon, could make certain – by all the traditional devices – that only the official candidate had much chance of succeeding. The result of the elections that were held in March 1852 was a foregone conclusion. Four legitimists, one independent, and three republicans (who refused to sit) were elected; the remaining 253 members were official candidates, chosen by the administration to uphold the Bonapartist cause in the constituencies. The labourers were not considered unworthy of their hire: in the same month the salaries of the prefects were doubled. 'The dictatorship with which the people has entrusted me ceases today', declared Louis Napoleon in an official pronouncement on 30 March. It was only to cease, in the humiliation of Sedan, eighteen years later.

The possibility of failure seemed far removed at the outset. The new régime was lucky in the stars under which it was born, for the lean years in European economy were at an end and the new government was able to take advantage of a rising tide of economic activity. Shares rose rapidly in value on the Paris market. The Bank of France reduced its interest rate to 3 per cent. A triumphal tour of a regenerated France in the autumn of 1852 by Louis Napoleon was followed by the proclamation of the Empire and a plebiscite in which 7,800,000 voted yes and 250,000 no.

Even allowing for two million abstentions this was a decisive endorsement of France's new ruler. Yet what kind of man he was very few knew. Aged forty-four in 1852, he was still almost completely an unknown quantity to the country that had entrusted its destinies to him. The son of Josephine's daughter Hortense Beauharnais, and Napoleon's brother Louis, the un-Napoleonic appearance of Napoleon III, as he chose to be known, and the adventures of Hortense subsequent to his birth, had led to doubt being cast on his paternity, though almost certainly without justification. He was brought up by his mother, after she and Louis had separated, among the flotsam and jetsam of the Empire in exile. It was the drifting, raffish life, in Germany, Italy, England, Switzerland, of a cosmopolitan adventurer. Queen Victoria, when she met the new Emperor, remarked that unlike Louis-Philippe, who was 'thoroughly French', Louis Napoleon was 'as *unlike* a Frenchman as possible', and much more German than French in character. She was a shrewd judge and meant it as praise.

The first political action of the young Louis Napoleon was in Italian, not French, politics. He joined an abortive Carbonari rising in 1831 and had to fly the pursuing Austrians in disguise. Possibly the tutorship of Philippe le

Bas, son of the Robespierrist, had aroused his youthful idealism. His first political declaration – the *Rêveries politiques* of 1832 – proposed the regeneration of France by a peculiar combination of Napoleon II and the Republic. Only after the death of the duc de Reichstadt was it possible for Louis Napoleon to put forward the Bonapartist claim on his own behalf.

It is difficult to know at what stage he began to feel he was a man of destiny. Queen Victoria, when she met Napoleon III in 1855, was impressed by his genuine belief that all he had done and did was only in fulfilment of his destiny. But if a superstitious belief in his fate deceived him, it need not deceive us or lead us to underestimate his real abilities. Chance had not dealt Louis Napoleon many cards apart from his name. He was no orator and wisely chose to listen rather than speak, unlike Louis-Philippe, whose garrulity was a legend. The charm which he could exercise over other men, and even more over women, owed little to advantages of appearance. Greville describes him as 'a short thickish vulgar-looking man'. Practically all the Bonapartes, of course, were rather vulgar. In addition, Louis Napoleon had no taste in literature or art. It would be an interesting question whether the official art of the Second Empire was, or was not, more boring, pretentious, and vapid than that of the First. That there was no originality in Louis Napoleon does not perhaps matter, for originality is not normally conducive to political success. On the other hand, like the first Napoleon he had a great capacity for picking up other men's ideas; his mind was immensely receptive. It can hardly be denied that between his election in 1848 and the *coup d'état* in 1851 he played his cards with great shrewdness and beat the politicians at their own game. He had more natural generosity and humanity – when his ambitions did not get in the way – than most dictators; and his sympathy for the lot of the French working-man went beyond the mere requirements of the cult of popularity. If we say that in the last resort he had no moral scruples, this is to refer to his single-minded devotion to the quest of power, in which he gave those who observed him the impression, if not of the frantic possession of a Hitler, at least of a quieter, but equally unswerving kind of somnambulism. Louis Napoleon's taciturnity gave the illusion of depths that were not there. It is difficult to dislike him; but equally difficult to respect him.

Napoleon III never became more than an adventurer, even when he was on a throne; and for all his triumphs he never seems to have enjoyed them. Perhaps he was already prematurely old when success came. Perhaps he had trained himself to sacrifice everything else, including happiness, to success in his chosen objectives. Only in some such way can his marriage be explained. Evidently the new Emperor would have to marry if he was to perpetuate his dynasty. Negotiations for one or two minor royalties had proved abortive when, unfortunately, Louis Napoleon's roving eye was caught by a Spanish beauty in transit through Paris. She was of noble birth, twenty-six years old, and a notorious virgin. It was a challenge and he attempted his usual gambit of seduction, which totally failed. Even fairly mature Spanish grandees were not easily seduced, especially if there was the prospect of something better. In January 1853 it materialized in the form of marriage. 'She has played her game with him so well,' wrote the British ambassador, 'that he can get her in no other way but marriage.' But though she was beautiful, an admirable model for a fashionable painter like Winterhalter, with all the dignity that Napoleon III himself sometimes lacked, and in the end exhibited courage and greater force of character than the Emperor, Eugénie was a bad choice in almost every other respect. She was not very intelligent, but very religious, or at least clerical in a Spanish way. Her influence, and that of her friends, over the policy of the Second Empire was almost invariably unfortunate. There were personal difficulties too. Her mother, it turned out, did not live up to her daughter's standards: she collected debts and lovers. Eugénie, on the other hand, proved to be one of nature's virgins, incapable of responding to the Emperor's sensuality, and he periodically resorted to Miss Howard, now created comtesse de Beauregard, and subsequently to many others. After the birth of the Prince Imperial in 1856, which nearly cost the Empress her life, marital relations ceased.

However, the succession was secured, so far as the life of one heir could do so, and the element of loyalty to a dynasty, though a very new one, could begin to play a rôle in politics. Bonapartism was more than mere attachment to a name. An opponent might say that it was a synthetic substitute for real political principles, a combination of inconsistent and irreconcilable objectives, of value only as propaganda. But among the supporters of Napoleon III there was one group, with which he himself had considerable sympathy, which – so far as its ideas went – could supply the Second Empire with a policy and some sort of working philosophy behind it. These were the Saint-Simonians, now more or less recovered from the père Enfantin's aberrations. Saint-Simon as the John the Baptist of Positivism may be left where he belongs, in the classes on moral philosophy of the *écoles normales*. 'It seems', writes one *normalien*, 'that his best title to fame is in having transmitted from Condorcet to Comte the idea of a positive policy founded on social science.' A better claim may be found in the implications of his well-known parable. Suppose, Saint-Simon says, France were to lose suddenly its fifty leading scientists of all kinds, artists, architects, engineers, doctors, bankers, merchants, ironmasters, industrialists in every branch, masons, carpenters, and workers in every craft – it would immediately sink in the scale of civilization and become inferior to all those countries of which it is now the equal. On the other hand, suppose it kept all its leading men of science, arts and crafts, commerce and industry, but lost the whole royal family, all the ministers and counsellors of state, the prefects, judges, archbishops, bishops, and all other ecclesiastical dignitaries, and in addition the ten thousand wealthiest landed proprietors living solely on the income from their property – the loss would undoubtedly grieve the French, being a humane people, but it would not materially affect their prosperity or their position in the world. In other words, Saint-Simon was asserting the primacy of the productive classes in society, of economic over political ends. It was also a protest against the dominance of the conservative propertied classes which was established by the Revolution.

Saint-Simon died in 1825, but his disciples continued and systematized his ideas of economic progress. The problem before France, as they saw it, was stated by Michel Chevalier in *Des intérêts matériels en France* in 1838. The new ruling class, he says, has won political power only in alliance with the people. If it is not to be overthrown in its turn it will have to meet the material demands of the people. This can be done only by means of the development of credit, communications, and education. The events of 1848 went a long way towards justifying this analysis, but they also showed that the position of the propertied classes was stronger than he supposed and that they had no intention of adopting Chevalier's remedy, or any other, except that of crude repression. They viewed the Saint-Simonian idea of the expenditure of large sums by the State to counter economic depression with horror. The Saint-Simonians themselves were not unaware of the strength of the opposition to their ideas and looked to strong government as the only means of economic and social reform. It was natural, therefore, that they should have welcomed the coming to power of Louis Napoleon, who himself had been attracted by the novelty and promise of Saint-Simonian ideas. They provided him with an economic programme, and with some of the personnel to put it into practice. The expansion of credit, railways, industry, trade, even the rebuilding of Paris, for which there had been a Saint-Simonian plan in 1832 – in fact, practically all the major economic developments, and therefore nearly all the real and lasting achievements of the Second Empire – derive from the inspiration of Saint-Simon and his followers. Though on a smaller scale and in a more restricted field, Saint-Simon might almost be called the Bentham of nineteenth-century France.

The key to economic progress in France lay in the growth of credit, as the Saint-Simonians correctly saw. It is sometimes assumed that the Second Empire was promoted, in their own interests, by the financiers. The truth is rather, on the contrary, that the financiers were promoted by the Second Empire. The affiliations of most high finance were with the old order of Orleanism or with the conservative republic. The only names that stand out on the side of Louis Napoleon are those of the Péreire brothers and Achille Fould. Existing banks and orthodox financiers catered mainly for the wealthy and conservative *rentiers*, interested principally in government loans. For the growth of industry new banks were needed. The Comptoir d'Escompte, founded in 1848 and developed with the encouragement of the Emperor, was primarily a commercial bank. Later it developed considerable colonial and Far Eastern interests. The Crédit Foncier, founded in 1852, was given a monopoly of mortgage finance, and its moderate terms facilitated the extensive rebuilding of the towns of France during the Second Empire. The Crédit Agricole dealt in farm mortgages and other agricultural finance; it ran into difficulties later, but this was after 1870. Private banks were also developed, the most famous being the Crédit Mobilier of the Péreire brothers, Saint-Simonians, who plunged heavily in French and foreign railways, a French steamship line, and government loans. Later, in 1863, the Crédit Lyonnais was set up; conducted with the traditional caution of the Lyonnais businessmen, it has flourished to the present day.

A wave of economic expansion followed the establishment of the Empire. It was concentrated particularly on the development of railways. After a slow beginning, the companies were rationalized by being reduced to six, and the pace of construction was so accelerated that by 1859 France had nearly three times as great a length of line as in 1851. By 1870 France had almost as extensive a network of lines in operation as Germany or Great Britain. Railway development stimulated, of course, the production of coal and iron. The consumption of coal was trebled, and the use of horse power in industry quintupled, between 1851 and 1870. The average price of steel was practically halved. The greatest of the iron-works, at Le Creusot, was bought by the Schneider brothers in 1836 when its annual production was 5,000 tons; in 1847 it was 18,000, and the increased pace of growth under the Second Empire is shown by the rise from 35,000 tons in 1855 to 133,000 in 1867. In the same period the foreign commerce of France practically trebled.

Meanwhile the growth of the French population had slackened, so that the increased wealth of the country was not swallowed up by the excess of mouths. Moreover the shift from the country to the town continued. The proportion of urban population grew from 24 per cent to 31 per cent, and this probably represented a rise in the average standard of life in the countryside, for it was the landless labourers and the poorest element there which declined most. The growth of railways, which played their part in facilitating the movement from the country, also broke down some of the traditional rural isolation.

The share of the state in providing the actual finance for this general economic development should not be exaggerated. Up to 1860 the public works programme was financed mainly by private investment. Budgetary expenses for this purpose were indeed smaller than they had been under Louis Philippe; whence those developments in which for one reason or another the private investor was not interested – roads, canals, ports – languished. The same was true of agriculture. The peasants, whose votes had established the Second Empire, were those who profited least from it. They were suspicious of all new methods; the legal structure of France protected the small proprietor in his jealous independence of any interference, and the subdivision of the land prohibited any general or co-ordinated schemes of improvement.

The programme of public works which Louis Napoleon inaugurated was in his mind a continuation of the policy of the First Empire. He himself wrote of Napoleon I, 'The public works, which the Emperor put into operation on such a large scale, were not only one of the principal causes of domestic prosperity, they even promoted great social progress.' While these motives were certainly present to the mind of Napoleon III, the propaganda value of public works was also not absent, particularly if they could be effected in full view of the public. The improvement of Paris, in continuation of the work of Napoleon I, was therefore among the first projects to be taken in hand after the *coup d'état*.

The need to render Paris, like all the other great urban agglomerations of Europe, habitable, was patent enough; but it would be a mistake to attribute the improvements solely to the pressure of hard facts. Reforms, in Paris as in London, did not come about by the automatic pressure of circumstances; they were the conscious achievement of the disciples of a Saint-Simon and a Bentham, and in France the result of deliberate government policy. It was not confined to the capital: at Lyon, the prefect Vaisse effected an almost equally dramatic transformation.

The first attempt of Napoleon III, after the *coup d'état*, to promote a policy of public works was frustrated by the conservative financial ideas of the officials in charge, but in 1853 one of the most energetic of the prefects was brought to Paris. This was the Alsatian Protestant, Haussmann, who had hitched his administrative wagon to the rising star of Louis Napoleon as early as the presidential election of 1848. As a godson of Prince Eugène, Haussmann had almost an hereditary claim to be regarded as a Bonapartist. Forceful and cunning, ambitious, unprincipled, formidable in bulk and character, he was the ideal agent for the Second Empire in a grade a little lower than the highest. He was to be Prefect of the Seine from 1853 to 1870. Such a man did not shrink from unorthodox, but up to a point justified, financial methods. The theory behind them was simply that the new values created by the reconstruction of the older sectors of Paris would themselves pay for the work that had to be undertaken.

The scope of Haussmann's demolition and reconstruction is amazing. He gave Paris eighty-five miles of new streets with wide carriage-ways and pavements shaded with trees. Private enterprise lined them with houses and shops, to a height and with a façade prescribed by the authorities, and in a style that represented Haussmann's idea of architectural beauty, for the Prefect of the Seine had the born philistine's conviction of his own impeccable artistic taste. Viollet-le-Duc, apart from the injury he did to Notre-Dame, was kept out of the rebuilding of Paris by Haussmann, who was neither romantic nor medieval. His passion, like that of Napoleon I, was for vistas. The place de l'Étoile looks very fine from the air: it is a pity that it is not normally seen from that angle. Napoleon III, indeed, reproached Haussmann that in his love of straight lines he neglected the needs of traffic. The new railway stations, for example, were left without adequate approaches.

The best things in the re-planning of Paris were due to the influence of Napoleon III. His memories of London inspired the creation of many squares and other open places. The Bois de Boulogne, which had been a rather dull royal forest, cut across by long straight avenues for the hunters, was given by the Emperor to the city. At the instigation of Morny a race-course was created at Longchamps; it rapidly became a fashionable social resort, the profits on which largely paid for the transformation of the uninteresting *bois* into a landscaped park. A similar treatment was accorded to the Bois de Vincennes on the east of Paris. Napoleon III was also responsible for the construction of the Halles, the great central market, as a functional structure of metal and glass.

Apart from the long straight roads he drove through Paris, and the vistas they afforded, Haussmann's greatest achievement was in the drainage of the city. The sewers of Paris before him are luridly described by Victor Hugo in *Les Misérables*. By the end of the Second Empire the visit, especially of the great sewer which Haussmann liked to call his Cloaca Maxima, was a tourist attraction. A further virtue of the sewers was that they had been built without tearing anything else down, for much of old Paris and many fine and historic buildings were sacrificed to make it a Second Empire city. A sentimental regret for what was lost, and even an aesthetic distaste for what replaced it, would neither, perhaps, be justified if a fine modern city with improved living conditions had been built. But the tradition of urbanism, the Florence of the Medici, the Paris of Louis XV, the Nancy of king Stanislaus, had now come down to the boulevard Malesherbes and the place de l'Opéra. Behind the state-prescribed façades of Haussmann's streets the builders could put up what they liked, and often new and more imposing slums replaced the older and more picturesque ones. Running water was only supplied at the option of the owner of a building, who often decided that it was an unnecessary luxury, since it involved the payment of a water rate. The function of the grand new sewers must not be mistaken: they were to remove the rain-water from the streets and prevent flooding. Sanitary, or rather insanitary, refuse still had to be carted away by an army of men at night in the traditional fashion, or sunk in cess pits, or deposited illegally in streets and gardens. Another, equally unpleasant, aspect of the city was the large area taken up by decaying bodies. Haussmann is not to be blamed for this; his plans for a great municipal cemetery outside Paris were successfully resisted by those who were determined that when they could do no more mischief there alive, they should leave their dead bodies to pollute the air and drinking water of the city.

The attention that was paid to Paris was not given to its surroundings. The Wall of the Farmers General (on the line of the present outer ring of boulevards), with its sixty gates, was now no longer the effective limit of occupation. A shift of population was taking place to the large area between this wall and the fortifications of the Orleanist Monarchy. Railway works and factories attracted a suburban population; and many of those who continued to work in Paris were drawn outwards by the cheapness of living in what was becoming a huge, poverty-stricken, higgledy-piggledy encampment of shacks. However, in the great enterprise of Haussmann good and bad were mixed up together, and his achievement suited his day and generation. Contemporaries who began by opposing and went on to mock his efforts, came to admire the results.

The crown of them all was to be the new Paris Opera, built by Charles Garnier, inspired by the eighteenth-century Bordeaux Opera, and calculated for the gratification of a society even richer and more luxurious than the eighteenth-century mercantile aristocracy of Bordeaux, as well as for a less chaste artistic taste than that of the age of Louis XV. Within and without it was loaded with decoration in all the styles known to history. A separate carriage-way led into a private entrance to the imperial box, for Napoleon remembered the attempt by Orsini and the murder of the duc de Berry. A huge entrance hall and elaborate stairs, for the arrival and reception of foreign or French notabilities; a foyer for the circulation of the fashionable throng; an auditorium surrounded by boxes to preserve the privacy of wealth and rank or facilitate amorous intrigue; a stage as deep as the auditorium, on which the most grandiose spectacles could be presented – such was the Paris Opera, a worthy setting for the luxury and splendour of Second Empire society, where Napoleon III and his Empress might shine amidst the wealthiest *nouveaux riches* and the most beautiful courtesans of Paris. This was a dream picture: in 1871 the Opera was still unfinished. It was completed, with the constitutional laws of the Third Republic, in 1875.

The Second Empire was the real bourgeois monarchy, an age of plutocrats without the culture or taste of an eighteenth-century Farmer General, of fashionable priests without the religious feeling of a Lamennais or a Lacordaire, of well-disciplined academics without the intellectual distinction of the Orleanist scholars, of glittering *demi-mondaines* whose possession was one of the chief forms of ostentatious expenditure and signs of worldly success. The fashionable painters and writers were even more insignificant than usual in modern times. Apart from Daumier's cartoons, Millet's paintings exhibiting the dignity of labour, and Courbet's bourgeois-shocking realism, the only painters of real distinction were the rebels of the Salon des Refusés in 1863 who, rejected by official art, founded the great impressionist school of the Third Republic. The most lasting artistic creations that belong properly to the Second Empire are the comedies of Labiche and the operettas of Offenbach. What was on a higher level represented either a survival of the romanticism of the early century, or a direct or implied protest against the new society and its standards. Victor Hugo, fulminating in exile from the Channel Isles, launched *Les Châtiments* against 'Napoléon le Petit'. The cult of realism that is associated with the Third Republic developed in fact under the Second Empire, which recognized its enmity when the publications of *Madame Bovary* and the *Fleurs du Mal* were prosecuted in 1857.

If we want to see the spirit of the Second Empire at its best and most triumphant, we must look at the Exhibition of 1855, organized in imitation of the Great Exhibition of 1851 in London, but representing none the less a genuine aspiration after economic progress and pride in the beginnings of achievement.

4. L'EMPIRE C'EST LA PAIX

AN age of materialism and money-making was opening, selfish and – especially after the June Days – hag-ridden with class hatred, but all classes were striving, with varying success, for the same thing – a higher standard of living. The desire for adventures, either domestic or foreign, if it ever existed, was over. Nationalist historians have represented a nineteenth-century France constantly harking back to the military glories of the First Empire. Nothing could be more misleading. There were many grievances against the July Monarchy, but its lack of bellicose ardour was not one of the causes of the 1848 Revolution. If the left-wing republicans and socialists aroused the opposition of the nation under the Second Republic, it was not least because of the fear that they might involve France in war with Europe. Louis Napoleon had judged the desires of the country rightly when he proclaimed, *l'Empire, c'est la Paix.*

They had not changed by 1853, when the Russian occupation of Moldavia and Wallachia led to a Russo-Turkish War. France was involved because she claimed to be the protector of Roman Catholic interests in the Near East, and a quarrel over the custody of the Holy Places had been the occasion, if not the cause, of the Russo-Turkish war. The French Emperor was indignant at the Russian aggression and at what seemed to him a humiliation for France; but though clerical support might have been expected, the country as a whole entered the Crimean War not only without enthusiasm, but with patent reluctance. However, confused as were the events leading up to the outbreak of war in March 1854, the responsibility of Napoleon III for them was comparatively slight. Nor can he be held personally responsible for the incompetence with which the war was conducted, particularly by his British ally.

The news of the fall of Sebastopol in September 1855, after much disappointment and disillusionment, was greeted in France with an outburst of rejoicing. It was assumed to mean peace, and if it had not meant peace, opposition to the continuance of the war would have been widespread. The Peace Congress was held at Paris in the spring of 1856. It was a triumph for Napoleon III, though what France gained by the war it is difficult to say.

If the Crimean War was the result of accident, the same can hardly be said of the next war that the Second Empire was involved in. The legend of Napoleon I as the liberator of Italy, the early association of Louis Napoleon with the Italian Carbonari, and his genuine nationalist ideals, given his obstinate, fatalistic habit of clinging to the ends he had once set himself, made it certain that the Emperor would endeavour to do something for Italy. Cavour was fully

aware of this and played on Napoleon III in all the ways
he knew. The insane attempt by the Italian revolutionary,
Orsini, to assassinate Napoleon III and Eugénie as they
arrived at the Opera, which killed eight people and injured
many more, was just the thing to appeal to the over-clever
mind of an ex-conspirator as an opportunity to turn it to
precisely the opposite ends from those that any reasonable
calculation could have anticipated. Orsini, of course, had
to be executed, but first he had to play the rôle, which his
appearance and the Emperor cast him for, of the romantic
patriot. Through his would-be assassin, Louis Napoleon
was able to proclaim indirectly his allegiance to the ideal of
Italian liberation.

The next step was the secret conference with Cavour, in
July 1858, at Plombières, where, in the absence of his
ministers, the Emperor reached a verbal agreement envisag-
ing war against Austria. The Italian war, which was now
planned, shows even more clearly than any of the other
wars of the Second Empire, that they are not to be attributed to pressure from below, or to the French desire for
glory, so beloved of historians, or to a supposed need to
cement the Emperor's authority. They were the necessary
result of his foreign policy, which he kept largely in his own
hands, partly through belief in his star, and partly because
he never fully trusted any of his ministers. This was why,
says Émile Ollivier, 'he adopted the custom of dealing
directly with the ambassadors on important occasions, to
the exclusion of his ministers.' The meeting at Plombières
was followed by a year of declarations which seemed to
make war inevitable, yet which, under the pressure of
French and European opinion, stopped short of actually
provoking it. There is a possibility, indeed, that Napoleon
was playing an insidious game of bluff, which would be
characteristic of him, and hoping in the end to achieve
something without war. His last-minute agreement to a
European congress to discuss the future of Italy, though he
pretended to those who wanted war that it was not intended
seriously, casts some doubt on the sincerity of his bellicose

gestures. The cunning of Cavour and the folly of the Austrians robbed him of the choice and in April 1859 war began.

Despite these equivocations, the Italian War was essentially the Emperor's own. The ministers were opposed to it; the clergy and those who followed their lead, the peasantry and most of the better-off classes, were against it. Only the enemies of the Emperor, the republicans and their clientele in the towns, viewed it with favour. The Emperor had seemed to be working for war by all the methods he could, with little regard for scruple, or even for French interests, as if he were infatuated. It was the even greater folly of the Vienna government and the Austrian ultimatum that gave him the chance to bring France into the war on a temporary wave of anti-Austrian sentiment. Whatever the feelings of the peasants who furnished the mass of the troops, their departure for the war brought cheering crowds into the streets of the cities; and when the Emperor himself, leaving Paris from the Gare de Lyon, had to pass through the workers' quarter of Saint-Antoine, there were scenes of great enthusiasm.

Perhaps as a Bonaparte, Napoleon III was expected to be, and may – though this is more doubtful – have expected himself to be, a military genius. Really, considering his total lack of military experience, the fact that he did not get his armies into a complete mess, indeed into rather less of a muddle than professional generals had done in the Crimean War, or than the Austrian generals did with the troops opposed to him, is very much to his credit. The Austrians, who had advanced into Piedmontese territory, were defeated first at Magenta, which saved Milan, and then at Solferino, after which the French and Piedmontese were on the point of invading Venetia.

It is unlikely that this luck would have lasted, and there were other considerations which called for serious reflection. Things were not turning out quite as Napoleon III had expected. Revolutions in the smaller Italian states were throwing them into the arms of Piedmont. The revolt of the papal province of Romagna increased the opposition of the French clericals to the war. Prussia was mobilizing on the Rhine. The Austrian forces were now in a stronger position, resting on the famous fortresses of the Quadrilateral. Solferino had brought enough glory and bloodshed for both the Emperor and his people. As after the fall of Sebastopol, only now even more so, there was a general cry for peace. All this might easily have been anticipated, but it apparently took Louis Napoleon by surprise. He reacted quickly by opening negotiations with Francis Joseph, and less than three weeks after the battle an armistice was concluded at Villafranca.

By its terms, Lombardy was to be ceded to France, for her to transfer to the Kingdom of Sardinia; but Austria was to keep Venetia, and in the Italian states which had revolted their former rulers were to be restored. Since he had failed to unite all Northern Italy to Piedmont, Napoleon could not claim the cession of Savoy and Nice to France, which had been part of the agreement with Cavour. The fact that the other Italian states were united to the Kingdom of Sardinia in the course of 1860, and that France could consequently annex Savoy and Nice, was a purely adventitious gain, but it meant that at the last minute the Emperor's luck had held. Though some clerical and right-wing support was alienated, and the Foreign Minister, Walewski, whose sympathies were with the papal cause, had to resign, republican and left-wing opinion – which presented a much more serious opposition – became more favourable to the Empire. The real miscalculation of the Italian war lay in its effect on the European situation, but this was only gradually to be revealed.

Napoleon III was much more interested in asserting the rôle of France among the Great Powers than in developing imperial ambitions outside Europe. In the colonial, as in every other field, it is difficult to trace a consistent policy through the aberrations of the Second Empire. The Emperor began with a prejudice against Algeria, which he called '*un boulet attaché aux pieds de la France*'. His romanticism, or his national ideas, or perhaps even his idealism, brought about a drastic reversal of policy in 1863, when, in a public letter to the Governor General, he condemned the confiscation of native land for the colonists. 'Today', he declared, 'we must convince the Arabs that we have not come into Algeria to oppress and despoil them, but to bring them the advantages of civilization. ... Algeria is not a colony properly speaking, but an *Arab kingdom*. ... I am just as much the Emperor of the Arabs as of the French.' One result of this new orientation of French policy was a drastic diminution in colonization, and attempts to introduce large-scale capitalist enterprise which failed. The government of Algeria continued to be in military hands until 1870, when a parliamentary enquiry condemned the system and the government restored the authority of the prefects.

Senegal, considered of secondary importance, had the good fortune to be governed from 1854 to 1865, with a brief gap, by one of the wisest colonial administrators France has had. This was Faidherbe, an engineer captain in 1854, who established a system of indirect rule and extended French authority inland. When he retired, he had wrested large populations from the overlordship of the Moors and sketched out the plan of an extensive and prosperous colony. He established the pattern of pacification, organization, and assimilation which was to be continued with remarkable success for many years. In 1857 the port of Dakar was founded. Attempts to develop the native agriculture of Senegal were markedly successful. A cadre of able colonial administrators was built up. Altogether, in Africa under the Second Empire we can see the beginning of the modern problems of colonial government, and tentative answers, emerging sometimes through the influence of the Emperor, and sometimes in spite of him.

In the Far East French missionaries and merchants led the way, to be followed by small expeditionary forces. An Anglo-French punitive force in 1860 occupied Pekin, burnt the Summer Palace, and looted everything it could lay its hands on, to show the superiority of European civilization.

A French force annexed Cochin-China in 1862 and a French protectorate was established over Cambodia.

Nearer home, Turkish massacres of Christians in Syria led to a French expedition there in 1860, which afforded the occasion for international recognition of France's traditional interests in the Levant. Finally, it was in 1859 that Ferdinand de Lesseps began the construction of the Suez Canal, in spite of English opposition. The most ambitious of the overseas projects of Napoleon III was to be in Mexico, but this must be dealt with later, at the moment when the reckoning was sent in.

This colonial expansion was carried on without any suggestion of rivalry or conflict with Great Britain. This is all the more remarkable because French opinion, throughout the Second Empire, was even more than normally Anglophobe. At the Congress of Paris it was remarked that an uninformed observer might have thought the Russians the allies and the British the recent enemy. Yet Napoleon III was determined not to make the mistake of his uncle and allow himself to be drawn into hostilities with Great Britain. This determination, in the light of his European ambitions, was undoubtedly wise, and perhaps all the more so because it ran counter to the dominant trend of French opinion, while in England anti-French feeling was so strong that coastal fortifications were constructed and corps of volunteers enlisted for defence against France.

After the Italian war, the Emperor began seriously to reflect that perhaps after all the Empire ought to mean peace. Fear of further wars was beginning to weaken confidence inside France. He had by now thoroughly stirred up Europe and shattered the status quo. This may have been one reason for the negotiation of the Cobden Free Trade treaty with Great Britain. It was intended as a gesture of reassurance. In a letter published in January 1860, Napoleon announced that peace would be used to develop national wealth and improve the conditions of the agricultural population and the workers. At the same time he had a genuine belief in the benefits to be derived from the adoption of Free Trade principles. Chevalier had persuaded him to accept the plan for a commercial treaty with England before Cobden met the Emperor. It had not been a difficult task, for Napoleon III had a genuine interest in the well-being of the populace of France, and believed that a reduction in the traditionally high French tariff wall would promote it.

He kept his plans secret from those ministers who were not likely to agree with them. Walewski, who was out of sympathy both with the Italian and the commercial policy, was removed from the Foreign Ministry in December 1859. In January 1860 Napoleon published a letter to his Minister of State, Fould, in which he announced measures for the improvement of French agriculture and industry with the aid of government loans, in preparation for the commercial treaty. Because the Legislative Body, weak as it was, would not abandon protective duties quietly, the Emperor resorted to a reduction by executive action. Cobden and Chevalier negotiated the Anglo-French free trade treaty, which was signed in January 1860. The French industrialists, fanatical protectionists, reacted with combined panic and fury. Petitions were got up; manufacturers descended on Paris to protest – those from Rouen even chartered a special train – but all to no avail. By the terms of the treaty France agreed to bring absolute prohibitions of import to an end, and to reduce her tariff to a maximum of 30 per cent within two years and 25 per cent in five years. Great Britain practically abolished all customs dues on imports from France, except for those on wines and spirits. In actual fact the French government went further than it had promised in reducing customs rates.

Commercial treaties followed with other states. In matters of trade the Second Empire was the only liberal régime France has ever known. It did not seem to harm French prosperity. The small iron works, still dependent on wood, the iron mines of the North, rapidly being worked out, were hurried to their end by foreign competition, but British competition brought down the price of iron and so stimulated the growth of railways and the introduction of machinery.

On the other hand, the hopes of a period of international peace to be promoted by the adoption of a free trade policy were hardly fulfilled. In the sixties the Second Empire was entering on a period of misfortunes and mistakes. Though he had his long-term objectives, the actual policy of the Emperor had always developed as a series of lucky improvisations. Now his luck was changing, or perhaps we might say that the unpaid debts resulting from earlier gambles were coming in for payment. He was less equal to them than formerly, because a disease of the kidneys and bladder was increasingly weakening him and sapping his capacity for decision.

In the fifties Louis Napoleon had built up the prestige and influence of France in European councils with considerable success. What this meant was that France was returning to the position among the Great Powers that her population, wealth, and military potential justified. It is also fair to say that for a number of different reasons the competition inside Europe was not formidable at this time, while the Emperor sedulously avoided any serious dispute with Great Britain. But in the sixties the situation began to change, partly as a result of Napoleon III's own actions. His semi-romantic, early nineteenth-century ideas of foreign policy were no longer appropriate in the harsher climate of blood and iron that was sweeping over Europe; and also it must be admitted that, in the age of Cavour and Bismarck, Louis Napoleon was out of his class.

There was another, and perhaps more fundamental, cause of the failure of French foreign policy in the sixties. France could now only maintain her prestige and keep up her relative position among the Great Powers of Europe by preparing for, and facing the possibility of, eventual war. But by 1860 the French nation had fought in ten years two more wars than it wanted. The Emperor himself had his fill of war and moreover was well-informed of the strongly pacific trend of public opinion. This was perhaps the decisive factor, which needs to be emphasized. Napoleon III never forgot that he had been brought to power by the masses of the people. His authority had not been created by, nor did it depend on, the army. There was no great party machine, as in modern fascist and communist dictatorships, to hold the people down. His was a personal and plebiscitary dictatorship, and what the people had given the people might take away. The Emperor was therefore almost pathologically conscious of his dependence on public opinion, and lacking the machinery – apart from a press of which the known subservience was the measure of its lack of influence – or the modern techniques for manufacturing opinion, he had often, indeed too often for the well-being of the country, to follow it. The problem was to discover what the public, in so far as a public existed, was thinking. Here the Second Empire had to fall back on the method of earlier régimes, by relying on a continuous flow of reports on the state of opinion from its own administrative agents.

Dependence for information on those who have a vested interest in representing the situation in the most favourable light, for naturally they do not wish to cast discredit on their own services or their efforts to influence opinion, can prove very dangerous, and leave a government – as it left Louis-Philippe and Guizot – in sublime ignorance of their own isolation from the country. The stronger the government, the greater the danger of this. The governments of the Second Empire were weak, though the régime was not equally weak. The prefects and other officials would doubtless generally have been anxious to provide the answers that their superiors wanted if they had known what these were, but often they did not; and particularly in his later years the Emperor was genuinely trying to discover what public opinion demanded, in order to satisfy it. Sometimes, it is true, he initiated policies under the impression that they would win popular favour, and then found it difficult to liquidate them when this proved a miscalculation. But he was no longer prepared, as he had been when he assumed responsibility for the Italian War and the Treaty of Commerce, to swim against the tide.

When Poland revolted against Russian rule in 1863 the Emperor followed opinion faithfully in first alienating Alexander II and sacrificing what was almost a Russian alliance by protesting against the suppression of the Poles, and then exhibiting his weakness by doing nothing to follow up the protest, beyond proposing a congress. Great Britain, suspecting French ambition to recreate a Polish client state in Eastern Europe, refused to support this proposal. The next year, when Prussia and Austria seized the duchies of Schleswig and Holstein, it was Great Britain that proposed the congress, and Napoleon III, in a futile hope of extracting compensation from Prussia on the Rhine, who refused his support. Neither France, nor Great Britain, of course, was prepared to fire a shot in support of the smaller nations of Europe; in these circumstances their notes and diplomatic manoeuvres could not be anything but useless gestures.

In 1866 came the Austro-Prussian War, in preparation for which Bismarck had played Napoleon III like a cynical animal trainer with a greedy but rather stupid beast, enticing him into the desired position with the proffer of a choice morsel – of not clearly specified territory on the Rhine – but all the time intending to snatch it away at the last moment. Louis Napoleon, of course, was not foolish enough to count on Bismarck's gratitude for the reward of his neutrality. He believed that Austria was the stronger of the two Germanic powers, and with his old pro-Italian and anti-Austrian obsession, gladly saw Italy join in on the side of Prussia to redress the balance and wrench Venetia from the Austrian Empire. His miscalculation was basically due to the fact that the Austrian Empire was still for him what it had been for Napoleon I, the real enemy in Europe. Prussia, on the other hand, was seen as the weak state defeated at Jena and a natural ally of France. French opinion also, as Bismarck had assured himself through his informants in France in advance of the war, was determined that France should keep out of it. Louis Napoleon even contemplated an alliance with Prussia and Italy against Austria; and when Thiers in a brilliant speech warned France against a policy that was setting up a united Germany and Italy as dangerous rivals to France, Napoleon went out of his way to repudiate this view and proclaim his belief in the primary interest of France in smashing the Vienna settlement of 1815. After the rapid Prussian victory, the foreign minister, Drouyn de Lhuys, and the Empress were for immediate war, and this was the moment when France might have resorted to war with the best chance. Unfortunately, although French sentiments were now anti-Prussian, the habit of sitting on the side-lines and cheering or booing without intervening in a dangerous game had gone on too long to be changed overnight. France was still profoundly pacific and Napoleon had done nothing to prepare French opinion for the necessity of resisting Prussian aggression. At the critical moment he was ill, and his strongest minister, Rouher, was opposed to armed intervention. All the Emperor could fall back on was the notorious 'policy of *pourboires*' – territorial compensation to be extracted by weakness from strength – the left bank of the Rhine, Belgium, Luxembourg. What Great Britain, the German states, and the states involved in the proposed bargain, when it became known – and Bismarck saw to it that it did – thought of these proposals need not be said.

Meanwhile the French garrison, kept in Rome under pressure from the French Catholics but withdrawn in December 1866, had been brought back in October 1867. A small French force assisted the papal troops in repelling Garibaldi at Mentana. This completed the antagonization of Italy. Between 1863 and 1867 Louis Napoleon succeeded in alienating practically every state of any importance in Europe.

Outside Europe earlier colonial successes had led up to a much more ambitious scheme to undo what Napoleon III might well consider the mistake that Napoleon I had made in selling Louisiana. As always, a series of accidents seemed to mark the path of Napoleon III to the end which, when he had attained it, could be seen to have been in his mind all the time. A moderately reforming and anti-clerical government in Mexico under President Juarez having repudiated the foreign loans incurred by its predecessor, in 1862 a debt-collecting Anglo-Franco-Spanish expedition was sent to Mexico. When the other two contingents withdrew, a French force remained at Vera Cruz to experience a defeat at the hands of Juarez' men. This, of course, had to be avenged for the sake of French honour and imperial dignity. Reinforcements were therefore sent out, which captured Mexico City and organized an Assembly of Notables. This offered the throne of Mexico to a Habsburg prince, Maximilian, put forward by Napoleon III. The Civil War meanwhile prevented the United States from opposing the breach of the Monroe Doctrine.

A mixture of motives inspired this attempt to establish a client state of France in the Americas. To the expected extension of national power and prestige was added the hope of economic gain – perhaps a persistence of the legend of the wealth of the Indies. Morny had a more personal hope of gain in the form of a commission of 30 per cent on the repayments to a great Swiss creditor of Mexico. There was strong Catholic support for a plan which promised to overthrow the anti-clerical Juarez government; at Rome the French campaign was proclaimed a crusade. The French expedition proved a much bigger military commitment than had been expected; in the mid-sixties nearly 40,000 of the best French troops were tied up on the wrong side of the Atlantic, when the balance of Europe was being changed. The situation was not improved by the fact that the French general, Bazaine, quarrelled with the other leaders of the imperial forces, married a young Mexican girl, and may have had ambitions of setting up as a ruler on his own. Guerrilla warfare dragged on with a continued drain of men and money – the adventure rapidly becoming intensely unpopular in France – until the end of the American Civil War announced the end of the French intervention in

Mexico. In 1867 the French troops were withdrawn, while Maximilian remained to be shot by the Mexicans, and his Empress went mad. It was a tragic end to a squalid and foolish adventure. Worse was to follow, but before tracing the foreign policy of Napoleon III through to the final catastrophe, it is necessary to say something of the concurrent decline of his authority at home.

5. TOWARDS THE LIBERAL EMPIRE

LITTLE has been said so far of the politics of the Second Empire. But the impression should not be given that apart from its foreign and colonial adventures, the only thing that really counted in its history was economics. The politics of a dictatorship, like that of an absolute monarchy, normally consists of mere court intrigue. If this is increasingly less true of the Second Empire, that is because it was rather a weak and half-hearted dictatorship. The simple preservation of parliamentary forms is not particularly significant; nor can we learn much from the elections, at least in the earlier years. Dictatorships, since they cannot tolerate opposition, normally suppress it by force, as the Second Empire did in the beginning. But Napoleon III also liked to pretend that it did not exist. This belief was made the easier by the fact that the majority of the nation undoubtedly supported him to the end. However, nothing less than a hundred per cent support is really satisfactory to a dictator. To secure the appearance of almost unanimous support the Second Empire relied on electoral management.

After 1852, the next elections were held in 1857. Opposition was still weak and the government was supported by just over 84 per cent of those voting (62 per cent of the electorate) as against 83 per cent in 1852. The prefects and their subordinates secured the election of the official candidates in all except thirteen constituencies; and of those who succeeded without the blessing of the Minister of the Interior eight were independents whose opposition to the régime was very mild. The remaining five were republicans, four, including Jules Favre, Émile Ollivier, and Ernest Picard from Paris, and one from Lyon. The Party of Five, as it was known, counted for rather more than its minute size might suggest, because the eloquence of Ollivier and Favre, and the wit of Picard, made a striking contrast to the dull pomposities of most of the yes-men of the prefects. But the fact that these republicans had accepted a seat in the Legislative Body was already a long step in the direction of reconciliation with the régime. The Italian War, with which they sympathized, carried them still farther. By 1859 the Emperor felt his position so thoroughly consolidated that he offered an amnesty to all political exiles, with the solitary exception – and this is significant – not of any of the socialists but of the leader of the red republicans, Ledru-Rollin.

In 1860 the first step away from dictatorship and in the direction of a real parliamentary system was taken. Since the Empire was at the height of its success and under no necessity to make concessions, and the change was introduced against the advice of the ministers except Morny, it must be attributed to Napoleon III himself. His motives, as always, remain inscrutable. One possibility is that he may have found himself too much at the mercy of his ministers, having neither the expert knowledge nor the assiduity to examine and control all they said or did in his name. He now allowed the Legislative Body and the Senate to hold annual debates on the speech from the throne, in the presence of ministers who were to reply to them on behalf of the government. An official report of debates was also to be published.

In 1861 a further step was taken. The vote of the budget by sections, instead of *en bloc*, was conceded. Political life was reviving, and in 1863 for the first time the government went into the election faced by a real, if hopelessly divided, opposition. This only won 32 seats, 15 to the Catholic opposition and 17 to the left. The Empire still had rather over five million votes out of over seven millions, but the opposition obtained a vote of two millions, compared with under half that figure in 1852 and 1857. An ominous fact was that out of the twenty-two largest towns in France, eighteen had given a majority to the opposition candidates. Paris elected Thiers and eight republicans.

These elections had been managed by the devoted Persigny, who had followed the star of Louis Bonaparte from Strasbourg to the Tuileries. Minister of the Interior after the *coup d'état*, and subsequently Ambassador in London, he had returned to the Ministry of the Interior in 1860. It was characteristically inconsequent that Louis Napoleon should have put back into the key position this enthusiastic, authoritarian Bonapartist, just at the time when an attempt was being made to moderate authoritarianism. Persigny's ruthless application of the system of official candidatures in the election of 1863 could only have been justified by conspicuous and increased success. The absence of this was equivalent to failure, and the resentment that his methods aroused suggested that they were becoming anachronistic. So Persigny had to go, with a dukedom as a consolation prize.

The leading influence over the domestic policy of the Emperor for the next two years was to be that of Morny, the most brilliant, unscrupulous, and from a political point of view perhaps the ablest and wisest of the Emperor's collaborators. The duc de Morny had a special qualification for his rôle, since he was the Emperor's half-brother. He was the son of Hortense Beauharnais, Louis Napoleon's mother, by General de Flahaut, her lover, himself an illegitimate son of Talleyrand. This double illegitimacy was to add up to a great dignitary of the Second Empire, but already under Louis-Philippe, Morny had won a fortune by speculation and a seat in the Orleanist Chamber of Deputies. He, more than anyone else, perhaps even more than Louis Napoleon himself, was the architect of the *coup d'état*. He quarrelled with the Emperor over the confiscation of Orleanist property, which may perhaps be set off against some of his own rather dubious financial transactions. In 1854 he became President of the Legislative Body, and he believed all through that France must return to a qualified parliamentary régime, in which the position of Napoleon III would perhaps not be so very different from that of Louis-Philippe. Morny's charm, his capacity for managing men, his combination of bonhomie with the air of a *grand seigneur*, his dashing ways with women and with wealth, his shrewdness and essential sense of the possible, made him one of the chief assets of the Second Empire and an ideal agent for the transformation of the régime into what was to be called the Liberal Empire. Morny envisaged an imperial government freed from the incubus of the rigid authoritarians, the unimaginative conservatives; a parliamentary Empire, which should be led and managed by himself and in which the oratorical talent which he lacked should be supplied by some brilliant orator of the left, such as Émile Ollivier. Among a crowd of technicians, *fonctionnaires*, political managers, and general second-raters, he stands out as something like a statesman. If he had lived, his ability might increasingly have supplemented the failing powers of Napoleon III. His death, at the age of fifty-four, in 1865, was perhaps the single most disastrous event for the Second Empire in a period that was increasingly filled with disasters. It postponed the coming of the liberal Empire for five years, and meant that when it did come, it should be under much less favourable auspices.

The series of disasters in foreign and colonial policy bears witness to the strength rather than the weakness of the Second Empire. In all of them, it is true, public opinion was the accomplice of the Emperor, as it had been in December 1851; but a régime with less support could not have passed through them with such immunity, nor have been so little shaken by the growing opposition in France.

This opposition was now coming as much from the right as from the left. The relations of the Empire with the Catholics had changed markedly since 1852. At the time of the *coup d'état* a few bishops, like Sibour of Paris, saw ultimate dangers for the Church in too close an identification with the new régime. Lacordaire despaired, but most

Catholics welcomed it. Montalembert only hesitated for a few days; Veuillot was enthusiastic. Napoleon III paid part of the price for the support of the Church by increasing the financial contribution of the State to the Church, thus enabling clerical salaries and pensions to be raised. Legal recognition was accorded to congregations of women and a large loophole was left for congregations of men. Between 1852 and 1862, 982 new religious congregations were authorized. The Panthéon was restored to religious use.

Under state patronage the Church in France grew in size and vigour. Membership of religious orders increased from some 37,000 at the beginning of the Second Empire to nearly 190,000 by the end, mostly of course women but three times what it had been in 1789. This was not a mere numerical growth; religious zeal mounted as well as numbers. The episcopate was distinguished by scholars, administrators, politicians, theologians. The lower clergy, disciplined by their training in the seminaries and their total subjection to the bishops, showed none of the dangerous independence of the eighteenth century. The laity was kept in a state of religious zeal by a well-organized propaganda. Perpetual Adoration became general and the cult of the Virgin occupied an increasingly dominant position in religious worship. In 1854 the doctrine of the Immaculate Conception of the Virgin Mary, supported by the Jesuits and opposed by the Dominicans, was promulgated. Visions were seen and miracles happened. In 1858 the events occurred at Lourdes that were to make it the greatest holy place of modern Catholicism. In these circumstances where all the anti-clericals of the Third Republic were to come from seems a mystery.

Perhaps they might have been fewer if the liberal Catholics of the Second Empire had been more; but these were only a tiny minority. The organ of liberal Catholicism was *Le Correspondant* of Montalembert; and with such collaborators as Albert de Broglie, Dupanloup, Falloux, and Lacordaire, its intellectual distinction was guaranteed. On the other side were those for whom the *loi Falloux*, by which clerical control of education had been greatly extended, was not enough. The law was attacked bitterly by the Intransigents, the leader of whom was the powerful Catholic journalist, Louis Veuillot. Born of peasant stock, trained as a lawyer's clerk, as editor of *L'Univers* he was the voice of the Church militant and spared neither opponents nor allies. Any concession was a crime; persecution was a sacred duty. Veuillot was one of the athletes of faith: to call any happening a miracle was for him to render it *ipso facto* worthy of faith. The liberal Catholics were worse than infidels or heretics.

At the opposite pole to Veuillot was Dupanloup, Bishop of Orleans, a politician, a frequenter of salons and academies, and as restless and fervid a controversialist as Veuillot himself. Dupanloup had most of the intellectuals of the Church behind him. Veuillot had – what was more important – Rome; and through him French Ultramontanism was identified with the religious views that prevailed at the Vatican under Pius IX. The publication of the Syllabus of Errors in 1864, if it might easily have been foreseen as the inevitable recognition of the need to condemn and ban all liberal ideas, came as a shock to the French liberal Catholics. It aroused the latent Gallicanism of the French Church. The opposition to Rome was led by the Archbishop of Paris, Mgr Darboy, appointed in 1863 and destined to die before a Communard firing squad in 1871. The conflict between liberal Catholics and Ultramontanes reached its peak in 1869–70 with the Council summoned at Rome to proclaim the dogma of papal infallibility. Dupanloup agitated in press and pamphlet; Darboy tried to bring in Napoleon III against the papalists; but it was no time for the tottering Emperor to assert himself. Veuillot sent back from Rome brilliant reports for *L'Univers*, demolishing the enemies of the Pope. It was doubtless significant of something that the most powerful voice among the French Catholics was now that of a successful journalist. The victory of the Ultramontanes was complete.

It was during the Second Empire that the cleavage between the majority of French intellectuals and the Church, which had begun under Louis XIV, was renewed. Even the political alliance of the Church with the State began to wear thin before the end of the Second Empire. The Italian war alienated the sympathies of many Catholics, who manifested their dissatisfaction in the elections of 1863. The Emperor, in turn displeased, not only removed the pro-clerical Walewski from Foreign Affairs but appointed Victor Duruy as Minister of Education, to defend the interests of the lay University against the clericals and struggle for the emancipation of education from religion. Duruy cautiously modified the educational system, increasing the number of State schools and reducing the fees, as first steps towards free and compulsory education. He also introduced changes into the traditional syllabus, including a more secular education for girls. In these years, also, anti-clericalism was spreading and becoming more aggressive. Among the middle classes Freemasonry, now more or less purged of the misty illuminism of the eighteenth century, was one of the chief means by which it was expressed. And because of the alliance – however strained it had become – between the Church and the Second Empire, anti-clericalism was associated with republicanism.

The growing opposition, of both right and left, is much more interesting than the time-serving politicians and bureaucrats of the Empire. This should not lead us to exaggerate the size or strength of the oppositions. To the end there was no possibility that either could have obtained a majority in the country, still less have overthrown the régime. Their chief effect was in weakening its self-confidence, and in leading the Emperor, who was acutely conscious of changes in public opinion, to feel the need for concessions. Another factor in the situation was his own declining health, which both weakened his grasp and made him more conscious of the problem of the succession. As has been said, the death in 1865 of Morny, who might have been able to guide the régime into more liberal paths with the alliance of Émile Ollivier, delayed the changes which

Napoleon probably already had in mind; but in a letter of January 1867 he announced coming constitutional reforms. They may not seem to amount to very much – the chief were that the right of interpellating ministers in the Legislative Body was to be substituted for the debate on the address, that ministers were to speak in support of their legislative proposals, and that the control of the press was to be somewhat relaxed – but conservative resistance held up the new press law for a year.

Until 1868 the press had been kept by direct or indirect methods under effective governmental control. A paper could only be published with government permission and on depositing substantial caution money to meet the fines it might incur. For any article that the authorities disliked it could be warned, and after two warnings was liable to suspension. As well as banning the publication of hostile articles, the government also circulated favourable ones, which were reproduced throughout the country by journals which wished for official support. Most of them did, for it brought advantages in the form of access to information from government sources, such as in England *The Times* had, and also more direct forms of favour – the publication of official notices amounted to a disguised form of subsidy and outright payments were not unknown.

The press law of 1868 ended this administrative control of the press and allowed new journals to be established without preliminary authorization. It was much more dangerous for the régime than any of the constitutional reforms. Immediately there was a proliferation of new sheets, among them the notorious *Lanterne* of Henri Rochefort, which reached a sale of half a million by June 1868. After three months of calculated and brilliant, if irresponsible, insults against the whole Bonapartist establishment, it was suppressed by legal action. Another episode resulting from the relaxation of the press laws occurred in 1868, when the stalwart *quarante-huitard* Delescluze and another journalist started a fund in their papers to erect a monument to the deputy Baudin, who had been killed in the *coup d'état* of 1851. The government made the mistake of prosecuting them. The trial provided the opportunity for a young defence lawyer, just beginning his political career, to deliver a resounding denunciation of the crime of December and all who had been accomplices of it. Gambetta had made his appearance on the political scene.

Everything seemed to be conspiring against Napoleon III in the last, unhappy years of his rule. Economic progress, which had been the great idea, and up to a point the great achievement, of the régime, slackened. There was a severe crisis in the cotton industry in the sixties, attributable mainly to the effects of the American Civil War and to increased competition within France as a result of the development of rail transport. The silk industry suffered from a disease of the silk worm. In the vineyards the appearance of phylloxera in 1863, to become widespread after 1875, began to produce depression. The later sixties indeed belied some of the golden hopes which the economic development of the fifties had raised, though they did not undo the progress that had already been achieved.

The financial crisis was more dangerous for the régime. The Second Empire had been founded on credit, it flourished while the credit lasted, and began to break down when the springs of credit dried up. The steadily increasing threat of war undermined confidence increasingly in the eighteen-sixties. Monied men ceased to invest and left their money idle in the bank: this was known as the *grève du milliard* – the thousand million francs that went on strike. Those with capital to invest feared the adventurous disposition of the Emperor now that he had ceased to want adventures. With more reason they were alarmed by the deterioration in the international situation.

The great financial house which was most closely identified with the Second Empire was naturally the one which suffered most in this crisis. The Crédit Mobilier found in 1866 that its commitments had outrun its mobilizable resources. Its titles to property were still extensive, and given time and the cooperation of other financial houses it could have weathered the storm. But the adventurous methods introduced by the Péreire brothers had alienated the world of orthodox finance, which cheerfully allowed them to sink. In the course of 1867 their shares fell from 1,982 francs to 140, and their credit to the point at which the Legitimist lawyer Berryer, in a law-suit arising out of the crisis, could describe the Crédit Mobilier as 'the greatest gambling house in the world'. The Rothschilds and the more traditional bankers now took their revenge for the earlier triumphs of the Péreires; and the Emperor – for all their services to his régime – could only make a weak and unsuccessful attempt to come to their rescue. As soon as they had safely gone under for the third time, the Crédit Mobilier was refloated by rival houses. But in ruining the Péreires and launching a campaign against 'Saint-Simonian finance' the orthodox bankers had delivered a deadly blow to the already tottering credit of the Second Empire. Perhaps this was not altogether unintentional. They had been suspicious of Louis Napoleon from the beginning, and now they were beginning to believe that a parliamentary government might be more conservative and a better guarantee of property and wealth than an Emperor. As so often, we see the prefigured shape of a coming régime appearing behind the increasingly blurred outlines of the existing one.

The government that had to cope with this critical situation was one from which the paladins of the Second Empire had disappeared, but the party hacks, the official spokesmen, and – at best – the administrators remained. The Empire had not been able to renew its cadres or its leaders. Fould, uncommitted rival of the Péreires from the beginning, was at the Ministry of Finances. Haussmann ruled Paris. In 1863 Baroche added Cultes to Justice, and Rouher became joint Minister of State with Billault, who had been the voice of the Empire in the Legislative Body. Before the session opened Billault had died, and the chief burden was to fall on the broad shoulders of Rouher.

The question which contemporaries and historians have

asked themselves is whether henceforth Rouher or the Emperor determined the policy of the declining Empire. Ollivier called the minister the vice-emperor; the wits declared that France had not a government but a 'Rouher-nement'; high officials and foreign diplomats looked to him for the best indication of the policy of the Emperor. He had been a notable servant of the Second Empire from the beginning. With a capacity for hard work and intrigue, a determination pushed to the point of obstinacy in pursuing a fixed line of action, and the rather crude cunning of an Auvergnat, Rouher rapidly made himself almost indis-pensable to an Emperor whose own powers were noticeably weakening. With the close collaboration of Fould and Baroche, he built up a subservient clientele in the Legisla-tive Body. Yet he could never feel quite sure of his position: there were many rivals round the Emperor, and he could not afford to make a mistake or a concession. His position was essentially that of a political manager and an advocate rather than a statesman. He envisaged his task as one of defending a régime and implementing its policy, not of supplying the policy himself. Garde des Sceaux on the eve of the *coup d'état* of 2 December, Rouher had probably had a larger share in drawing up the Constitution of 1852 than anyone. He was thus committed to the Bonapartist idea from the outset, that is to a dictatorship which rested on universal suffrage – in other words to the official candida-ture and electoral management. By character, training, and conviction he was opposed to any liberal concessions. He could only hold his position and continue to function so long as the political system which needed him, and which he had done so much to create, lasted. The death of Morny left him free to pursue his own authoritarian tendencies, one sign of which was the appointment to the Ministry of the Interior of La Valette, who combined a heavy hand with a rather irresponsible head.

Yet the government of Rouher was essentially weak, as was shown when it was faced by the one really vital issue, that of rearmament. The series of military defeats inflicted on the Austrian Empire, begun – by Napoleon III's own act – at Magenta, and culminating at Sadowa, had changed the balance of power in Europe. In face of the rise of Prussia and the isolation of France, only a rapid French rearmament could redress the situation. A commission, appointed after Sadowa in 1866, revealed the weakness of the army – the exemption, in practice, of the sons of the better-off classes from military service; the reliance mainly on professional soldiers and only such as were attracted by the meagre pay and not worried by the dullness of life in barracks; the slowness to adopt the new weapon, the *chassepot*, which only began to be introduced in 1866. But when, early in 1867, the commission produced proposals which would have made military service less easy to avoid and created an effective reserve, there was an almost universal outcry. Government supporters in the Legislative Body feared for their seats; opponents saw a stick with which to beat the government.

Finance was the other major obstacle to rearmament. The earlier wars, colonial expeditions, the Mexican adventure, had still to be paid for. A programme of public works was needed to check the growth of unemployment. The government could not face, at the same time, extensive borrowing to modernize the army. Eventually a few relics of the proposed reforms were passed in the Army Law of January 1868, amid demonstrations of protest from the republicans in the cities, and even these reforms were not put into practice effectively. Throughout the years of increasing international tension the republicans and monarchists opposed rearmament. Napoleon III, who saw the dangers of the international situation, had not the strength either to avoid, or prepare for, the coming clash; and Rouher seems to have been pinning his hopes on a policy of peace at almost any price.

Although Rouher was the main target for the attacks of the opposition and a sufficiently large if pachydermous one, almost as fierce a fire was concentrated on another apparently permanent feature of the Second Empire. This was the prefect of the Seine, Baron Haussmann. Like the Péreire brothers and Rouher, what particularly singled him out for attack was his close association with Napoleon III; and again the attack was launched with the aid of the Rothschilds, as well as with ammunition furnished by Fould from the Ministry of Finances. For Haussmann, to rebuild Paris, had relied on unorthodox methods of raising credit. As building costs increased, and with the slackening of economic activity, speculators who were willing to invest in the property values his new roads created became less easy to find, he was driven to more and more daring expedients to finance his operations. When all these were exhausted, in 1868 he had to come to the Legislative Body to ask for retrospective sanction for a loan amounting to about a quarter of the whole French budget. Fundamentally, the financial position of the rebuilding of Paris was probably sound, but it had been achieved by daring methods which even a parliament still largely composed of official candidates could hardly accept. Rouher, who, like Fould, had no love for Haussmann, practically disavowed him. A future minister of the Third Republic, Jules Ferry, made his mark on the political scene with a pamphlet entitled *Les Comptes fantastiques d'Haussmann*. The Emperor did not yet abandon the prefect who had served him so well, but the fate of Haussmann, and of more than Haussmann, was to turn on the elections of May 1869.

In this situation the wisest policy for Napoleon III might have been to attempt to raise his régime above the electoral battle. There was, after all, no serious possibility of a movement to overthrow the Empire. Legitimists, Orleanists, conservative Republicans, men of property, and peasants, the Empire was still what divided them least. Napoleon III could have afforded to leave the election in 1869 comparatively free; but Rouher could not. He flung everything he had into the struggle, though his own unpopularity was such that his support was the greatest handicap he could inflict on his own candidates. Paris, Lyon, and all the big cities produced crushing majorities against the government. The opposition won some 3,300,000 votes (a million and a half more than in 1863) to 4,400,000 for the official candidates, and it yet remained to be seen how far the latter would be loyal to Rouher.

The Emperor, ill and exhausted, was in no state to enter on a stern struggle in defence of his minister. Persigny was warning him of the unpopularity of Rouher and Baroche; his always inconvenient relative, Prince Napoleon, was intriguing; the Legislative Body was evidently on the point of escaping from Rouher's control.

Unwilling to resign in time, the 'vice-Emperor' found himself, when Napoleon at last decided to yield to the demands of the opposition, faced with the bitter task of announcing the abandonment of his own policy and the concession of the parliamentary liberties which he had consistently and uncompromisingly refused. This was the end of the Bonapartist constitution that had been set up in 1852; and the building having tumbled down in ruins, it was inevitable that its chief architect should go. The same evening Rouher tendered his resignation: Haussmann was to follow him in January 1870. It is hardly necessary to enumerate the constitutional changes that followed, they were to endure so short a while.

The year 1870 opened with the choice of Émile Ollivier, whom Morny had picked out for the rôle five years earlier, as head of the first and last parliamentary government of the Second Empire. Ollivier had been chosen, partly doubtless in the belief that his eloquence would help to sustain the new régime, but partly because he was an *isolé*, not committed to any party and therefore supported by none. He was a dazzling orator, full of good intentions, enthusiastic for the liberal Empire, and convinced of his own ability to play the rôle for which he had been cast. Whether this belief was right or wrong, whether the liberal Empire could have endured, or how it might have evolved, was never to be known.

The new constitution was put into formal shape in April 1870: it established government by a cabinet responsible to

parliament. Evidence of the new spirit that it was intended
to introduce into the political life of France was a circular
of the Minister of the Interior to the prefects: 'You will take
care not to subordinate the administration to politics, and
you will treat with equal impartiality worthy men (*les
honnêtes gens*) of all parties.' The liberal reforms were submitted to a plebiscite on 8 May and approved by 7,358,000
votes against 1,572,000 with 1,894,000 abstentions. It was
a triumph for the Empire: republicans and monarchists
both recognized it as such. Napoleon III had obtained
practically the same number of affirmative votes as in 1852,
despite a long series of misfortunes. Although the towns
were the centres of opposition, it is claimed that the attachment of the workers to Napoleon III remained lively to the
end of the Empire. At any rate, when they did revolt it
was only after the Empire had fallen. In the early summer
of 1870, though the Empire was in process of evolution,
there seemed not the slightest danger of revolution.

6. THE PRICE OF DICTATORSHIP

NEMESIS was to come in the shape of war, not unjustly, on
an Empire that had denied its own promise that it was
peace. The complicated international manoeuvres that led
up to the Franco-Prussian War have been narrated many
times and given various interpretations. The offer of the
throne of Spain to a Hohenzollern prince, and its acceptance – after much hesitation – in June 1870, precipitated
the crisis that had been threatening ever since Sadowa.
French opinion was outraged, and the Foreign Minister,
the duc de Gramont, a light-weight to have to deal with
such a serious situation and an opponent such as Bismarck,
declared that a Hohenzollern king in Madrid would be a
casus belli. In spite of attempts, after the war, to suggest that
Napoleon III had dragged an unwilling country into war,
the evidence is strong that public opinion throughout
France felt that the time had come to make a stand against

Prussian aggression. France had been out-manoeuvred by Prussia too many times in the recent past to be in a mood to accept one more humiliation. The Empress and the court at Saint-Cloud expressed the general sentiments of the nation when they called for a firm stand, and if necessary war. The popular demonstrations in Paris were described by republican politicians after 1870 as 'organized by the police'. There seems to be no justification for this view. Nor should they be dismissed as the mere outburst of a frivolous populace. They were the natural reaction to the history of the previous ten years. Émile Ollivier himself is alleged to have declared, 'Enough humiliation: it is no longer Rouher who controls the government of France.'

However, Ollivier was no fire-eater, and when the acceptance of the Spanish throne was withdrawn by the Hohenzollern prince, he rejoiced that peace had been saved. Napoleon III, who knew the real weakness of the French army, and had been striving by personal approaches to the other European courts to secure a Hohenzollern withdrawal, without which, he realized, he could not avoid war, also believed that peace was saved. He counted without the French need, after years of humiliation, for a victory, if only on paper; and one seemed at last within grasp. Let France demand something more secure than a mere withdrawal, something in the nature of guarantees: the Legislative Body would probably have overthrown Ollivier if he had not done this, and it reflected a widespread opinion, at least among the politically vocal classes. What the peasants thought, or if they thought, cannot be known. Equally, what Ollivier would have done in the face of this movement of opinion cannot be known, for the liberal Empire was too new to permit the normal processes of a parliamentary and cabinet government to operate.

The crucial decision was taken not in parliament or by the head of the government, but at the Court of Saint-Cloud, and by a little, and in every sense irresponsible, group headed by the Empress, with the acquiescence of the Emperor. The only minister present was Gramont, who telegraphed immediately after the meeting at Saint-Cloud to Benedetti, French ambassador at Berlin, instructing him to demand a personal guarantee of the withdrawal of the Hohenzollern candidature from the Prussian King, which, it was added, he could hardly refuse '*s'il n'est véritablement animé d'aucune arrière-pensée*'. However much this may look like a deliberate attempt to snatch war from the jaws of peace, such an interpretation would be mistaken. The Empress and her entourage were still haunted by the insecurity of a dictatorial régime, which they felt to be more insecure than ever now that it had been launched on the experiment of liberalization. Only a striking diplomatic victory, they believed, could restore the tottering prestige of the Bonapartist cause. And the man over whom they expected to gain this victory was Bismarck.

The king of Prussia seems to have behaved with complete propriety, but of course refused Benedetti's demand for a declaration which would have been almost an admission of his own dishonesty. Bismarck, to whom the episode was reported, saw his opportunity and gave the press a short statement which read like a brusque rebuff from William I to Benedetti: there is no doubt that he knew what he was doing. This was the so-called Ems telegram. When it was published in France a wave of emotion swept through the country – the Empress, Gramont, Ollivier reflected the feeling that practically all the newspapers were proclaiming, and that was manifested on the boulevards of Paris and in the streets and squares of every town in France.

On the day after the interview at Ems, the Imperial Council met repeatedly, with the Empress present, and decided on mobilization. The Emperor was too incapacitated by illness to oppose the irresistible current of opinion, even if he wanted to; but when Ollivier reported to the Legislative Body, it was seen that the current was not quite as irresistible as it had seemed. Certainly it was resisted. The centre and the left envisaged the approaching war as an attempt to undo the concessions of the liberal Empire, which in part it was, and they had a spokesman in Thiers, who in private had already been one of the few in France to foresee defeat, and in public denounced a policy which involved shedding torrents of blood to avenge a few insulting words. Ollivier, whatever his earlier doubts, was now carried away by his own eloquence, and – in one of those phrases with which a man can damn his own reputation for ever – declared that he accepted the responsibility of war 'with a light heart'. On 19 July war was declared on Prussia.

The blunders of Napoleon III's foreign policy ensured that France should enter the war with no allies, but on the side of the government hardly anyone, except perhaps the Emperor himself, supposed that there was any need for them. *À Berlin* was the war-cry on the boulevards and the password of the army. There was a run on maps of Germany in the shops; it would have been unpatriotic, defeatist, and absurd to suggest that maps of France might be more useful. Yet from the beginning the French army was outnumbered, out-gunned, and out-manoeuvred. The mobilization was so muddled that the Prussians, unexpectedly even to themselves, were able to take the offensive at once. The French, nominally under the supreme command of the Emperor, who was suffering cruelly from his illness and could only sit his horse in agony, experienced a series of defeats – at Wissembourg, Fröschwiller and Forbach – in the first week of August. Alsace was lost and Lorraine invaded. After these initial defeats the Emperor was coolly pushed out of his nominal supreme command by the generals, who were more responsible for them than he was. In his place they chose Bazaine, an unpleasing intriguer, disgraced for misbehaviour in Mexico, which was almost his only qualification for the position. He withdrew with a large army on Metz, where the Prussians cut him off by a victory at Gravelotte. Meanwhile the Emperor, with Marshal MacMahon, was gathering a new army on the Marne at Châlons.

When the news of the defeats reached Paris, the Empress, left behind as Regent, summoned the Legislative Body, which called for the dismissal of the ministers and generals whom it held responsible for the defeat, and the appointment of a new government chosen by the Assembly. Eugénie at least had the courage of her lack of judgement and did not yield to this. She appointed a Bonapartist ministry in place of the defunct government of Ollivier, but it was patent to everyone that only a military victory could save the Empire. In a forlorn hope, MacMahon and the Emperor led their army in the direction of Metz, where Bazaine remained in a state of inaction that was later to bring the charge of treachery on him. His motives were at least peculiar – but then he had always been what he looked, rather a peculiar individual. In their turn, MacMahon and Napoleon found themselves penned in at Sedan. Under the bombardment of the Prussian artillery a continuation of the struggle meant only futile slaughter of the encircled troops. On 1 September, beaten and broken, the Emperor surrendered with 84,000 men, 2,700 officers, and 39 generals.

At Paris, recently so gay with optimism, opinion was reeling under the report of defeat after defeat. The news from Sedan brought revolutionary crowds out into the streets. Eugénie and the Prince Imperial fled to England. The Second Empire disappeared: it had become such a phantom that the mob was not even concerned to take revenge on its adherents. Napoleon III was perhaps never less hated or more pitied than in his fall. The Legislative Body, to anticipate a revolutionary movement from the extreme left, proclaimed a provisional Government of National Defence. It was headed by General Trochu, already military governor of Paris, and it included the leaders of the parliamentary opposition, but not Thiers. Far too shrewd to allow himself to be put in a position of responsibility for what he foresaw as inevitably a humiliating defeat, Thiers undertook instead a futile mission to the courts of Europe to plead for intervention.

The usual kind of vulgar libels were produced by the Parisian journalists against Eugénie, as formerly against Marie-Antoinette. Now it was '*la femme Bonaparte, ses amants, ses orgies'*. But there was surprisingly little anti-Bonapartist demonstration. Patriotic enthusiasm and a belief that, as in 1792, the republic would spell victory, excluded other emotions. Of course, the political machine of the Second Empire collapsed. The new Minister of the Interior, Gambetta, replaced all the prefects of the fallen régime. He began preparing for a national war. The size of the National Guard in Paris was doubled, and at the end of the month it contained 360,000 men. By this time Paris had been surrounded by German forces, which had pushed on beyond the city and occupied all France north and east of Orleans except for Paris. The Government of National Defence was now deprived of contact with the rest of the country and with its own delegation at Tours, whither Crémieux, a venerable survivor of '48, had been sent, on the ground that he was the oldest.

When it became evident that a more energetic leadership was needed, it was decided to despatch Gambetta, on 7 October, across the German lines by balloon to Tours, where he assumed the functions of Minister of War along with those of the Interior. The son of an Italian immigrant and a Frenchwoman from Gascony, and born at Cahors, Gambetta was a southerner by birth and upbringing. His comparatively humble origins left their mark in his uncouth appearance and manners, which did not conceal his charm and ability or diminish his oratorical powers. In all these respects he reminded his contemporaries – and perhaps was not sorry that they should be reminded – of another great Frenchman in another time of troubles, Danton. An early career in the law led on to politics, and in 1869, at the age of thirty-one, Gambetta was elected to the Legislative Body as a member for Belleville, on the strength of the radical programme of political reform known as the Belleville programme. In the autumn of 1870, as heir of the *quarante-huitards* and of the Jacobins of '92, he believed that even in this crisis the republic could save France and hurl back the invader.

To second him at the improvised Ministry of War

Gambetta chose the engineer Charles de Freycinet, as cool as Gambetta was excitable, but equally determined. The two civilians summoned from the soil of France huge new armies in a way that the generals could never have done; but to train and arm them time was needed, and they had hardly begun to take the field before another military disaster occurred. Bazaine, passive in Metz, intriguing with Bismarck for the restoration of the Empire, perhaps hoping to march his troops back to suppress the republic in Paris, playing, as formerly in Mexico, an equivocal rôle, capitulated with 173,000 men. The only military objective left now – and it was a forlorn hope – was the relief of Paris. The army that Gambetta had formed on the Loire, under the command of a Bonapartist general with a reputation for ruthlessness, d'Aurelle de Paladines, won an initial victory at Coulmiers and on 7 November reoccupied Orleans. A full-scale sortie from Paris, attempting to join forces with the army of the Loire, was driven back, but already d'Aurelle de Paladines had decided that he could go no further and had been dismissed by Gambetta. His army was now split by a German counter-attack into two forces, one led inadequately by Bourbaki, and the other with skill by Chanzy. In the north-east Faidherbe was struggling to contain the German advance with temporary success.

The sudden, unexpected, heroic resistance of republican France, after the imperial armies and generals had crumpled up so ignominiously, had taken the Prussian command by surprise; but when they recovered from the shock and deployed the forces freed by the capitulations at Sedan and Metz, the result was a foregone conclusion. By January 1871, Chanzy had been driven back fighting from Le Mans to Mayenne. Faidherbe was in retreat. Bourbaki, sent to the east to threaten German communications, led his army into internment in Switzerland. The delegation at Tours, no longer safe there, withdrew to Bordeaux.

Resistance was concentrated now in Paris, where, in numbers at least, there was a formidable force. Trained troops of course were lacking, though a Mobile Guard of reservists had some military value and a small volunteer body of *francs-tireurs* combined courage with lack of discipline. Practically the whole male able-bodied population of Paris was enrolled in the National Guard, to the number of some 350,000 men, whose duty it was to man the defences of the city. There they became simply a semi-armed rabble, demoralized by lack of military training or occupation of any kind, for the Prussians had no intention of taking Paris by storm when it could so much more easily be starved into surrender. The circle round Paris had been completed on 25 September and the beleaguered population, much larger than was estimated at first, in a fever of patriotism and hope awaited relief from without by the new armies of Gambetta, joining with a victorious sortie from within. It had little information of what was happening in the rest of France, for while balloons could carry letters out of Paris, they could not, because of the prevailing westerly winds, return.

Shortage of food rapidly made itself felt. The poorer suffered greatly, and the lower middle class, whose small shops and trades were ruined, perhaps most of all. On the other hand, luxury restaurants remained open with full menus, apart from vegetables and sea fish, throughout the siege, even if exotic dishes such as kangaroo or elephant, and humble ones like cat, had to appear on the list. As winter came on, cold was as great an enemy as hunger. The trees in the Champs Élysées were cut down and a swarm descended on them to seize firewood, like the ragged army that daily prowled in the no man's land beyond the fortifications to bring back roots and greenstuff. The Seine began to ice over and soldiers were frozen at their posts. From cold and hunger the death rate mounted. The quest for food became a universal occupation. Edmond de Goncourt, walking in the dusk, hears a girl murmur – '*Monsieur, voulez-vous monter chez moi ... pour un morceau de pain.*'

At what Bismarck calculated to be the appropriate moment, on 5 January, the weapon of terror was added by the bombardment of Paris. It lasted several hours each night for twenty-three nights. About 12,000 shells fell on the city, killing or wounding some 400 persons, helping to found the modern German tradition of war, but having little effect on the spirit of resistance in Paris.

The extremists of the left, who had emerged from hiding or prison with the fall of the Empire, were now the leaders of republican patriotism. 'The Frenchmen of 1870 are the sons of those Gauls for whom battles were holidays,' declared Delescluze. Blanqui entitled the journal he founded *La Patrie en danger* and proclaimed the determination of the people to fight to the death and to save Paris at all costs. Believing as they did in the necessary victory of republican forces, defeat naturally was equated with treachery. When the Parisian offensive of 27 October was beaten back three days later, and at the same time arrived the news of the capitulation of Metz, the left-wing leaders called out the mob, invaded the Hôtel de Ville, and began to organize a revolutionary government. Loyal battalions were fetched up and brought the situation under control. There was a similar reaction to a final *sortie en masse* on 19 January, which failed with heavy loss. It has been regarded as an attempt by Trochu to demonstrate to the Parisians the hopelessness of the situation and so prepare the way for capitulation, but as he put himself at the head of the troops this may not be altogether fair to him. The defeat led to another march on the Hôtel de Ville, which was dispersed by the Mobile Guard. The transformation of the patriotic struggle against the invaders into a social struggle inside France was beginning. Elsewhere – in Lyon, Marseille, Toulouse – revolutionary communes had already been set up, but had been brought under control by Gambetta's prefects.

The propertied classes, who had most to lose from the continuance of the war, had long been ready to abandon the struggle. Thiers had all along believed in negotiating with the enemy, under the impression that the price of peace would be cheaper the sooner it was concluded. After the failure of the left-wing rising of 22 January the government in Paris felt safe in accepting the inevitable armistice. By its terms Paris was to capitulate and there was to be a three weeks suspension of hostilities to allow for the election of an assembly which could negotiate a peace. Gambetta, his policy of national defence having failed, resigned. Although he was elected by nine departments, the result of the elections was overwhelmingly against him. He recognized defeat and withdrew from France.

The electoral decree was issued on 24 January and the elections held on 8 February. To bring to an end the electoral management of the Second Empire, *scrutin de liste* was introduced in place of single-member constituencies. The new prefects had not the influence to make the election, and in any case had been instructed not to do so. The vote was largely a plebiscite for peace and against the dictatorship of Gambetta. Many electors were prisoners or in the new armies; over 40 departments were occupied by the enemy. The population, which could only look for guidance to its local notables and clergy, returned conservative lists everywhere save in Paris and some other large towns, in parts of the East, and in a few southern departments. There were 400 monarchists, 214 of them Orleanist, 182 legitimists mostly from the West and South-west; 78 moderates who were to become conservative republicans; 150 republicans, about 40 of a radical tinge; Bonapartism was reduced to a mere 20, only 4, and these in Corsica, daring to proclaim themselves as such. Some third of the new Assembly was *noblesse*; only 175 had ever sat in an Assembly before; their average age was 53.

It was an exceptional body, elected under exceptional conditions, for a single purpose – to make peace. The shadow of things to come might have been seen in the election as President of the Assembly of Jules Grévy, the republican who had warned in 1848 against the constitutional arrangements which opened the door to Louis Napoleon. Thiers, for whom the election had practically been a plebiscite, with 2,000,000 votes accumulated in multiple candidatures and election in 26 departments, was the almost inevitable choice as head of the Executive. France invariably looks to those it has known for many years when a national crisis emerges. Nevertheless, an overwhelmingly monarchist assembly had begun by placing in the key positions two republicans; and Thiers' three leading ministers, Favre, Picard, and Simon, were also republicans.

But there was more than one kind of republican in the minority of the Assembly. Paris had sent a group of deputies, including Louis Blanc, Victor Hugo, Delescluze, Ledru-Rollin, Rochefort, Quinet, whose names were like a roll-call of '48. To the monarchist majority they were intolerable and in fact were so little tolerated that some eight of them resigned. The National Assembly, under the leadership of Thiers, was determined to eliminate the danger from the left, and now this meant almost exclusively Paris. A court martial sentenced Blanqui and Flourens, as leaders of the 31 October rising, to death in their absence. The former Bonapartist, d'Aurelle de Paladines, dismissed by Gambetta, was put in command of the Paris National Guard. The Assembly was brought back from Bordeaux to Versailles instead of to Paris. Finally, Thiers gave orders for the 400 guns in the hands of the National Guard of Paris to be removed on 18 March. It has been described as a deliberate provocation, which Thiers never expected to succeed in any other respect; but he did not expect his troops from Versailles to fraternize with the Parisians, and he expected the National Guard from the middle-class quarters of Paris to give his policy support. This was to underestimate the effect of two fatal measures passed by the Assembly. The first had ended the moratorium on the promissory notes through which much of the business of Paris was conducted; the second was to make rents which had remained unpaid during the war immediately payable. These decisions seemed very reasonable to the landed gentry of the Assembly, to the financiers who had speculated in paper and rents, and to Thiers. They spelt ruin to the lower middle classes of Paris.

Thiers' attempted seizure of the guns was the spark which

set off revolution in Paris. After a riot and a few murders, he ordered the abandonment of Paris by all the legal authorities. The only organized body left in the city was the moderate Central Committee of the National Guard, which found itself obliged to take over the essential services, abandoned by Thiers' orders. Naturally those who came to the front in this emergency were the stronger and extremer leaders, bred in the red clubs which had flourished during the siege of Paris. The eternal conspirator, Blanqui, temporarily not the eternal prisoner, had been the inspiring genius of the most famous of the clubs, meeting in the Halles. His *club rouge* has been described as 'a chapel consecrated to an orthodox classical cult of conspiracy, in which the doors were wide open to everyone, but to which one only returned if one was a convert'. Blanqui himself presided over the cult, with 'his delicate, superior, calm countenance, his narrow, piercing eyes shot across now and again with a dangerous, sinister light' – an unusually favourable picture of the conspirator described by Victor Hugo as 'a sort of baleful apparition in whom seemed to be incarnated all the hatred born of every misery'.

The Blanquists were only a tiny fraction, the rest of the Parisian rebels felt the need to legitimize their position by holding elections. A municipal government, to be known by the historic but alarming name of Commune, was elected on 26 March. The name of the Commune was a memory of the year II, of the Jacobins of Robespierre and the *sans-culottes* of Hébert. It was a symbol beneath which the most opposed schools of revolutionary thought could rally. Four separate groups can be distinguished among its members – the pure revolutionaries, divided between Blanquists and Jacobins, the federalists following Proudhon, and the adherents of the First International. The conservatives or moderates returned in the first election of the Commune resigned, and after complementary elections there was a revolutionary majority of some 57 Blanquists and Jacobins, and a socialist and Proudhonist minority of about 22.

It is a mistake to regard the Commune as Marxist in inspiration; only one of its members can be described as a Marxist. Equally it was not a government of the working-class. Though there were 25 *ouvriers*, there were more than twice as many lesser bourgeois or professional men. The 'Declaration to the French People' issued by the Commune on 19 April represents the federalist tendencies of the minority. As soon as the active struggle began, the Blanquists, weakened by the absence of their prophet, who had been arrested and returned to jail as soon as danger began to threaten in Paris, and the Jacobins, headed by Delescluze, took control in a temporary alliance, to be followed, as in 1793, by bitter quarrels. On 1 May they set up a Committee of Public Safety by 45 votes to 23.

The second siege of Paris began on Palm Sunday, 2 April, by a Versailles army in a wretched state of disorganization and lack of material and morale. Its first military achievement was to shoot five prisoners. The forces of the Commune retaliated with a wild sortie in the direction of Versailles, which was easily dispersed with the loss of some 1,000 prisoners captured by the Versaillais, who picked out those they thought were the leaders and shot them. Given a small measure of capacity and unity, at the outset the Commune should have been able to take the offensive with success. It had many more men and guns than Versailles, and a base in the fortified camp of Paris which could be provisioned through the neutral Prussian lines. These advantages were gradually lost. While the leaders of the Commune talked and small bodies of men defended the forts, the life of Paris, theatres, concerts, the busy traffic of the streets, went on much as usual and far more normally than during the Prussian siege. Such changes as were deliberately debated and brought about by the Commune were hardly of major importance. The old revolutionary calendar was revived and May 1871 became *floréal* year LXXIX. The Vendôme column was pulled down in a great public ceremony.

Meanwhile the military strength of Versailles was growing. On 8 May a general bombardment of the fortifications began. The forts round the south of Paris, gallantly defended by isolated groups of men, fell one by one. On 21 May a section of the walls near the porte de Saint-Cloud was discovered to be undefended, and by nightfall the Versaillais had a large body of men within Paris. On the same day the Commune held its last official meeting, devoted typically to a trial of its own military commander. Both he and his successor had failed to secure a reasonable measure of military behaviour from the forces of the Commune. Now that Paris was at bay, the old Jacobin Delescluze proclaimed a war of the people, not conducted by staff officers and military discipline, but by the people, the *bras-nus*. And now that all was really lost the Communards at last began to fight in earnest, in the traditional way, the only way that the people of Paris knew. It was a street battle of barricades, which was to rage for seven days across the breadth of Paris from west to east.

The Versaillais, strong in the knowledge that they were defending order and public morality, throughout the fighting showed more barbarity than the Communards. Apart from the initial episode and the actual fighting, there were practically no shootings of opponents or suspected opponents in Paris until the last stages were reached, though hostages were seized. The Versaillais systematically shot their prisoners. This was one motive of the subsequent murders of hostages that accompanied the final battle in the streets of Paris; but also, it is true, there was a group of ruthless men among the leaders of the Commune, who had not distinguished themselves in the fighting but had had their eye on the hostages all the time. Now they had their chance and particularly chose priests, including the Archbishop of Paris, for their victims. To the horror of the street fighting and massacres on both sides was added fire. Incendiary shells from the Versaillais, the burning of buildings by the Communards to clear lines of fire or form a barrier destroyed much. The Tuileries and other public buildings were fired in a last act of defiance by desperate men, though the story of the *pétroleuses* is a mere piece of propaganda.

In its final phase the defence of the Commune degenerated into uncoordinated episodes of heroism or cruelty. Delescluze, in the dress of a deputy of '48, top hat, frock coat, and red sash, cane in hand, all being now lost, mounted a barricade to be shot. The last combat of any size was among the graves of the Cemetery of Père-Lachaise; and there, on the next day, against the wall that was to become a place of pilgrimage, 147 Communards were shot. Military justice continued to take its toll. The Versaillese lost about 1,000 dead in the fighting; the death roll of the Communards was probably not less than 20,000. Thiers had won a notable victory in the class war; the illusions of 1789 and 1792 had drawn the people of Paris into the bloodiest and most merciless of all its defeats; the Second Empire had ended in disgraceful surrender, revolution and repression, blood and tears; but it was an assembly of monarchists, under a conservative republican head of state, that first provoked and then put to fire and sword the people of Paris. It is a mistake to say that the repression of the Commune founded the Third Republic. That was founded in the attempt to undo the evil that accompanied the end of the Second Empire.

IV

THE THIRD REPUBLIC

1. THE MAKING OF THE REPUBLIC, 1871–89

THIERS settled with the Prussians even before he settled with Paris. All Alsace except Belfort, along with the southern part of Lorraine, the payment of what seemed at the time a huge indemnity, and occupation of the eastern departments till the indemnity had been paid – this was the price. Such was the desire for peace that the Assembly voted the acceptance of the terms without delay, on 1 March, and so reduced the period spent by the enemy army in Paris, which was to last until peace was concluded, to a single day. By the treaty France lost a population of nearly a million and a half, the iron mines and metallurgical industries of Lorraine, and the industries of Alsace. The amount necessary to pay off the indemnity was raised, by means of loans, far more rapidly than had been expected, and the last of the occupying forces left France in September 1873. In spite of this financial burden, aided by favourable world economic conditions the French budget was balanced by 1875.

The chief problem immediately confronting France after the war and the Commune was to settle its future form of government, and the only solution which seemed definitely excluded was the Bonapartist one. The Second Empire, with its political and administrative personnel, followed its predecessors into the increasingly overcrowded Valhalla of defunct régimes, whose ghosts haunt the French historical imagination. Bonapartist sympathies survived among the army officers, high ecclesiastics, and Corsicans, and, as under the Second Republic, the selfish policies of monarchists and conservative republicans subsequently revived

Bonapartist sentiments among those suffering under economic pressure. The death of Napoleon III, in 1873, left the young Prince Imperial as a more appealing representative of the dynasty; and however averse the governing élites might be to it, plebiscitary dictatorship had not exhausted its attraction for the people. What destroyed Bonapartism as a movement with a future as well as a past was the Zulu assegai which killed the Prince Imperial in 1879. No one else in the quarrelling and in some cases disreputable Bonaparte clan was a possible claimant to the heritage.

If the elections of February 1871 adequately represented the wishes of France, a restoration of the monarchy should have been a foregone conclusion. But apart from the fact that it was soon to be revealed how unrepresentative the Assembly was, the fatal division of monarchist forces stood in the way. The legitimist cause was embodied in the person of the comte de Chambord, posthumous son of the duc de Berry, *l'enfant du miracle*, brought up as he said himself to expect everything from God and nothing from man, devout to the point of mysticism, free from worldly ambition, lame, secluded, passing his life with his little court of exiles apart from the world in a castle in Austria, perhaps the noblest of his line and beyond doubt now the last, for he had no children. In this fact lay the opportunity for a deal with the rival house of Orleans, by which the comte de Chambord might occupy the throne while he lived, and on his death be succeeded in the due line of succession by his Orleanist heir. This seemed a reasonable plan to the comte de Paris, a very different kind of person, who knew the world and had perhaps profited from a study of the career of Louis Napoleon in preparing his own candidature. He had fought in the American Civil War, written a history of it and various books of travel, studied trade unionism in England. Unfortunately for his hopes it was quite out of the comte de Chambord's character to do a deal with anybody. He made this plain in a manifesto issued as early as July 1871, with the symbolic declaration that he would never abandon the white flag and fleur-de-lys of his ancestors.

Extensive decentralization, provincial liberties, universal suffrage 'honestly applied', parliamentary government – these he could and did promise; but the royal standard was an almost mystical symbol in his eyes. *'Français! Henri V ne peut abandonner le drapeau blanc d'Henri IV!'* This was his last word and it was fatal to the monarchy. For several years still the Orleanists, and some of the legitimists, vainly hoped for a compromise; but it was impossible for France to abandon the *tricolore* and the comte de Chambord was immovable. Perhaps, as well as his sincerely held principles, there was also on his part no great desire to abandon the quiet life of a country gentleman for the discomfort of Versailles, the bustle of Paris, and the dangers of a disputed crown. That it would have been no easy or peaceful restoration was indicated by the first elections to be held in normal conditions. These were the supplementary elections of July 1871, in which for 114 seats, 99 republicans, and only 9 Orleanists, 3 legitimists, and 3 Bonapartists were elected. Subsequent by-elections confirmed the trend. Between 1871 and 1874 there was a great change in the composition of the Assembly: 126 republicans, 23 monarchists, and 10 Bonapartists were elected.

By 1872, now that the issue of war and peace no longer stood in the way, Gambetta had returned to active politics to uphold the republican cause. Thiers had made up his mind that the republic was going to win and was cautiously throwing his influence on that side. Not quite cautiously enough, however, for there was still a monarchist majority in the Assembly which determined to free itself from the embarrassing old man. The monarchists forced his resignation in May 1873 and replaced him at the head of the state by Marshal MacMahon, with a leading Orleanist, the duc de Broglie, as head of the government. The monarchists had thus brought to an end the abnormal situation in which practically all authority had been concentrated in the hands of Thiers, and replaced it with parliamentary government.

De Broglie stood for a resolutely conservative policy, but some of the monarchists wanted much more than this. The religious revival that had begun early in the century was still strong. The masochistic tendencies of the French right asserted themselves as they had in 1815 and were to do again in 1940. The nation was called to repentance for the sins that had brought on it the disasters of the war. A popular religious movement was promoted by the rising order of the Assumptionists, who organized great mass pilgrimages to Lourdes and other shrines. The appeal for the erection of Sacré-Cœur on the heights of Montmartre over Paris, where Loyola and his first group of followers had met, had been launched in 1870; the foundation stone was laid in 1873. The Church obtained the passage of a series of laws putting it in a more favoured position than it had held even under the Second Empire. The growing cult of the Sacred Heart was linked with the sorrows of France, and with those of a Church whose head was now the prisoner of the Vatican. The restoration of the legitimate monarch in France, and the liberation of the Pope, became the joint aims of the more militant Catholics. To those who were less ardent, the prospect of war with Italy for the sake of the revival of the temporal power of the Pope, and a parallel agitation against the religious policy of Bismarck which threatened further hostilities with Germany, were alarming. The result, because of the close link between legitimacy and the Church, was that the monarchists were saddled with the joint incubus of clericalism and war-mongering.

Until legitimists and Orleanists had reached an agreement, the restoration of the monarchy was not practical politics. The provisional solution that the National Assembly found was the *septennat* of November 1873, by which MacMahon was to be head of the state for seven years. The monarchists hoped that before his term was over their difficulties would have been removed and a king could take his place, but if they thought time would work in their favour they were mistaken. The moderation of the republicans, including even Gambetta, and the extremism of the legitimists and clericals, had the effect of consolidating opinion on the republican side. In January 1875 a motion that 'the Government of the Republic is composed of two Chambers and a President' was defeated by only 359 votes to 336. It was followed by the famous *amendement Wallon*, notable for the terms in which it was proposed. 'My conclusion', ended Wallon, 'is that it is necessary to leave the provisional. If Monarchy is possible, show that it is acceptable, propose it. If on the contrary it is not possible, I do not say to you: decide for the Republic, but I say: recognize the government which is now established and which is the government of the Republic. I do not ask you to declare it definitive – What is definitive? But all the same do not declare it provisional.' The importance of this amendment was that it prescribed a method of electing the successors of MacMahon and so made the presidency of the Republic into a permanent institution. It was passed by 353 votes to 352, so that it could be said that the Republic was established by a majority of one vote.

The Third Republic never had a constitution. In its place there were a number of constitutional laws, passed to cope with practical issues as they arose, and, against all precedent, with little theoretical discussion. The monarchists and conservatives generally, knowing that they would lose heavily in an election, were anxious above all to avoid a dissolution and were therefore prepared to compromise. So it came about that the Republic was established by an Assembly which still had a monarchical majority. It naturally insisted on the retention of as many conservative elements as possible – a President chosen for a long term, re-eligible and not responsible to parliament; a Senate with powers theoretically equal to those of the lower house, and with one-third life members and the remainder indirectly elected by local governing bodies. The possibility of an easy transition from republic to monarchy was preserved by establishing a simple procedure for the revision of the constitutional laws. The balance of power between President, Senate, and Chamber was left unsettled, so that it could be tilted, when opportunity offered, in the direction of monarchy.

The practical working-out of the new constitutional laws was to have just the opposite result. The weakness of the monarchists was shown at the outset when the life senators were elected. The legitimists so hated the Orleanists that they joined with the republicans to exclude them from the Senate, at the price of electing 57 republicans out of 75. The completion of the membership of the Senate in 1876 produced a house in which republicans and monarchists were almost equally balanced. In the lower Chamber elections had produced 300 republicans (including 80 of the left) against 135 monarchists. MacMahon thus found himself faced with a republican Chamber of Deputies, and in this situation the plans of the monarchists produced exactly the opposite result from that intended by them; for, faced with a President elected by a defunct Assembly and a Senate chosen by indirect election, the Chamber could claim to represent the voice of the people.

If the monarchists accepted this situation they abandoned all hope of achieving their ends. Rather than do this they played their trump card – control of the executive. Mac-Mahon dissolved the Chamber on 16 May 1877, appointed de Broglie at the head of a new government, and prepared for new elections by a wholesale administrative purge. Over 70 prefects and 226 secretaries general or sub-prefects were replaced, and 1,743 municipal councils dissolved. The new prefects were largely Bonapartists, because only the agents of the former Bonapartist machine had the necessary experience of electoral management, but the task was to be too difficult even for them. The left replied with a policy of republican concentration under an alliance of Thiers and Gambetta, and when Thiers died in the middle of the campaign, instead of weakening them, it provided the opportunity for a great republican demonstration in which his sins were forgotten and only his patriotism remembered. A safe, moderate republican, Jules Grévy, took his place as the nominal leader. The attempt of MacMahon and de Broglie to make the elections was a total failure: the left won 326 seats and the right 207. The *coup* of 16 May had failed. In January 1879 the Senate also acquired a republican majority. After this decisive repudiation by the country there was nothing left for MacMahon to do but to resign. He was replaced as President by Grévy.

The crisis had done more than register the failure of the monarchists. In his first message the new President declared, 'Subject to the great law of the parliamentary régime, I will never enter into opposition against the national will expressed by its constitutional organs.' The balance of the constitution had been decisively shifted in favour of the Chamber and against the Senate and the President. The Senate was for long after this a mere 'theatre of the left-bank', not a stage on which the greater dramas of national life were enacted. Its influence gradually increased, but it was only in the last years of the Third Republic that it became practically the headquarters of the general staff of republican politics.

The presidency, on the other hand, never recovered from the failure of MacMahon's attempt to be an effective head of state. Presidents were elected by an absolute majority of the Senate and Chamber in joint session at Versailles, for seven years and renewable, though only two Presidents (Grévy and Lebrun) were re-elected. All Presidential acts had to be countersigned by a minister. The President could not be removed, though in fact two Presidents – Grévy in 1887 and Millerand in 1924 – were forced to resign. It became practically a constitutional convention of the Third Republic that no strong statesman should be elected President; Poincaré in 1913 was an exception attributable to the threatening international situation. The President's duties were mainly honorific: he has been described as an elderly gentleman whose function it was to wear evening dress in day-time. Yet he alone was in a position to provide continuity in policy – very necessary in a régime of rapidly changing governments, and his right to nominate the new head of the ministry made him the key figure when a government fell. His skill in manoeuvring could often determine whether a political crisis should be of short duration, or long and severe. But at best the President could do no more than grease the wheels of politics. After 1878 power resided in the parliament and chiefly in the Chamber of Deputies.

The years 1877 to 1881 mark the real foundation of the Third Republic. The defeat of the right in the legislative elections of 1877 was accompanied by a similar republican victory in the local elections, which has been called the *révolution des mairies*. After further elections in 1881, the republicans had a majority in 66 departmental Councils out of 87. This was quite as important as the changes in political personnel at the centre. It was the end of the rule of that *haute bourgeoisie*, which had dominated French political life under each successive régime for some eighty years, and the succession of the *petite bourgeoisie*. The smaller towns and the countryside had at last revolted from the rule of the notables. Correspondingly, the legislative elections of 1881 gave the republicans 467 members out of 557 in the Chamber, and strengthened the more radical elements among them. A series of other political changes marked the increasing republicanism of the régime. In 1879 the Senate and the Chamber of Deputies returned to Paris from Versailles. *La Marseillaise* became the national song, and the Quatorze Juillet the national holiday. A long campaign which had been waged in favour of an amnesty for the Communards sentenced to exile or deportation had provided one of the chief lines of cleavage in the republican ranks. In 1881 the wound was healed, so far as it could be, by the grant, thanks mainly to an intervention by Gambetta, of a total amnesty. In the same year a new press law abolished 'crimes of opinion', leaving only direct provocation to crime or disturbances of the peace, insults to the President, defamation and the like as press offences, and these to be subject to trial by jury. Another law freed the holding of public meetings from the need for official authorization.

The chief area of strategic conflict between left and right now shifted to the field of education. In 1879 a determined opponent of clerical control, Jules Ferry, became Minister of Education. He belonged to a distinguished family of the Vosges and had been a strong critic of the Second Empire and a member of the Government of National Defence. Though able and determined in character, he was too rigid and uncompromising to win popularity. Conservative in social matters, expansionist in the colonies, he was a convinced republican and fiercely secularist in educational policy. There was a general feeling, in republican circles, that French education did not cope with the requirements of the times. The disaster of 1870 was regarded as a victory for the German teacher. Whereas German schools provided instruction in the sciences and modern languages, French education, it was alleged, was still following the methods and aims of the seventeenth century. An attempt at modernization in 1872, by Jules Simon, was frustrated by the influence of the Church and particularly of the great cleric, Dupanloup. It seemed unlikely that reform would be possible so long as education remained largely in clerical hands; and as the clergy were in the main monarchist in their political sympathies this was another reason for fearing their influence on the educational system.

Ferry launched his attack with characteristic single-mindedness and vigour. He began by secularizing the Conseil Supérieur de l'Instruction Publique, expelling the bishops and other high ecclesiastics from it. He confined the granting of decrees and other educational qualifications to the State. Education in the public primary schools was made free and by a subsequent law compulsory. For the training of women teachers *écoles normales* for girls, which hardly existed as yet, were to be founded in every department. Religious instruction was excluded from the State schools: it was the coming of the '*école sans Dieu*', declared de Broglie. The bitterest struggle was waged over the proposal to prohibit from any share in running schools or teaching those religious orders which were not legally recognized. After a struggle, which sometimes involved the expulsion of members of the unrecognized orders from their schools by force, along with rioting by their supporters in the local population, and the dismissal of officials who refused to enforce the laws, some 300 unauthorized religious houses for men, with about 3,000 members, were dissolved. This was only the beginning of a conflict which was for long to embitter the politics of the Third Republic.

In spite of the success of the republicans their real leader, Gambetta, had remained excluded from office. Grévy reflected the hostility of the more conservative republicans against the man whom Thiers had damned as the '*fou furieux*'. It was the first of many occasions during the Third Republic when the reasonable, sensible, moderate, intriguing, little men, of whom Grévy was no unworthy representative, joined to exclude a man whose greater stature made him seem dangerous. Only in 1881 did Gambetta form a ministry. Perhaps his critics had been right in thinking him unsuited for the everyday task of government. His list of ministers was not favourably received and he had to resign in January 1882, less than three months after taking office. The same year he died, prematurely, at the age of forty-four, and many hopes and fears died with him.

In a second ministry, beginning in February 1883, Ferry continued the task of republican consolidation with the notable law on municipalities of 1884, which established the free election of *maires* by the local councils everywhere except in Paris. The full importance of this step can only be seen if the extent of the powers of the *maire* is known. He was, and is, the agent of the State for proclaiming and carrying out the laws and regulations of the central government; the registrar of births, marriages, and deaths; as a judicial officer he can denounce breaches of the law, and in default of the police commissioner prosecute them in the courts; he is the executive agent of the commune, he presides over the meetings of the local council, prepares its agenda, and draws up its budget. In the light of all this we can see why the Republic has been described as the régime of the elected *maire*.

Other laws passed at this time included a prohibition of any revision of the republican form of government, or of the election of any member of a family which formerly reigned in France to the Presidency; the abolition of life Senators as and when the existing ones died; the recognition of trade unions; and the re-introduction of a law of divorce. These were the work of Ferry and those moderate republicans whom their critics condemned as Opportunists. Ferry's achievement has seemed greater to historians than it did to his contemporaries, dominated by a personal hatred of the man. Hardly any other politician of the time aroused such bitter hostility; but it was not his domestic policy but his contribution to building a new colonial empire that brought about his downfall.

The left in France was naturally opposed to military expeditions, and the right regarded overseas commitments as a diversion from the task of revenge against Germany. The creation of a colonial empire by the Third Republic is difficult to explain except in terms of the personal policy and influence of Ferry. Coming from the industrial Vosges and from a family of industrialists and financiers, he could envisage the rôle of colonies in providing markets for surplus manufactures and a source of supply for raw materials. It is true that he only produced this explanation of his policy after his two ministries had been overthrown, in 1881 and 1885, on colonial issues, and it was in a sense a justification after the fact. The first of Ferry's colonial acquisitions is to be explained more easily in terms of rivalry with Italy. At the instigation of French colonists in Algeria, a protectorate was established over Tunisia in 1881 to prevent its annexation by Italy. Ferry's second great colonial commitment was also hardly the result of deliberate choice. The Second Empire had established a foothold in Indo-China. Trouble with pirates and the loss of a small French force there turned a minor expedition for police purposes into a substantial war with China for the possession of Tonkin. The credits required for the expedition were resented and there was a heavy loss of life from disease. As the

colonial war dragged on it became more and more unpopular in a country that was not interested in colonial
expeditions and had unhappy memories of the Mexican
adventure. When, in 1885, the report arrived of a French
reverse in Tonkin, the enemies of Ferry saw their opportunity. Led by Clemenceau from the extreme left, they
shouted him down with cries of 'Tonkin-Ferry' and hurled
him from office. The Tonkin affair was soon after concluded successfully, but Ferry's reputation never recovered
from the attack.

He fell at a time when political and economic developments were leading up to the first great crisis of the Third
Republic. Economic conditions, which had given the
Republic a good start in the seventies, became much less
favourable in the eighties. The boom had reached its height
in 1880 to 1881. At the beginning of 1882 one of the leading
banks, the Union Générale, established under Catholic
influence to challenge the financial dominance of Protestants and Jews, suspended payments. Speculations in
central Europe had brought the bank into conflict with
the more powerful Rothschilds from which it emerged the
loser. The failure of this Catholic financial venture, a panic
on the Bourse, and bankruptcies, were perhaps not unconnected with the growing agitation against Jewish financiers.
Also, for the first time under the Third Republic there was
a deficit on the budget in 1882, which continued until 1887.
A general industrial slump, in which prices and wages fell
and unemployment rose, followed the financial crisis. The
conclusion was drawn that economic depression was the
result of the weak and unstable policies of republican
governments, whereas in fact it was their cause.

The republican parties therefore entered the elections of
1885 in unfavourable conditions. They were disunited
because of the growth of a left wing, now beginning to be
called Intransigents or Radicals, who were hostile to the
social conservatism as well as to the colonial policy of the
dominant Opportunists. The right, on the other hand, as
a result of the deaths of the Prince Imperial in 1879 and of

the comte de Chambord in 1883, were left with only one candidate for the throne, the Orleanist comte de Paris. It is true that the more rigid legitimists never reconciled themselves to his claim, and the Bonapartist tradition was to develop in a different direction, but for the moment the monarchists were less divided than usual. Throughout the history of the Third Republic the strength of the right in the country was greater than their generally inferior position in the Chamber of Deputies would lead one to suppose, and this permanent inferiority was partly responsible for their tendency to flirt with revolution. In 1885 they obtained 3,500,000 votes against 4,100,000. The obvious danger forced the usual electoral coalition on the republican parties, who in the second ballot won 383 seats against 201 for their opponents. In December 1885 Jules Grévy was re-elected President. However, the Opportunists could only continue to form the government with the aid of the more radical left and were to that extent at their mercy.

The left wing was responsible for the miscalculation which now endangered the Republic. The leading personality among the radicals, Clemenceau, put a protégé of his, General Boulanger, whose actions had attracted to him left-wing sympathies unusual for a general and whose martial air and panache aroused the enthusiasm of the crowd, into the Ministry of War in January 1886. The attention that Boulanger in his new office paid to the welfare of the troops increased his popularity, which was not diminished by German attacks on him for verbal fireworks directed against Germany. The Opportunists becoming alarmed, in May 1887 he was dropped from the ministry; but he was now a national figure, round whom opposition, from left and right, began to rally. Popular discontent, arising from economic difficulties as much as anything, found a cause to concentrate on in November 1887, when it was revealed that the President's son-in-law, Daniel Wilson, had been turning the Élysée Palace into a market for the sale of decorations and other favours in the presidential gift. Grévy, though discredited by these revelations, clung to office until he was forced out. The obvious successor was Ferry, but the popular hatred that had been built up against him was such that his nomination might well have provoked a revolution. Instead, therefore, Sadi Carnot, a worthy moderate republican and the bearer of a great republican name, was elected.

The situation was still dangerous, for the right had now taken up Boulanger. They saw in his popularity a lever with which they might overturn the republic. The episode that followed is a watershed in the history of French politics. It marks the end of the old-fashioned monarchist tradition, whether of Legitimists or Orleanists, and the beginning of a new nationalist, plebiscitary, anti-parliamentary tendency based on an appeal to left and right against the centre, and relying on the cult of a man rather than a policy. Summed up, it was bonapartism without a Bonaparte. The government gave Boulanger and his new supporters their opportunity by forcing him into retirement from the army in March 1888. He had now lost the support of most of the radical leaders, but not necessarily of their voters. On the extreme left Blanquists were attracted to a potential dictator. Many socialists, in their enmity to the conservative republic, favoured Boulanger, and unemployment brought the workers on to his side. Rochefort, once editor of *La Lanterne*, who had returned to France with the amnesty of 1880 and as editor of *L'Intransigeant* conducted a guerrilla war against the Republic, contributed his clientele. Boulanger was backed by a committee of monarchists and Bonapartists, his campaign was financed by the legitimist duchesse d'Uzès, and he had much support in the army and the church. In a series of by-elections he won overwhelming majorities culminating in a victory by 244,149 to 162,410 in the Paris election of January 1889.

When the Paris result was announced, huge excited mobs surrounded Boulanger crying '*À l'Élysée*'. The Ligue des Patriotes, founded in 1882 by Paul Déroulède with the intention of reviving French national spirit by a mass appeal, was ready to give the lead, which many would have followed, for a *coup d'état*. It is difficult to see what but his own faint-heartedness stopped Boulanger from seizing power. He has been charged with losing his head in this crisis and with an unmilitary preference for parliamentary methods. This is to forget that apart from Louis Napoleon, who had the First Empire and the Napoleonic tradition behind him, there was as yet no modern precedent, outside Latin America, for this kind of dictatorial seizure of power. Possibly Boulanger may have realized – what was certainly true – that his supporters were so diverse that they could never have agreed on a coherent policy. If they had seized power, they would not have known what to do with it. It is more difficult to explain why he gave up the game altogether. When a comparatively weak government began legal proceedings against Boulanger and he believed himself in danger of arrest, he fled the country. With his flight the whole movement collapsed. In the elections of September 1889, conservatives and Boulangists could win no more than 210 seats: the republicans gained 366. Among them the Opportunists with some 216 were the dominant element, for the radicals suffered because of their flirtation with Boulanger.

2. THE TRIUMPH OF THE REPUBLIC, 1889–99

THE next ten years was a period of confused and changing policies, which superficially could be described in terms of personal rivalries and the political intrigues of parties and factions, though to do so would be to miss the whole significance of the decade. But a straightforward – if that is the appropriate description of a period which witnessed so many twists and turns – summary of political developments is perhaps necessary in the first place, though it will tell us little of what was really significant in these years.

The new Chamber, in September 1889, continued to support the cabinet of republican concentration which had seen the end of the Boulangist crisis. It was 'replastered', to use the French term, twice, under different leaders, but achieved nothing in particular until November 1892, when under a nondescript republican premier, Loubet, it had to face a new crisis. Two survivors of the Boulangist movement, the author Maurice Barrès, who had become a deputy for Nancy in 1889, and Édouard Drumont, editor of the anti-Semitic journal *La Libre Parole*, now discovered in the affairs of the Panama Canal Company an opportunity to renew the attack on the Republic. After his triumph with the Suez canal, Ferdinand de Lesseps had launched a company to drive a canal through the isthmus of Panama. This proved a much more difficult, and therefore expensive, undertaking than had been expected. To raise new money the Panama Company resorted to issuing shares repayable by lot, which required the passage of a special act of parliament. In spite of the new money, the Company went bankrupt, and in the subsequent enquiry accusations of bribery of politicians by the Company were put forward. In the middle of the enquiry the Jewish financier, the baron Jacques de Reinach, involved in the charges, committed suicide, and Cornelius Herz, another financier with political connexions, fled the country. Governments fell, ministers had to resign, the names were published of deputies who, it was alleged, had received payments from the Panama Company; the editors of national papers were also on the list of payees.

The most violent storm fell on the head of Georges Clemenceau. Though he came from Catholic and royalist Vendée, Clemenceau's ancestors, small proprietors and doctors, were anti-clerical and Jacobin. La Reveillière-Lépeaux, regicide and director, had been a cousin. Clemenceau's father narrowly escaped deportation under the Second Empire. He himself was *maire* of Montmartre during the siege of Paris, and one of the *maires* who attempted to mediate between the Commune and Versailles. In the Chamber of Deputies he became the most feared of the guerrillas of the left, notorious for his violent speeches, vitriolic articles, and duels. Now he was to fall a victim to the kind of onslaught he himself knew so well how to launch. Suspicions that he had been the power behind Cornelius Herz were crystallized in a speech by Paul Déroulède. Everyone knew who was the guilty man, Déroulède proclaimed, but they dared not say it for they feared three things – his tongue, his pistol, and his pen. 'I defy all three and name him: it is M. Clemenceau.' A duel naturally followed, which was bloodless, but the fatal blow had been struck. Clemenceau was hounded out of public life with cries of 'Aoh yes!' for to the charge of Panama corruption was added, to sink him beyond hope of rescue, that of being an English agent.

The republican majority, having shed its more compromised members, got over the Panama affair as well as it could. The elections of August 1893, in which there were many abstentions, returned a majority of about 310 moderate republicans, some 150 radical republicans, and a small group of independents or socialists on the extreme left – these last the electoral witness of rising social unrest. The republican cabinets of the next few years had to govern amid a wave of violence which culminated, in June 1894, in the assassination of Sadi Carnot. Casimir-Périer, who replaced him as President, only held office for six months, after which, frustrated at the powerlessness of the presidency, he resigned. In his place was chosen the amiable man-of-the-world, Félix Faure. Scandals connected with a railway company brought down the first government of his presidency in October 1895. For the first time a radical cabinet was formed, under Léon Bourgeois, in November. It was undermined by its attempt to introduce financial reforms, including an income tax, and in April 1896 was replaced by a cabinet of moderate republicans under Méline, who had no such dangerous ideas. General elections in May 1898 once again proved that despite all the faults of the republican parties the country remained republican. But now a new crisis had unexpectedly arisen. In January 1898 Zola published in Clemenceau's journal an open letter *J'accuse*, and the Dreyfus affair broke.

Before this, however, and behind the petty political manoeuvring of the nineties, major developments had taken place, which fundamentally changed the meaning of right and left. First, the old right, the monarchists, whether legitimist or Orleanist, ceased to be an effective political force. The Boulangist movement showed the pattern of the future right, in which neither Church nor King, nor the inherited traditions of the old monarchist parties, was to have much real part to play.

There had been, however, after the failure of Boulangism, an attempt to refashion the right on different lines, which must be described. This was the Ralliement. Its first outward manifestation came in November 1890, when Cardinal Lavigerie, Archbishop of Algiers, at a dinner to officers of the Mediterranean fleet, called on Catholics to put their political efforts on a constitutional basis by frankly accepting the Republic. This was an astonishing pronouncement from a former strong legitimist, but it was not an individual eccentricity: it was a declaration of papal policy, as was made evident when the Pope issued his Encyclical *Au Milieu des Sollicitudes* in February 1892, which advised French Catholics to 'rally' to the Republic and defend the interests of the Church by participation in political life. Leo XIII was alarmed at the growing divorce between the Church and modern society. With the progress of secularization he saw France slipping out of the fold. He also saw a danger in the identification of the Church with the wealthier classes, which had already gone a long way towards duplicating the social cleavage in industrial society with a religious one. By the Encyclical *Rerum Novarum* of May 1891, the Pope called on Catholics to adopt a positive attitude to the problem of wages and hours and the social welfare of the workers. The heirs of the Social Catholics of half a century earlier, such as the legitimist Albert de Mun, welcomed the new move. As an example of what it might mean in practice may be taken the case of a young cavalry officer named Lyautey. Under the influence of the new school of Catholic thought he put forward, in an article in the *Revue des Deux Mondes* in

1891, a new rôle for the army, now composed mostly of conscripts spending their time in peaceable manoeuvres or kicking their heels in barracks. The Army, said Lyautey, should be a school of citizenship and the officer an educator. All that an attempt to put his ideas into practice with his own squadron gained for the young officer was a severe reprimand and the advice to transfer himself and his unsuitable ideas to the colonies. Curiously, the first steps towards putting his ideas into practice in France were taken after 1901 by the anti-clerical War Minister, André.

As an effort to reconcile the Catholic Church and the Republic, the Ralliement proved almost a complete failure. Faced with the choice between the advice of a Pope (which another Pope might reverse) and their deeply ingrained hatred of republican ideas, most of the monarchists and Catholics remained irreconcilable. Even the bishops closed their ears to the appeal from Rome. There is this to be said for them, that it was not a mere matter of accepting republican institutions, but also republican symbols and dogmas, which were profoundly secularist and anti-clerical. On the republican side, while the moderates were prepared to accept the support of Catholics, the radicals feared them even when they brought gifts.

The failure of the Ralliement meant that the conservative and monarchist right ceased to be a real force, or to have more than a nuisance value in French politics. Even though the monarchy was still a flag that was waved, a different party now fought under the same banner and directed its efforts towards a different objective. The logic of the situation made it a revolutionary party, and being this it had to adopt a revolutionary pattern of behaviour. It still found its allies naturally in the two great professional bodies which had not been conquered by the Republic – the Army and the Church. Hence militarism and clericalism became the marks of the new right. From Bonapartism it had inherited a contempt for parliamentary government and from Panama had learnt the cry '*À bas les voleurs*'. It took over from the Opportunists a belief in the colonial mission of France, which it added to the hope of revenge on Germany and the recovery of Alsace-Lorraine. Therefore it stood for war, as well as, and perhaps partly as a means towards, the overthrow of the régime. It drew its support largely from the urban middle classes. Never more than a revolutionary minority, with only a small representation in parliament, it could provoke a permanent feeling of insecurity by continual agitation. Henceforth the Republic had always to live on the brink of a threatened *coup d'état*, and the conservative elements that should have provided ballast for the State were weakened by the existence of a revolutionary party on their right, which might capsize the ship by a sudden lurch at any moment.

The conservatives, properly so-called, were now to be found among the right-wing republicans, and the minority Catholics of the Ralliement naturally gravitated towards them. This alliance was, however, not without its harmful effect on the original social ideals of the Ralliement; for the conservative republicans who were now changing the title of Opportunists to that of Progressivists, had taken over from the Orleanist and Second Empire notables the defence of property. The bitter class struggles of 1848 and 1871 were now a historical memory, labour was beginning to organize itself, and socialist parties were effecting a breach in republican politics. But the wealthy propertied classes were still prepared to resist all concessions and to do no more to improve the conditions of the lower classes than they were compelled to; and in a nation so largely made up of peasant proprietors and independent craftsmen, pressure from organized labour was bound to be weak. The particular social situation accounts for the backwardness of social legislation in France. Even the reforms that were passed into law often remained ineffective for lack of the machinery to put them into practice. The compulsory worker's *livret* was ended in 1890; in fact it had fallen into disuse much earlier, for it involved obligations on employers as well as those on their workers. A law of 1892 establishing labour conciliation remained unapplied. Even such modest reforms as were passed usually were so only after a prolonged struggle and much delay.

Freedom of individual enterprise, however, did not involve any dogmatic adherence to ideas of free trade. Without much difficulty an alliance of agriculturalists and manufacturers, aided by the slump of the late seventies, secured the abandonment of the liberal commercial policy of the Second Empire. In 1881 a tariff law imposed duties of between 10 per cent and 30 per cent on imported manufactures. Agriculture, which had been suffering from bad harvests and the competition of overseas products, demanded protection in its turn. Its cause was championed by the Minister of Agriculture, Méline, whose campaign reached a successful conclusion in 1892 with the introduction of a tariff covering practically the whole of agricultural and industrial production. The system of high protection provided a platform on which small men and big, peasant proprietors and great agriculturalists, craftsmen and capitalists, could stand together, under the impression of rich and poor uniting to defend their common interests against cheap food and cheap manufactures.

The interests of the propertied classes were even more closely touched by the question of taxation. In 1895 and 1896 proposals were tabled for progressive death duties and a progressive income tax, with a compulsory declaration of income to be officially checked. Some such way of making French tax methods more modern, more elastic, and more equitable was badly needed, and it had been part of the programme of the radical wing of the republicans. The moderates and the right reacted almost unanimously against the proposal. Here, again, the small businessman and the peasant provided the rank and file of the army that fought in defence of the social irresponsibility of wealth. The radical cabinet had to resign, and Méline, who had already been the agent of class interests in his protectionist campaign, became premier with the task of defending the interests of property against the new tax proposals. This was practically the only policy of his cabinet, but it was enough to guarantee it a solid majority for over two years, from 1896 to the elections of 1898.

No cynicism was needed to conclude that the poorer population of France would only gain those concessions or improvements in its conditions that it could win for itself by its own efforts. But the methods by which it hoped to achieve something were changing. The revolutionary tradition of *journées* had led the populace of Paris to bloody disaster twice in a quarter of a century. It was enough. When Delescluze died on the barricades a whole tradition passed away with him. This was the end of the *bras-nus*: only romantic Marxist historians, and a few Blanquists, continued to cherish the legend of the *journées* and the barricades. The excitement of the descent *dans la rue*, of joining in a surging mob swirling through the streets, beleaguering the Hôtel de Ville, breaking into the Legislative Assembly, now passed from left to right. Boulangism was the first sign that the threat of revolution in France was henceforth to come from the opposite end of the political spectrum. That the peasants had ceased to be a revolutionary force had been demonstrated in 1848; indeed 1789 had seen the last Jacquerie except on a very small scale. After 1871 the craftsmen and small employers also moved out of the revolutionary ranks of the left. What remained was a growing, but still – in relation to the whole population – small, wage-earning proletariat of factory and mine, disciplined by its conditions of life, lacking the initiative or the political instincts of the master craftsmen and the middle class, more capable of the dumb, passive resistance of the strike than the active effort to overthrow governments and seize power by *journée* or *coup d'état*, lacking also the middle-class leadership that can usually be traced in the revolutionary mobs of the past. What the industrial proletariat was capable of, what indeed it was conditioned to accept, was organization in trade union or political party. The nineties saw the real development of the trade unions, or *syndicats*, and the Socialist party or rather parties, though the previous decade had been one of preparation for them.

After the Commune, of course, left-wing leadership had been temporarily eliminated from France. In 1879 a very moderate workers' movement formed the Fédération des Travailleurs Socialistes. Its leaders were called the 'Possibilists'. A great change came about with the return of the exiles of the Commune in 1880. Jules Guesde, who had been converted to Marxism, split the Federation by founding, in 1882, the Parti Ouvrier, with its chief support from the areas of mines and heavy industry in the North-east and the Centre. Older traditions were still strong, however. The ideas of Proudhon appealed to the craftsmen; and a small party of Blanquists survived, though this was to be weakened by the divergence of some of its members into Boulangism.

Even the Opportunists recognized that a new force was appearing in French politics after 1880. They offered it a concession in 1884 by the law permitting the legal formation of trade unions, or, to use the French term which is not without significance, *syndicats*. Although now legal, they were bitterly opposed by employers and the State. Officials, including the railway workers, were excluded from the right of forming *syndicats*. The two main tendencies in socialist politics were reflected in union organization. Under Guesdist influence a Fédération Nationale des Syndicats was formed for political action in 1886; in opposition, Bourses de Travail, founded in 1887 as popularly controlled centres of mutual aid, workers' education, and employment exchanges, formed a national federation in 1892. The period from 1889 to 1892 was one of economic progress, when the membership of the *syndicats*, 140,000 in 1890, multiplied by three; then, in a period of economic recession, it rose very slowly and was still only 580,000 in 1899 – this in a country with a total population of some 39 millions. This modest progress of the *syndicats* was marked by strikes, violence on both sides, and repression. In 1890, May 1 was recognized as the annual Labour Day. On its first anniversary, in 1891, an incident in which the troops fired on a crowd produced nine dead and over one hundred injured.

The situation darkened when 1893 brought an industrial slump, and about this time also the infection of anarchism, hitherto not much more than a literary freak, broke out in France. The anarchists upheld a doctrine of propaganda by action, in which bombs were the chief form of conversion, though a knife was used to kill President Carnot in June 1894. The disease worked itself out after a year or two, but provided a justification for the cabinet of Casimir-Périer to pass what the left called the '*lois scélérates*', imposing severe penalties on press offences and on provocation or organization of attacks on persons or property.

The extreme left was now in a better position to defend itself politically. Socialist and syndicalist agitation had created an effective workers' vote, which in some constituencies could materially influence or even decide the elections. The result was the arrival in the Chamber of Radical-socialists (strictly 'socialist radicals') and even of Socialists. The latter appeared in appreciable numbers for the first time in 1893. There were forty-eight, divided into a number of different groups and including Millerand and Jaurès. They were too few to be more than a small weight in the parliamentary balance, but the main lines which socialist and syndicalist developments were to follow can already be detected in outline.

In twenty-five years from 1871 the Third Republic had already outlived every other régime that France had known since 1789. Politically republican institutions seemed to have been consolidated. The social problems still remained and a hard-fought struggle was evidently ahead between the intensely conservative propertied classes and the growing class of employees. The agricultural population, which had been suffering from a prolonged depression, had not yet awoken to the use of its potential political power to secure better conditions, but even this was to come. These issues, however, could be fought out by ballot box and in the debating chamber: they did not threaten the stability of the régime.

Though the ideology of the socialists was revolutionary, they were already beginning to show their capacity for being absorbed by the parliamentary system. The real danger arose from the fact that there were still influential elements, which have been mentioned above, which remained unreconciled to the Republic and fundamentally opposed to its ideology.

The Ralliement, by its very failure, had underlined the hostility of most of the Catholics to a political régime which was fundamentally secular and seemed to be the deadly enemy of religion. Though the political personnel was now overwhelmingly republican, the higher ranks of the administration continued to be recruited from families of the *haute bourgeoisie* which, whatever their origins, now had, or were rapidly acquiring, Catholic connexions. Literature in France has always tended to lean towards the opposition, and the opposition was now on the right. New pre-fascist ideologies were growing up, which may loosely be called nationalist, and which appealed to the new generation of writers, angry young men in revolt against the boredom of a régime that had lasted for a quarter of a century.

One of the most important new facts was the change in the composition of the officer class in the Army. The older legitimist families had abandoned the Army, as well as all other forms of government service, after 1830; while the sons of the wealthy bourgeoisie avoided a career that brought neither gain nor social prestige. However, this situation did not last. Gradually, during the Second Empire, the status of the Army officer rose and recruitment from aristocratic families revived. This tendency was intensified, rather unexpectedly, in the early years of the Third Republic, perhaps assisted by the agricultural depression, which made a profession more necessary for the sons of the old landed proprietors. The result was that by the end of the century, when in other fields the republicanization of the State was becoming effective, the higher ranks of the Army were an almost solid conservative, monarchist, and

Catholic monopoly. There were the ingredients here of a dangerously explosive situation, though no one could have guessed in advance that was to be the spark that would set it off.

This came in 1894, though the train that led to a nation-wide conflagration was a long and slow-burning one. In September 1894 a list of French military documents apparently handed to the Germans was rescued, in the normal process of collecting information, from a waste-paper basket in the German Embassy. The famous *bordereau* was examined by the counter-espionage branch of the French Army, which operated under the title of the Statistical Section and was practically a law to itself, being answerable only to the Chief of Staff. It followed its own ways – rather eccentric and devious ones, be it said – in blithe freedom from all outside control. The dominant influence in the little office – its staff only numbered some seven altogether – was a career officer who had risen by his own ability from the ranks, one Major Henry, a heavy and powerful peasant type, brave, ruthless, and – as it turned out – with peasant cunning and an extraordinary gift of invention that accorded ill with his blunt, bull-like appearance.

It was evident from the *bordereau* that there was a spy at work in the French officer corps, and looking for a culprit, the Statistical Section hit on the name of Captain Alfred Dreyfus. Member of a wealthy, textile-manufacturing family of Alsatian Jews, which had chosen French nationality in 1871, Dreyfus entered the Army as an artillery officer, and had recently been seconded to the War Office in Paris. The evidence against him was not merely negligible but entirely non-existent. Even the writing on the *bordereau*, the one material fact, did not resemble Dreyfus's hand. In the whole story, while we meet, naturally, with some ingenious rogues, what strikes one most is the monumental stupidity that was exhibited, not least in the Intelligence branch, by the Army. What settled the fate of Dreyfus was the fact that he was a Jew and as such a rare –

possibly unique – phenomenon on the General Staff. Anti-semitism, formerly, in so far as it existed in France, a prejudice of the left and the people, under the Third Republic had moved over to the right and become a mark of those who were, and therefore of those who wished to be regarded as, socially superior. The chief propagandist of anti-semitism was the journalist Edmond Drumont, who founded in 1892 a paper called *La Libre Parole* to spread his ideas. One of the earliest features was a series called 'Les Juifs dans l'armée'. In 1886 he gave the anti-semites a text-book in *La France Juive*, and in 1889 founded the Anti-semitic League.

The one part of France in which anti-semitism was indigenous – it had appeared in 1789 and again in the Revolution of 1848 – was Alsace. Now not only was Dreyfus an Alsatian Jew, but the head of the Statistical Section was also Alsatian: this may have helped him to settle on Dreyfus as the guilty man. He reported his discovery to the War Office. The Minister, General Mercier, who was to play a sinister rôle from beginning to end of the affair, ordered a court-martial. It might have been thought that the absence of evidence would prove a difficulty at this stage. By now, however, the press was on the scent. With its usual determination that justice shall be done, or at least seem to be done, and a victim be found, it proclaimed that a rich Jewish traitor was about to buy himself immunity for his crimes. The War Office being anxious not to provide any opening for such a suspicion, the conviction of Dreyfus became a political necessity. Major Henry, who was a practised hand at producing forged papers to be planted on foreign agents, supplied the necessary evidence. Though the result was rather crude, it was good enough for a secret court-martial which had a profound conviction of the guilt of the accused. Dreyfus was unanimously found guilty and sentenced to be cashiered and deported for life. There was a good deal of public indignation that he was to escape being shot. The War Ministry did not really deserve this criticism. Enraged that Dreyfus had refused to commit suicide as a gentleman should when found out, or even to confess, although promised better treatment if he would do so, General Mercier ordered him to be sent to the severest possible solitary confinement in Devil's Island. The order was faithfully carried out for the next four years.

The case was now closed, but there was still a desire to get to the bottom of the crime. What was the motive of Dreyfus? What was he after? It could hardly be money for he was a wealthy man. Efforts were made to uncover a woman. A secret love nest was in fact ferreted out, but it proved to be only a mare's nest, belonging to quite a different Dreyfus. Moreover staff papers continued to disappear and the invaluable waste-paper basket of the German Embassy produced another document, this time an express letter – the *petit-bleu* – addressed by name to a French officer named Esterhazy. There was now a new head at the Statistical Section – Major Picquart, yet another Alsatian – who had represented the War Office in the trial of Dreyfus. Put on the track of Esterhazy by the *petit-bleu*, Picquart obtained specimens of his writing and discovered to his astonishment its similarity to the writing on the *bordereau*. One might have thought that this would be the end of the case: it was only the beginning. Major Henry rapidly appreciated the danger of the situation and proceeded to manufacture some better evidence against Dreyfus for Mercier to use. The War Office also became alarmed, and before he could cause trouble by any more inconvenient discoveries Picquart was removed from his position, sent to Tunisia, and subsequently ordered to the fighting area where there was at least a chance that his inconsiderate activities might be brought to an end.

Major Henry's mind was still not at ease, and his alarm was shared by two highly placed members of the War Office, General Gonse and the Marquis du Paty de Clam, who had taken part in the original investigation of Dreyfus. Gonse was a good office man, and as it turned out prepared to lie through thick and thin to cover up for the office. Du Paty de Clam had been a dashing young officer and evidently still fancied himself as something out of a romantic novel. Henry, who was obviously the brains of the triumvirate, now had the fantastic idea of using Esterhazy, with a promise of protection, to consolidate the case against Dreyfus. Esterhazy was a notorious debauchee, permanently in debt, and known to the foreign attachés, if not to the Intelligence branch, as prepared to do anything for money. But he was also the son of a French general, had himself formerly been a member of the Statistical Section, and had an imposing aristocratic air. Because of the discovery of the *petit-bleu* it was not possible to avoid a court-martial, which took only three minutes to acquit him. Esterhazy's sardonic imagination was now added to the cruder cunning of Henry, and more and more officers were entangled in a web of forgery and false evidence so complicated that even its inventors began to lose the threads.

The family of Dreyfus had all this while been struggling unavailingly to re-open the case. They had obtained only a little outside support and that chiefly from other Jews; but Picquart, who had already sacrificed his career to his sense of justice, was trying from a distance to prevent his suspicions from dying with him. He therefore sent a statement to a friend in Paris, who, armed with this, approached the eminent Alsatian senator, Scheurer-Kestner, who was convinced by it of the need for a retrial. Scheurer-Kestner interpellated the government in December 1897 but received no satisfaction. Indeed, Méline prematurely announced, '*Il n'y a pas d'affaire Dreyfus.*' This made it an affair on the political level. Public interest was now aroused: evidently something mysterious was going on. It burst on the general public in January 1898, when the novelist Zola, who had already been sufficiently interested to write one or two articles expressing his concern, published in Clemenceau's *L'Aurore* an open letter to the President of the Republic – the famous *J'accuse* – indicting the War Office of a judicial crime. The Office and the government fought back – they could do nothing else – even though it meant bringing out some of the secret evidence against Dreyfus.

Zola was tried, found guilty, and eventually took refuge in flight to England. Picquart was charged with indiscipline and dismissed the service. Surely the case was now closed.

The case may have been closed, the Affair had just begun. Press and public opinion were aroused and a campaign for revision of the sentence on Dreyfus was started. For some, justice and the fate of an innocent man were at stake; for others it was a heaven-sent opportunity for a campaign against the enemies of the Republic. A petition calling for revision of the judgement on Dreyfus was signed by leading writers and artists – Lanson, Seignobos, Brunot, Viollet, Blum, Langevin, Anatole France, Proust, Halévy, Briand, Herr, Péguy, and many others. The League for the Defence of the Rights of Man was founded. Naturally, the majority of those who took an active part in the campaign for revision were anti-clericals, freemasons, Protestants, and Jews. The Army, monarchists, Catholics, nationalists, found themselves attacked by all those they hated most. The veil that had been cast over old grievances was rudely torn aside. Recent attempts at reconciliation went for nothing. The *anti-dreyfusards* had most of the press behind them and the campaign against the revisionists was waged without mercy. In its journal *La Croix*, the Assumptionist Order carried the Church into the struggle with a raging, tearing campaign which did much to stir up anti-clerical feeling on the other side. The question, wrote one commentator, is not whether a wretched individual is guilty or innocent, it is whether the Jews and the Protestants are, or are not, the masters of this country. The factions of the right had the incitement and the stimulus to fight back against enemies whose political control of France had seemed unshakeable, and in anti-semitism they had a symbol, a flag, a common cause to bind them together. Anti-Jewish riots broke out in many towns; in Algiers there was widespread looting of Jewish property.

The line between *dreyfusards* and *anti-dreyfusards* did not invariably coincide with other divisions; old associations were broken and families split. The political parties of the left at first tried to keep themselves uncommitted. The Radicals were anti-revisionist, the Socialist groups unwilling to be outbid in patriotism by the Radicals, and themselves not uninfluenced by anti-semitic feeling. A manifesto drawn up by Guesde and Jaurès called on the proletariat not to enlist in either of the clans of a bourgeois civil war. Jaurès, however, soon found his sense of justice stronger than his socialist ideology and became one of the leading advocates of revision. The small party of Catholic reformers was committed by Albert de Mun to the defence of the Army, but there were also Catholic *dreyfusards*, though neither side was particularly willing to draw attention to their existence. One who could not be ignored was Péguy, for whom the stake in the Affair was not the physical safety of France, which the Army and the politicians imagined themselves to be defending, but its spiritual salvation.

Politically, the fate of Dreyfus had come to be bound up with the survival of the Third Republic. The attempt to pretend that this was not the issue collapsed with the resignation of Méline in June 1898. The War Office had so far played its cards with complete success – this was not so difficult since Major Henry was always there to provide it with extra aces whenever they were needed. General Mercier, in particular, fought each move in the direction of revision with every weapon he had. The fanatical obstinacy of the War Office has led some historians to the supposition that there was somebody much more powerful than Esterhazy involved in espionage, who was determined to use the supposed guilt of Dreyfus to cover himself. Indeed it does seem possible that a second spy had been at work, though beyond this we cannot go. Whatever the reason, in its anxiety to beat down all criticism the War Office committed the tactical blunder of prosecuting Picquart, perhaps forgetting that since it had already expelled him from the Army this involved an examination of the case against him in a civil court. It was now discovered that one of the documents presented to the Court was a blatant forgery. Major Henry, whose capacity for covering up one forgery with another had at last come to an end, was put under fortress arrest. He was a brave man; he had done his best for the Office without thought of personal reward. Realizing he could do no more, he cut his throat that night. Esterhazy, realizing that *his* game was up, fled to England.

In fact the game was not yet up. To admit the innocence of Dreyfus would be to incriminate the War Office, the aristocracy, and the Church. The Ligue de la Patrie Française rallied intellectuals, artists, poets – Charles Maurras, Émile Faguet, Mistral, François Coppée, Heredia, Lemaître, Rambaud, Jules Verne, Léon Daudet, Forain, and many others – in their defence. The most powerful writer among the *anti-dreyfusards*, Maurice Barrès, converted what had become a defensive struggle against the revisionists into a mystical offensive on behalf of the nation. The country seemed on the verge of civil war.

What saved it was perhaps that spirit of *fonctionnairisme* with which the Army, like all the other great organizations which emerged from the Consulate and Empire, was imbued. Its officers in the last resort were servants of the State, bound by an oath to whoever held the legal authority of the government. Hence, of all the revolutions or *coups d'état* between 1815 and 1958, none was made and none was prevented by the Army. The revolutionary move had to come from civilians. The poet-politician Paul Déroulède, who had founded his Ligue des Patriotes for such a purpose, saw an opportunity to exploit the feverish state of public opinion early in 1899, when the President, Félix Faure, collapsed in the Élysée and the arms of a terrified lady friend. His funeral was used by the Ligue des Patriotes to stage an attempt at a *coup*; it was a farcical failure.

The tide was now running fast the other way. There is no need to recount the delaying tactics by which one barrier to revision after another was set up. In September 1898 the case of Dreyfus was referred to the appeal court; in June 1899 it decided for a new trial, and Dreyfus, in total ignorance of everything that had happened since his trial, was brought back from Devil's Island, white-haired and broken. He was to be tried again, before a new court-martial, at Rennes. It was no better conducted than the former trial: the generals and colonels lied like troopers in defence of the honour of the Army. By five to two the court reached the ridiculous verdict that Dreyfus was guilty of treachery with extenuating circumstances and sentenced him to ten years' detention. It was clear that no Army court would admit to an error of justice. A presidential pardon was therefore issued. A retrial before the Appeal Court in 1906 quashed the Rennes verdict, but the case was really over in 1899.

In the summer of 1899 it had seemed that the republican order was breaking down. A trivial incident in June proved the turning-point. In the course of a visit to the races at Auteuil by the new President, Loubet, a royalist baron knocked his hat off with a stick. This was going too far. It was only a straw but it came at the end of a history that had aroused intense passion. At last the republicans, moderates as well as the extremer factions, had had enough. The compromising, appeasing cabinets that had held office so far during the Affair came to an end. In June 1899 a cabinet of republican defence was formed under Waldeck-Rousseau. The new premier was a distinguished lawyer with a clear mind, a cool temperament, and a cold manner. He was a moderate in his political views, but added a sense of justice to his sense of order, and he was capable of giving the country what it needed most, a government that would govern. Perhaps only Ferry, among the politicians of the Third Republic, had an equal sense of authority, and Ferry aroused too many enmities. Waldeck-Rousseau drew his ministers from the whole gamut of republican politics. Their names are worth remembering, for it was a cabinet of strong men, not afraid of taking decisions, chosen for what they were rather than for the number of votes they could bring with them. General de Gallifet at the Ministry of War, hated by the left as the 'executioner' of 1871, was balanced against the socialist Millerand, even if the latter's acceptance of a ministerial post aroused resentment among other socialists; Delcassé was at the Quai d'Orsay, Caillaux at the Ministry of Finances; Lépine, strongest and most popular of Prefects of Police, brought Paris back to order.

The Waldeck-Rousseau cabinet obtained a majority of only twenty-five, but the new premier was not deterred from taking energetic measures. The appointment of the new Minister of War was a stroke of genius. Gallifet was a professional, in the best sense of the word, not a political general like Mercier, and free from any inclination to play at politics. His reputation with the Army put him beyond attack on that side and enabled him to quell all symptoms of unrest in it. To subject the Church to republican discipline was to be a longer and more costly process. But the critical decade had passed. The Affair, though at a heavy price both at the time and in drafts on the future, had ended in the triumph of the Republic. It was to survive for another forty years, and then only to be overthrown by a foreign enemy.

3. CONSOLIDATION OF THE REPUBLIC, 1900–10

THE struggle for justice in the Dreyfus affair had united, as perhaps nothing else could have done, the republican forces in France. Under a premier of character, like Waldeck-Rousseau, this meant justice not only for Dreyfus but also – of a retributive kind – for the enemies of the Republic. One of the first steps of the new government was to order the arrest and trial of those who had attempted to exploit the affair in the interests of revolution. Something also had to be done about the Assumptionist Fathers, who in their papers had been conducting a Holy War against the Republic and the Jews. They had been rather unwise in thus putting themselves in the forefront of the political battle, for as an unauthorized congregation they were in a weak legal position if the government chose to take action against them. Not without provocation – one of the last efforts of the Order had been to subsidize opposition candidates in the elections – it did take action, and the Order was dissolved.

Waldeck-Rousseau was not anxious to extend the attack to those religious bodies which had not flung themselves into the political struggle. He put forward, in November 1899, a scheme compelling religious congregations to apply for legal recognition. It also included certain steps for assimilating clerical and lay schools, so that, as he said, there should no longer be '*deux jeunesses*' in France. It is doubtful if the Church would have accepted such proposals in any case, but the plan was diverted from its original intention. One of the basic weaknesses of the parliamentary system of the Third Republic was that no government had control of its own legislation. Its proposals were seldom voted on in the form in which they were presented; they automatically went into the machine of the Commissions of the Chambers, from which they might emerge in an almost unrecognizable shape. Thus Waldeck-Rousseau's proposals, when they became law on 1 July 1901, had been vastly changed. By the new law each congregation had to apply for legal authorization or be dissolved, and no member of an unauthorized congregation was to be allowed to teach. However, the law was applied with moderation and did not seem likely to provoke serious opposition.

The country registered its approval, after a close electoral struggle, in May 1902. The government won some 370 seats against 220 held by the opposition, though once again the division was a much more even one than these figures might suggest, for in actual votes there was only some 200,000 difference between the two blocs. But they were now divided by the whole gulf of the Dreyfus affair. The bitterness of the feelings that had been aroused by the series of attempts to overthrow the Republic, and the moral revulsion against appeals to violence and anti-semitism, were now added to the traditional anti-clericalism, and a strong element of class hostility coincided with the religious cleavage. The aristocracy was pretty solidly Catholic, the wealthier middle classes and higher officials had also largely abandoned their former scepticism or indifference. On the other hand the lower middle classes and lesser officials retained all their fervid anti-clericalism, and the breach between many of the workers and the Church was becoming total. The attitude of the peasantry varied greatly. In the South there was wide-spread anti-clericalism; elsewhere – for instance in Brittany, the Vendée, Normandy, and Lorraine – the Church was still deeply rooted. The particular form which anti-clericalism took among the middle and lower middle classes was Freemasonry, which was also closely linked with radicalism in politics. The number of Freemasons has been estimated at some 50,000, though as it was a secret society its actual membership cannot be told accurately; but each one of these was a confirmed anti-clerical and the whole body exercised a far greater influence than its numbers might suggest.

The more violent anti-clericals regarded the election of 1902 as their particular victory. Waldeck-Rousseau was not the man to give them what they wanted; but he was in poor health and indeed died two years later. Unwilling to yield to pressure from the left, he resigned in June 1902 and his place was taken by a second-rate, elderly senator named Combes, indicated for such high office only by the fact that as an ardent anti-clerical himself he might be expected to hold an anti-clerical majority together. No one has a good word to say for this product of a seminary education who would have made a good narrow-minded and vindictive bishop in a backward diocese, for Combes was originally intended for the priesthood. He added to the *odium theologicum* the petty malignancies of small-town politics and carried both into national life. The corrupting influence of clericalism and anti-clericalism on French public life can be seen fully displayed, the first in the Dreyfus affair and the second in the ministry of Combes. With Combes all other national interests were sacrificed to the cause of anti-clericalism. Congregations asking for legal recognition under the new law found, with a few exceptions, their requests rejected; 81 congregations of women were dissolved and 54 of men. A law was passed to prohibit all congregations from teaching, and to dissolve all actual teaching congregations within five years. It is surprising that such legislation, though it produced demonstrations especially in the Catholic West, did not lead to more violent resistance.

Combes found a reaction more worthy of him in Rome, where the enlightened Leo XIII had been replaced by Pius X who, as his name indicated, was to take up the tradition of Pius IX, aided by a young and uncompromising Secretary of State, Merry del Val. The conflict, which the policy of the French government had prepared, was precipitated by an official visit of President Loubet to the King of Italy. A protest by the Vatican against the visit leaked out and the French government had to recall its ambassador to the Vatican. The action of the Papacy was widely resented in France, and the French cabinet's retaliation was endorsed by a vote of 427 to 95 in the Chamber. The conflict was exacerbated by differences between Rome and Paris over the appointment and dismissal of bishops. Finally, in November 1904, Combes, not very reluctantly, tabled a law for the Separation of Church and State.

Though his majority was weakening, it still held together, and it was in fact not his anti-clerical legislation that brought down the government of the 'petit père' Combes, but the indiscretions of his Minister of War, General André. One of Gallifet's reforms had been the reorganization of the Army Council and the attribution to the Minister of War of all promotions and appointments in the Army. This was obviously a desirable measure, on condition that it was put into effect with discretion, which was the quality André lacked. He had been chosen as the only general with strong republican sympathies, and had suffered throughout his career for his views. It was therefore with enthusiasm that he set about breaking down the Catholic and monarchist monopoly of the higher command. Its fantastic behaviour in the course of the Dreyfus affair did indeed suggest that drastic changes were needed, and Gallifet had taken the first steps towards them. André turned the tables with a vengeance. Promotion now went only to those who could demonstrate their sound republican and anti-clerical sentiments. This was not altogether unreasonable in a Republic, though it was not guaranteed to improve the morale or quality of the Army command. To obtain the necessary information, André organized, with the aid of informers, especially Freemasons and often from the lower commissioned or non-commissioned ranks of the Army, a great collection of *fiches* on the religious affiliations of the officer corps. In October 1904 his system was revealed by an employee of the Masonic Grand Orient, and public indignation was such that the Minister had to resign. Combes followed him in January 1905.

The question of Separation was still on the agenda. A new ministry put it in charge of the supple and conciliating young socialist, Aristide Briand, who secured the passage, in October 1905, of a Law of Separation which, it was hoped, would offend as little as possible the religious feelings of the Catholics. It went back to the Constitution of the year III, when the State recognized absolute liberty of conscience, and did not recognize, or contribute to the finances of, any religion; but each religion was to be allowed to keep its property, including its religious edifices, on condition of forming a legally recognized association to manage it. Rome was in no mood for a compromise and would have none of this. By an Encyclical appropriately beginning *Vehementer* the Pope repudiated the proposed arrangement. In France, although the application of the law met with strong opposition in Catholic areas, the elections of May 1906 kept the anti-clerical majority in power.

As a result of Vatican intransigence the French Church was not able to form the 'religious associations' provided for by the law, but it kept the use of its churches by a tacit understanding with the secular authorities. By a series of concessions Briand established a *modus vivendi* with the

French bishops, who were themselves the object of severe disciplinary measures by Rome, directed to crushing out any taint of 'modernism' deriving from the influence of the abbé Loisy. The attempt by another Catholic, Marc Sangnier, to follow in the path of the Ralliement by founding a party which should have mildly democratic sympathies and advocate the cause of social reform, with the name of *Le Sillon*, also fell under the Papal ban as 'placing authority in the hands of the people and tending towards the levelling of classes'. Papal control over the Church in France now greatly increased. One result of Separation was to enable the Papacy to appoint bishops who were less prepared to compromise with the State. The poverty which fell upon the lower clergy made their recruitment more difficult, while at the same time it helped to ensure that only those with a real religious vocation entered the priesthood. The *curés* and *vicaires*, who in the nineteenth century had represented a privileged class in the villages, perhaps gained more respect now that economically they were no better off than their parishioners; whereas the *instituteur*, the teacher, who had been one of themselves to the village people when he was a downtrodden usher, eking out a meagre living by acting as bell-ringer, clerk, and general drudge to the *curé*, now that he was a better-paid official of the state seemed to represent a superior and alien element.

On the whole, Separation, while it temporarily exacerbated, in the end tended to reduce, the tension between Church and State. The majority of the Catholics were not yet reconciled to the Republic, but with the decline of clerical interference in politics the violence of anti-clerical sentiment inevitably declined. The discredit resulting from the methods and narrowness of Combes was to some extent wiped out by the moderation of Briand and the uncompromising policy of the Vatican, and the Republic emerged from the crisis strengthened.

In October 1906 the man who had been the *bête noire* of the right, Clemenceau, for the first time formed a government, himself taking the Ministry of the Interior, with

Briand at the Ministry of Education and Religion, and – a defiance to the opposition – Picquart, now a general, at the Ministry of War. This was a more 'advanced' government than France had as yet known, radical in complexion, with socialist members. When Clemenceau met the Chamber he presented it with an impressive programme of social and political reforms, including many which had been held up while the Church and State dog-fight had been going on. One of the first steps of the new parliament was to increase the pay of its members from nine to fifteen thousand francs, which put a cry into the mouths of the opposition – the deputies became the *quinze mille*, but after this its reforms proved disappointingly few. Socialist pressure had induced a rather belated beginning of social reform when Millerand was at the Ministry of Commerce in the Waldeck-Rousseau government. A system of arbitration, labour councils, and inspectors of labour was established. A maximum eleven-hour day, made legal in 1900, was reduced in 1904 to ten hours. A proposal to introduce an income tax, put forward by Caillaux in 1907, was passed by the Chamber of Deputies in 1909, doubtless aware that the Senate could be relied on to reject it, as it did.

The period from 1906 to 1914 was, apart from a wave of unemployment in 1908, one of economic progress and industrial development. Along with this went a rise in the membership of the trade-union Confédération Générale du Travail from some 715,000 in 1904 to nearly a million in 1909. In 1905 the socialists amalgamated to form a single party. The move to the left was intensified in the elections of 1906, when the right could only secure 174 seats, against 90 Left Republicans, 115 Radicals, 132 Radical Socialists, 20 Independent Socialists, and 54 S.F.I.O. (Section Française de l'Internationale Ouvrière). What weakened the left was the cleavage between the industrial and the political movements. Socialism in the Chamber, under the predominant influence of Jaurès, was parliamentary and reforming, while the C.G.T., under the influence of former Blanquists and anarchists, and the more recent influence of Georges Sorel's *Réflexions sur la violence* (1906), repudiated collaboration with the parliamentary socialists, and advocated revolutionary syndicalism and the Sorelian myth of the General Strike. A Labour Congress in 1906 embodied these ideas in the Amiens Charter. The following years were marked by a series of revolutionary strikes, often of a violent nature, including in 1909 one of the postal services and in 1910 of the teachers. The government retaliated by sending troops to protect non-strikers, by arrests and imprisonment. Violence spread, in 1907, to the vineyard owners of the South, who reacted to over-production and a fall in the price of wine by violent outbursts, in one of which the prefecture at Perpignan was looted and burnt. The government of Clemenceau, though relying on a majority of the left, suppressed these movements ruthlessly, but it remained for his successor, Briand, to invent and put into use the decisive weapon, when he smashed a strike of railwaymen in 1910 by the device of mobilizing the strikers.

By 1910 the wave of revolutionary syndicalism had been defeated. The tradition of revolt had once again frustrated reform, but the backwardness of French social legislation is not to be attributed exclusively to this factor. The influence of a *haute bourgeoisie* with a weak social and a strong property consciousness, which had made social relations during the nineteenth century an open or covert class war, was no longer unchallenged in politics; but the rise to political power of the great body of peasant proprietors, shopkeepers, and small employers had not produced a balance of power favouring the interests of the unpropertied. Nevertheless the pressure for the creation of a more equitable society was steadily increasing.

Similarly, the structure of a society dominated at the top by the official and professional classes and *rentiers*, and at a lower level by peasants and small employers, was not favourable to economic progress. France was still predominantly an agricultural country. French production of coal in 1913 was one-seventh of British or German production. In iron and steel she produced less than a third as much as Germany. In population France, so long pre-dominant in Europe, had been overtaken. In 1871 the population of France, at 36 millions, had been well above that of Great Britain and only slightly lower than that of all Germany. By 1914 France had grown only to 39½ millions, Great Britain was 45 millions, and the German Empire 67 millions. Various explanations have been given for the stagnation of the French population, such as the influence of the rule of the division of inheritance among all children, generalized by the Napoleonic Code, or the persistence of a high rate of infant mortality, not unconnected with the absence of social reforms. The slowness of economic growth was probably another factor. However, the comparison with more industrialized nations should not be allowed to conceal the actual economic progress that was accomplished in France. Although agricultural methods were still very con-servative, France was second only to the United States and Russia in the production of grain, and produced more wine than any country except Italy. Under the Third Republic the production of coal had more than doubled, that of cast-iron had quadrupled, and of steel been multiplied by twelve.

If French economy suffered from lack of capital, the savings of the French flowed out to fertilize the rest of the world, nearly one-quarter of the foreign investments being – for reasons not unconnected with high politics – placed in Russia. The franc had been stable for a century and the budget was balanced. What French production lacked in quantity it made up in quality. France was still, what Louis XIV and Colbert had made it, the world's chief producer of luxury goods – fine fabrics, *haute couture*, perfumes and cosmetics, *objets d'art* in general. The race of craftsmen still survived and there is no irrelevance in adding that Paris under the Third Republic was more than it had ever been before the artistic capital of the world.

It is significant of an age of individualism that the public arts of architecture and town-planning, which had reached a high degree of excellence under the *ancien régime*, con-tinued to decline. The only advantage that the official architecture of the Third Republic has over that of the Second Empire is that there is possibly less of it. Ecclesiastical architecture, unfortunately, flourished. Sculpture did not develop beyond the romantic tradition. It reached a mastery of expertise in the immensely popular and powerful work of Rodin (1840–1917). A less dramatic but persisting appeal is to be seen in the lovely nudes of Maillol (1861–1944). Sculpture, however, like architecture, was largely dependent on the commissions of nineteenth-century officials and bourgeois, who, unlike their predecessors of the previous century, were notably lacking in taste.

Painting would equally have suffered from the philistinism of society if it had not been a comparatively cheap art, which the artist could pursue for his own pleasure and that of a few friends. France, of course, had an Academy art, like Great Britain, of painters whose works, having gratified a generation of town councillors and men of property, now clutter up provincial museums, and whose names are forgotten. The mid-century had not been a period of great distinction in art. A pastoral spirit, like that of the Berrichon romances of George Sand, illumined the poetic landscapes of Corot (1796–1874) and the Barbizon school. The growth of a social conscience had appeared in the paintings and cartoons of Daumier (1808 – 79), in the harsh realism of the socialist and Communard Gustave Courbet (1819–1877), and the unsentimentalized and affecting peasants of Millet (1814–75). A combination of realism with a purer interest in pictorial values appears in such paintings as the *Déjeuner sur l'herbe* (1863) of Manet, whose naked girl at the picnic seemed so much more shocking than all the romantic odalisques who had preceded her, or in his *Bar aux Folies Bergères* (1882).

Manet forms the link with the great school of the Third Republic. The Impressionists inaugurated an artistic movement which casts a glow over the society which in their own day rejected them. Paris of the Third Republic, damned by the Hôtel de Ville and Sacré-Coeur, is saved by the painters it despised or ignored. A roll of honour of artists decorates its days – Monet, Pissarro, Sisley, Degas, Gauguin, Seurat, Toulouse-Lautrec, le Douanier Rousseau, and the great names of Cézanne, Renoir, Matisse. To see in this galaxy of artists an element of greatness about the Third Republic is obviously justifiable. To go beyond this is perhaps not justifiable, but it is tempting to see also the reflection of an intensely vital society, full of colour and character, in which the individual vision mattered most, a fundamentally stable society in which experiments were possible because they were firmly rooted in tradition, and which through them rose to the achievement of a great classical art.

The Third Republic came to its greater musicians more slowly. Offenbach had delighted Second Empire society, but after him the world of music was bestridden by Wagner. In France, Bizet, César Franck, Massenet, Saint-Saëns could hardly challenge his genius. A new note was heard in 1902 with the production of *Pelléas et Mélisande* by Debussy. Soon after, Ravel joined him, and with composers such as Gabriel Fauré, Paul Dukas, Erik Satie, the Third Republic had a school of music of its own, not unworthy to be mentioned along with its great painters.

In letters the great names of the first half of the century had been succeeded by somewhat of a hiatus during the Second Empire. Romanticism, when the gloss had been worn off, was felt to be meretricious and false. A period of 'realism' in literature followed; its greatest figure, Flaubert, produced an exposure of romantic love in *Madame Bovary* (1857), which was also a detailed anatomy of life in a provincial town; and a picture of Paris from the Orleanist monarchy to the Second Empire in *L'Éducation sentimentale* (1869). None of the other realists of this time has left work that counts besides Flaubert's masterpieces. Notable writers appeared later in the century under the label of Naturalism, which was merely Realism pushed to a more brutal extreme and given a scientific theory by Taine. Vice and virtue, proclaimed Taine, are but products like vitriol or sugar; the three factors of race, environment, and conjuncture (which he called moment) determine absolutely the character of men and nations. The novelist therefore is really a kind of social scientist registering and recording the facts of social life which added together explain the men and women of his day. The Goncourt brothers applied this theory to writing the social and artistic history of the eighteenth century; they recorded the literary history of their own time; and they produced under the Second Empire a series of novels describing on the basis of a careful documentation the more sordid aspects of French life. They were followed on a monumental scale by Zola, whose *Les Rougon-Macquart* is the natural and social history of a family under the Second Empire. It appeared in twenty novels between 1871 and 1893 and its characters – all drawn from the same family circle and revealing in combination after combination the same hereditary traits – range from the scheming Senator or financier and the dissolute high society of the Empire to the degraded and wretched victims of social injustice and their own vices and follies, at the bottom of the social scale. Sheer power carries Zola's sordid concerns and pseudo-scientific theories into the rank of literary art. The other naturalists are lighter in weight. Guy de Maupassant, a disciple of Flaubert and Zola, probably still remains the greatest master of the *conte*. The other important contributor to *Les Soirées de Médan* (1880), a naturalistic symposium in which Maupassant published *Boule-de-suif*, was J.-K. Huysmans, but he was to move on to the higher realms of decadence and religious mysticism.

Naturalism may be regarded as in some sense the reflection in fiction of positivism in philosophy, for one of the strongest influences over French thought after 1871 was that of Taine. His scientific attitude to society played a part in the development of an important school of sociology, in which the greatest name was that of Émile Durkheim. Renan, expelled from his chair at the Collège de France in 1863 when he published his *Vie de Jésus*, which adopted an unduly rational attitude to religion, was, along with Taine, one of the prophets of the new generation of the Third

Republic and the exponent of a sort of scientific idealism, which can be seen in *L'Avenir de la science*, written as early as 1848 but only published in 1890.

The need to cultivate science seemed to be one of the lessons taught by the defeat in the Franco-Prussian War; and in science the Third Republic was distinguished by such names as those of Henri Poincaré, the mathematician, the Curies, famous for their work on radium, the chemist Berthelot, Pasteur, whose Institute was founded in 1888. Littré, the compiler of a famous dictionary, was trained in medicine and upheld a positivistic materialism. The same spirit produced a school of critical historians. Fustel de Coulanges, with an implicit faith in the document, declared that he did not write history, but history wrote itself through him. The critical work of historians like Lavisse, Seignobos, Aulard, Halphen, Lot, dominated historical scholarship. The historians of the Académie Française, though they included at first an Albert Sorel, rapidly sank to the level of rather good journalism.

Of course, the art of the Third Republic was as yet only for a small *élite*, and the new scientific and critical spirit also had its limitations. It dominated an influential intellectual class but was hardly at home in the educational system. Tradition was still too strong in French schools for their predominantly literary culture to be undermined by science, and to the literature of the Third Republic we must return. In poetry, as in other arts, there is a sort of pause after the ebb of the flood-tide of romanticism. It was occupied by the Parnassians, who aimed at writing an objective, classical verse, free from the passionate concern of romanticism with the self. From Gautier they took the doctrine of 'art for art's sake'. They included Leconte de Lisle, Sully Prudhomme, and José-Maria de Heredia, whose sonnets are still the most read achievement of the school. But like Naturalism and Positivism, its capacity for development was limited. A more fecund influence than Gautier's was that of Baudelaire. His *Fleurs du Mal* appeared, long before a time when it might have been appreciated and understood, in 1857. Baudelaire died in 1867, but he belongs to the generation that succeeded him, which began to put forth its first fruits when Verlaine met Rimbaud in 1871. Verlaine published *Romances sans paroles* in 1874. Rimbaud's own *Le Bateau ivre* was of 1871. In 1876 Mallarmé wrote *L'Après-midi d'un faune*. Symbolism had begun its conquest of the world of poetry, to be continued through Valéry into the heart of the twentieth century.

On a lower level the new age in literature belongs to the decadents and mystics of the *fin de siècle*, to employ a common but not very meaningful piece of literary jargon. The critic and novelist Rémy de Gourmont contributed to the spread of Symbolist ideas, but his novels, mixing a physiological naturalism with a superficial mysticism, exhibit the weakness rather than the strength of the movement. The half-Dutch Joris-Karl Huysmans contributed to *Les Soirées de Médan* in 1880, and was one of the first to write in praise of the impressionists in *L'Art moderne* of 1883, and to appreciate Mallarmé. He moved on from a naturalism which tried to outdo Zola to literary Satanism and the cult of black magic, sacrilege, and aesthetic orgies, in *À rebours* (1884). From this he progressed, like the hero of *Là-bas* (1891), to religion, becoming for a time an oblate in a Benedictine abbey. The transition from decadence to religion was also illustrated in the mystical Catholicism of Léon Bloy, who in his apocalyptic writings preached destruction on existing society and the coming of a new age. Another Symbolist who found the route back to Catholicism was Paul Claudel, but though he was born in 1868 he only became recognized with *L'Annonce faite à Marie* in 1912 and he really belongs more to the post-war years. This could also be said of Gide, who sprang from Symbolism. A very different figure is Charles Péguy, socialist, patriot, and Catholic, killed in 1914 on the Marne, who has left a legend behind him to which left and right can both look back.

With Péguy we approach a more politically committed literature. The growing pressure of politics can be seen in the life and letters of Anatole France. In him can also be seen the effect of the Dreyfus affair in forcing a political commitment. Anatole France's erudition, his scepticism, irony, moderation, the patina of the past with which he misted over nearly everything he wrote, the sense of being too consciously a literary man, have robbed him of much of the adulation that he received in his life-time. His fine novel of the French Revolution, *Les Dieux ont soif* (1912) could be disliked equally by those who favoured the revolution and the counter-revolution. *L'Île des pingouins* (1908) and the four volumes of *L'Histoire contemporaine* (1896–1901) were too understanding to political enemies, too lukewarm to friends, and altogether too humane, to appeal to the generation that followed him. A lesser literary figure was Romain Rolland, but his reputation has also suffered and for similar reasons. He devoted himself to the literary interpretation of music, combined with a fervent belief in internationalism, and particularly, as exemplified in his long novel *Jean-Christophe*, of the kinship of France and Germany.

More violent commitment is to be found among the authors of the right. Maurice Barrès, after his involvement in Boulangism, became the chief advocate of a mystic nationalism. The nation had its roots in race and province. As a Lorrainer much of Barrès' writing was inspired by local patriotism. In *Les Déracinés* (1897) he portrays the disillusionment of a group of young Lorrainers robbed of their traditions by the indoctrination of a Kantian school-master, and of their roots in their native soil by trans-plantation to Paris. But his literary interests, even if dominated by ideological passions, were never completely subjected to them. Charles Maurras, after an early literary career in which he endeavoured to model himself on a coldly classical rejection of emotion, in the course of the Dreyfus affair adopted a passionate political commitment, and devoted himself to the propagation of a doctrine of integral nationalism. Along with his collaborator Léon Daudet, he founded in 1899 the journal *L'Action française*, which became a daily paper from 1908. In its columns he conducted an unremitting war, with all the weapons of slander, personal attacks, incitement to violence, against the Third Republic, its politicians, and particularly the Jews and aliens who, according to Maurras, dominated it. By the influence of his bitter but brilliant pen, and of the organization of the *Camelots du roi*, Maurras exercised considerable influence over successive generations of rightwing students. The stone-deafness which afflicted him for much of his life may have assisted him to isolate himself from political reality and create a fixed, dogmatic, monarchist theory which he inculcated with remorseless fanaticism over a space of nearly half a century. The daily denunciation of the Third Republic and all its works, the uncompromising advocacy of a return to monarchy by the path of revolution, and the exploitation of the anti-semitism of the nationalists and Catholics, gave the movement of the Action Française more political prestige than its small numbers justified. It was to be more dangerous after the First World War, but to write the history of the Third Republic up to 1914 in terms of the noisy political journalism of the extreme right would be a distortion of perspective. The spirit of its greater literature would also only be distorted by an attempt to interpret it in terms of the politics of the day.

That there was something in common between Symbolism, Impressionism, and the music of Debussy, Fauré, or Ravel, can easily be felt. Perhaps it is an artistic vision which transcends physical reality but never abandons the world of the senses, which intensifies the concreteness of sensations by isolating them, and at the same moment combines the objective clarity of external observation with the oneness of internal vision, which sees beauty in everyday scenes and happenings, and love even in the unlovable. Time has only magnified their achievement, and even if the society of their own day failed to realize their greatness, the Third Republic cannot be robbed of a reflected glory.

There was also, it is true, a last, fading trail of romantic

melancholy in all these painters and poets and musicians.
A feeling of transcience, of impermanence, as though something were coming to an end, becomes stronger, indeed
becomes the dominant note, in the greatest writer of them
all. Marcel Proust, born with the Third Republic in 1871,
only produced the first volume of *À la recherche du temps
perdu*, in 1913. When he completed the work, and his
genius was recognized, shortly after the First World War, it
was clear that indeed something had come to an end. The
best known philosopher of the pre-war years had also been
concerned with the problems of time and transcience, but it
was really the spirit of optimism of the years before 1914
which led Bergson to *L'Évolution créatrice* (1907) and the
conception of an *élan vital* inspiring all life. The problems he
posed were perhaps more significant than his solutions;
at any rate Bergson and his brilliant literary style have long
been out of favour with philosophers. But even these have
their feelings, and fashions in philosophy are as much a
reflection of the emotional atmosphere of an age as its
fiction. The optimism, the belief in their world that is
radiant in the Impressionists, persistent in spite of everything in the Combray of Proust, assumes a more abstract
form in Bergson, but by it he belongs to a Republic in
which, after so many uncertain and changing régimes,
France seemed at last to have found the security of firm
achievement and confident trust in the future.

4. THE COMING OF THE FIRST WORLD WAR

THE internal problems of France before 1914, though
serious, were being faced, and with the promise of gradual
solution. Political divisions could still arouse intense feeling,
but there was little danger of the social and political fabric
breaking down in open violence. The one major threat to
the achievements of the Third Republic was war with
Germany, and even this danger, despite an increasing
nationalist cult of *la revanche*, seemed to be receding. France

during the Third Republic had recovered its position in the world of Great Powers with remarkable success; a system of alliances had been built up which enabled her to enter the conference room on equal terms with Germany; and despite the agitation on the right, and a genuine, if fading, regret for the lost provinces, there was no serious thought of aggressive war to recover them. The international situation, of course, was far too complex to be summed up briefly. All we can do here is to attempt to trace in outline the evolution of French foreign policy under the Third Republic.

In the first years after 1871 clerical agitation kept both Germany and Italy concerned with the possibility of a French attempt at intervention in either country in support of the Roman Catholic Church against the State. This was never a very serious danger, and the republican victory in the elections of 1877 eliminated it as a source of international tension. The condition of almost total isolation that the Republic had inherited from the Second Empire came to an end when French representatives took their seats at the Congress of Berlin. It was understood, in the course of conversations at the Congress, that the other Powers in Europe would not regard colonial expansion by France as a threat to their security. Indeed, it was felt that the diversion of French interests outside Europe might take the French mind off Alsace-Lorraine and help to stabilize the international situation. Algeria was the obvious first objective; for the French advance there, though punctuated by Algerian revolts, had gone on continuously. After 1871 the European population was increased by the emigration of a considerable number of Alsatians, as well as Italians, Spaniards, and others. By the end of the century there were some 665,000 Europeans in Algeria, rather less than half of them French, and about two and a half million native Algerians. Tunis came under French control in 1881, when Ferry used a minor frontier incident as an excuse for sending an expeditionary force against the Bey of Tunis and establishing a French protectorate. Far to the south, Madagascar was occupied in 1885, and subsequently annexed in 1896.

After the fall of Ferry in 1884 over the supposed failure of his Indo-Chinese schemes, a protectorate was established over Annam; and in 1887, Cochin-China, Annam, Cambodia, and Tonkin were united under French rule in an Indo-Chinese union to which Laos was added in 1899. In western Africa, from the basis of Faidherbe's conquests in Senegal, French rule was extended north and east until it met the French forces coming down from the Mediterranean possessions. On the other side of Africa France found a foothold in Djibouti.

Serious international complications only arose when French and English interests clashed in Egypt. A debt-collecting Anglo-French fleet had sailed to Alexandria against Colonel Arabi in 1882, but the Chamber of Deputies was unwilling to see France entangled in a war in Egypt alongside the English and left the liquidation of the affair to the latter. The point of collision was to be reached by land when, in 1898, a small French force under Colonel Marchand met the troops of Kitchener at the old Sudanese strong point of Fashoda. Feeling was intense, but to send French reinforcements to Marchand was practically impossible, and the French Foreign Minister, Delcassé, was not prepared to go to war for the sake of a large area of what Lord Salisbury called light agricultural territory. He was already looking to Great Britain as a potential ally against Germany. Therefore Marchand was given the order to withdraw and French and British zones of influence in the Sudan were delimited.

By now the room for expansion in the extra-European world was much more restricted. In Africa only Morocco remained, and French intervention here was to produce a series of international crises. But before this the attention of French governments had been drawn back to Europe. The inherent contradictions in the Bismarckian system made it increasingly difficult for Germany to keep in step with Russia and Austria. Russia at the same time provided an opportunity for French diplomacy, as the needs of the Tsarist government did for French finance. In 1888 the

Russian government borrowed 500 million francs on the French market. Other loans followed, stimulated by an extensive Russian-subsidized campaign in the French press. Franco-Russian friendship was further promoted when, in 1891, the French fleet paid a formal visit to the Russian naval base at Cronstadt, returned by the Russian fleet the following year. In January 1894 a Franco-Russian defensive alliance was announced. The *rapprochement* with Russia was immensely popular in France, which no longer felt itself isolated. Whether it was ultimately in the interests of France is – as with the Austrian alliance of the eighteenth century – a matter for doubt. Some of the wisest minds came to fear that Russia might turn the alliance to her own exclusive interests without any consideration for her ally; and if she made a serious mistake she might drag France down with her. Such doubts hardly existed in 1896 and 1897 when the Tsar and the French President exchanged highly successful visits.

After this, France was swallowed up in the Dreyfus affair and its sequel, and too preoccupied with the domestic problem to pay much attention to foreign affairs, which were left for seven years, under five successive premiers, in charge of one Foreign Minister. Delcassé was hard-working, pertinacious, secretive, and a passionate enemy of Germany, determined to build up a counter to the now decaying Bismarckian system. His aim was, without damaging the Russian connexion, to bring Great Britain into the French alliance, to restore friendship with Italy, and to consolidate the French position in the Mediterranean by securing control of Morocco. Only Delcassé's unreasonable optimism could have conceived the possibility of achieving such incompatible ends, and it must be said that if he did achieve them it was partly owing to the maladroitness of German diplomacy.

The key to the whole situation was Morocco, which British concern that no other great power should hold the southern shore of the Straits of Gibraltar had preserved in its native state of anarchy. French intervention there could only take place by agreement with Great Britain, but, to add to Delcassé's difficulties, the British government, uneasily conscious of its isolation at the time of the Boer War, was looking towards Germany, while French opinion was violently Anglophobe. Fashoda was not quickly forgotten. The right-wing press alternated anti-British and anti-semitic cartoons, repulsive enough to have satisfied the most exacting demands of the Nazis, who did indeed make use of them in their propaganda forty years later. Delcassé's approaches to the British government had therefore to be made cautiously and under cover, by way of the French ambassador in London, Paul Cambon, who was also convinced of the need for the alliance. An exchange of visits by Edward VII and the French President Loubet in 1903 did something to replace the mutual hostility of their two countries by a more cordial atmosphere. In 1904, behind the innocuous terms of an entente, were negotiated secret clauses by which France and Great Britain recognized each other's freedom of action respectively in Egypt and Morocco.

To the German government it seemed time to put a limit to the rapid improvement in France's international position. The defeat of France's ally Russia in the Far East, and the unrest produced in the French Army by the policy of the Combes government, made this seem a favourable moment for intervention. The Emperor Wilhelm II was therefore sent to Tangier, where he insisted, in a speech that was calculated to resound through Europe, on the independence of the Sultan and the maintenance of German interest in Morocco. This could be regarded as a demand that France should repudiate the policy of Delcassé, who was prepared to reject it formally. But his influence in the French Parliament, which he had almost abandoned for work in his bureau, had greatly diminished. His resignation in June 1905 could be regarded as a German triumph, but an international conference, held at Algeciras in 1906, recognized as well as the general international interest in Morocco, the primary rôle of France there.

This was a rebuff to Germany, and the progressive military occupation of Morocco by French troops followed. In 1908 an affair of German deserters from the French Foreign Legion produced another international incident. In 1911 a further French military advance brought the sending of the German gun-boat, the *Panther*, to Agadir, to reinforce a German demand for territorial compensation in the French Congo. The French and German Foreign Offices were by now prepared to work up a nice little war between them, but the French Premier Caillaux and the German Foreign Minister Kiderlen-Wächter chose to compromise: Germany recognized a French protectorate in Morocco, and France ceded part of the Cameroons to Germany. This reasonable solution aroused the nationalists on both sides to fury and Caillaux was driven from office in January 1912.

The international situation, which up to this point had never been more than a minor sub-plot in the history of the Third Republic, now takes the centre of the stage. Three times, in 1905, 1908, and 1911, Germany had rattled the sabre – not, it is true, without some cause on each occasion, but the effect was cumulative. Not that the French attitude was aggressively bellicose. While there was a vociferous nationalist minority, especially in Paris, which was well represented in literature and the press, the nation as a whole and its political leaders were patently anxious to preserve peace. On the left a strong vein of pacifism had developed. Under Jaurès the Socialist Party was wedded to the illusion that the international action of socialism could prevent the outbreak of war.

Naturally, the other parties did not share this optimistic belief, and it did not require any aggressive intentions to be alarmed about the international situation in 1912, when the position was increasingly threatening in the Balkans. Foreign policy pushed domestic issues into the background. The cabinet of the left under Caillaux fell in 1912 and the Chamber turned to Poincaré for a government of national union. Poincaré was a dry, hard, unsympathetic little man from Lorraine, inexorable in the pursuit of his personal ambitions and the policy he regarded as right for his country. His intelligence, honesty, unflagging energy, patriotic ardour, and combination of republicanism and anti-clericalism with conservative views on social and financial questions, made him the essential man for the crisis. The premiership was only a step to the presidency, which Poincaré attained, with the support of the right, in February 1913.

The international sky continued to darken. An increase in the effectives of the German army led to the introduction of a law reviving the three years' military service in France, whereas since 1905 the period of conscription had been two years. In spite of the violent opposition of Jaurès and Caillaux, the law was passed in July 1913. It could only be paid for, like other measures of military preparation, by new taxation, and this was to put more of a strain on the patriotism of the conservatives than it could stand. The French bourgeoisie remained, like its predecessors of the *noblesse*, willing to sacrifice everything rather than accept an equitable system of taxation. Caillaux's attempt now to revive the income-tax proposals of 1909 added to the intense hatred which he had gained by opposing the three years' law. A fanfare of wrath, probably orchestrated by Poincaré from the Élysée, blew round his head. His own capacity for equivocation and making enemies did not help him. Ruin came when Mme Caillaux assassinated the editor of *Le Figaro*, who had played a leading part in the campaign. Judging by the press and Paris, France was on the point of being carried away on a wave of nationalist and bellicose ardour.

The legislative elections that came in 1914 revealed the true sentiments of the country. The noisy nationalists of *tout Paris* kept the support of the traditional conservative and Catholic crescent stretching round from the Vendée, through Brittany and Normandy, with a gap in the industrial regions of the North-east, but strengthening again in the border departments of the East. For once there was a clear-

cut issue between left and right, and the line of cleavage
was not confused, as was usual, by an active clerical and
anti-clerical issue. The right set up Caillaux as a bogey-
man, with his *grand fonctionnaire* personality and association
with high finance, which went so ill with his presidency of
the Radical Socialist party. Opposition to the three years'
law was denounced as unpatriotic. On the other hand the
left was at least excusable in believing the seriousness of
the international situation to be exaggerated when it found
the right unwilling to pay an extra sou for the defence of
the country. The election proved that even in the existing
state of international tension French opinion was profoundly pacific and non-aggressive. Memories of 1870
were fading, colonial conquests only really interested a
small minority, the political consolidation of the Republic
seemed completed and the task of social reform ready to
begin. To the left, the threat of war seemed obviously a fifth
ace smuggled into the hand of the right and smacked
triumphantly on the table to take the electoral trick; the
idealistic radicals and socialists refused to believe it could
be true. The country was so little warlike that it agreed with
them. The result of the elections was a crushing victory for
the left with 104 United Socialists, 24 Republic Socialists,
and 172 Radicals and Radical Socialists. On the right were
37 members of the Republican Federation, 23 Liberal
Action, 15 Right, and 44 Independents, 119 in all. The
centre and the centre left included 66 Radical Left, 23
Republican Radical Socialist Union, 7 'Dissidents', 53
Republicans of the left, and 32 Democratic left, making a
floating vote of 181. This catalogue well illustrates the
leading features of the French political system: the dominance of the group system; the bias to the left, so strong that
the real left only began where parties ceased to label themselves as such; the inability of the members of the extreme
right to present a coherent programme and their disposition
to disguise themselves as independents; and the dis-
proportionate influence that could be exercised by small
groups in the dead centre of French politics, which were in

a position, by throwing their votes on one side or the other, to bargain for office and set up and destroy governments at will.

An unusual element in the political situation at this time was the presence of a President who was not content with the normal restricted rôle. Despite the verdict of the electorate, Poincaré was determined to maintain the three years' law. After failing to obtain a premier from the right, he accepted the socialist Viviani, who agreed not to press for the immediate reversal of the law on condition of the Senate's lifting its *non possumus* on the income tax. The tax was in fact voted in principle, though the details were not to be worked out until 1917, by which time France had accumulated a colossal burden of war debt. With the three years' law respited, President and Premier, on 16 July, took ship for a state visit to the Czar arranged earlier in the year.

Nobody knew that the event that was to lead to a World War had already occurred. On 28 June 1914, some Jugoslav criminals (or nationalists) brutally murdered the Austrian Archduke Francis Ferdinand and his wife at Serajevo. The situation evolved at first slowly, while the peaceful populations of Europe went about their work and their pleasures in the warm summer weather. It seemed that this crisis would be got over, as had so many others in the recent past, peacefully; but there were those, in Vienna and Berlin, who thought otherwise. When Poincaré and Viviani left Russia, on 23 July, their visit concluded, they did not yet know of the Austrian ultimatum, on the same day, to Serbia.

It is not necessary to summarize here the fatal events of July 1914, through most of which France could only stand by and watch passively the moves on the international board that were leading her helplessly and inexorably to war. That the most pacific Chamber the country had ever known should have led France into a World War was ironic. One might be tempted to push the blame back earlier on to that policy of the Russian alliance which tied France to the support of her Russian ally; but in fact the struggle of the great military despotisms of Germany and Austria-Hungary against Russia was written on the tablets of fate – or only avoidable on the supposition of quite different governments in the three countries. In such a struggle Russia was bound to be defeated, and to assume that after this victory the Reich would abandon the path of conquest, and that the German eagle would settle peacefully on its perch, side by side with the rather clamorous but essentially domesticated Gallic cock, would have been to expect the impossible. Whether France would stick to her alliance with Russia, and equally what the entente with England would amount to in practice, did not really concern the directors of German policy. They viewed British military potential with contempt, and the French, even if they got as far as honouring their commitments to Russia, as a decadent race of immoral artists and corrupt politicians. The great German General Staff had its Schlieffen plan, according to which the German army, by disregarding an old treaty of neutrality and marching through Belgium – obviously justifiably because Belgium could offer no serious opposition – would be able to turn the flank of the French army and crush resistance within a few weeks.

On 28 July Austria-Hungary declared war on Serbia. The next day Poincaré and Viviani landed at Dunkirk. On 31 July Germany, having issued an ultimatum to Russia, called on France to declare what she would do in the event of war between Germany and Russia. This seemed a clever move: if France replied with a declaration that she would stand in shining armour beside Russia (as Wilhelm II had in relation to Austria-Hungary a few years earlier) this could be presented as a threat of aggression; if on the other hand the French offered to remain neutral, then Germany intended to demand the occupation of Toul and Verdun as a guarantee. Viviani escaped the trap by replying evasively that France would consult her interests. Public opinion was now becoming excited in all countries. In France, mounting nationalist fervour, fed by years of irresponsible agitation, led to the assassination of Jaurès by a fanatic. There was no widespread movement. Small chauvinist demonstrations were easily suppressed by the police. *La revanche*, or the thought of recovering Alsace-Lorraine, hardly entered into the mind of the French people, whose only thought was the preservation of peace. The government had one other concern: what would be the attitude of Great Britain if Germany attacked? The entente, even the military and naval conversations, were far from binding her to intervene. A personal letter from the French President to King George V asked for an assurance that Great Britain would not remain neutral if the Central Powers attacked France, but the British government refused to commit itself. The probability is that the German and Austro-Hungarian General Staffs were already so far determined on war, and that such civilian opposition as there was in high places in Germany had been so effectively stifled, that no action by the British could have prevented war; but it was a reasonable conclusion for the French to draw after the catastrophe that a clear statement of the British position (which unfortunately was far from clear) might have averted it. This was to have much influence on French policy after 1918.

The French government could only wait on the course of events, and take such precautions as were possible to safeguard itself from any possible charge of French aggression. When the French Cabinet acceded to the demand of the General Staff that covering troops be sent to the frontier, on 30 July, it was only on condition that they be kept ten kilometres behind it, to prevent the development of any incidents. The Commander-in-Chief, Joffre, agreed to this, though he protested strongly against the failure to call up reservists and the order that only those troops who could do so by moving on foot should take up their war-time stations. On 1 August the order for mobilization was given: on 2 August Germany occupied Luxembourg and German patrols crossed the French frontier. Joffre was now given freedom of action, but while ordering the repulsion of incursions into French territory, he instructed his commanders not to pursue enemy troops into Germany. He believed that the Germans would attack France without a declaration of war, as indeed they did, but not from the direction anticipated. In 1914 there was still a general expectation that treaties would be kept until they were formally denounced. It is difficult to think back now to a time when the German disregard of Belgian neutrality was a shattering blow to normal conventions of international behaviour, something that no other Great Power – or so it was believed, and perhaps rightly then – could have done, or hardly so blatantly. On 2 August the German government demanded the right of passage for its troops through Belgium, on the ground of its knowledge of French plans to invade Germany from the same quarter, which was a patent lie. The next day Germany declared war on France, alleging with equal mendacity French attacks on Germany. German policy had achieved what a little earlier would have seemed the impossible – a stubborn if hopeless Belgian resistance to the German army, a declaration of war by Great Britain on 4 August, and the entry of France into the war with total national unity from extreme right to extreme left.

The Third Republic in 1914 had no Fifth Column. In the armed camp that Europe had become by 1914, with the atmosphere of tension created by the irresponsible nationalists of all countries, and given the interlocking and opposed systems of alliances, it is all too easy, and correct in a sense, to present the outbreak of the First World War as the result of an international anarchy to which all countries contributed, and the responsibility for which was so divided that if there were any guilt all were equally guilty. To the French in 1914 this would have seemed nonsense. They understood, for they had been through a struggle over the same issue themselves, that Germany was a country where the General Staff could override the civil authorities, and the executive was largely independent of the legislature; its government had repeatedly used the threat of war as a diplomatic instrument. Other countries had their wild men. France was particularly afflicted by the 'integral nationalist', anti-Semitic, war-mongering elements in the conservative and Catholic sectors of opinion; but the pacifist and defensive sentiments which prevailed in French policy on the eve of the First World War reflected a general national temper, which had gradually risen to dominance with the triumph and consolidation of the democratic Republic. It was difficult for civilized, humane men of the stamp of Jaurès to believe that the rulers of a great European power could be so wicked or irresponsible, and their subjects so passively obedient, as to plan and put into operation, or accept without question, a major war. More pessimistically, a Delcassé or a Poincaré had believed in the inherent aggressiveness of the German state; but their contribution to the increase in French defensive capacity, in arms and allies, was in no way intended as a preliminary to starting a war on Germany. This is not to deny that the increasing strength of France and her allies was perhaps the decisive factor in provoking war, for 1914 seemed to the Central Powers the moment at which war might be launched with a maximum prospect of rapid success. It is difficult to see what France could have done that would have averted the war, short of repudiating her treaty bonds with Russia and recognizing German military and political hegemony over Europe. This was not contemplated in 1914. No one could have been expected to know that the coming struggle, and even ultimate victory, would be almost as fatal to the ideals and achievements of the Third Republic as defeat could have been.

5 · THE FIRST WORLD WAR

THE *union sacrée* for which Poincaré appealed on the outbreak of war met with practically universal acceptance. All divisions in the nation disappeared. The Ministry of the Interior, which had a list of extremists to be interned in the event of war, wisely took no action. Monarchists and republicans, employers and trade unionist workers, and peasants, rich and poor, were united in defence of the *patrie*. The peace-time battle of clerical and anti-clerical was forgotten. Priests joined up and fought side by side with laity. Most remarkable of all, defeats were not to be followed by the cry of treachery.

The man of the moment was the Commander-in-chief Joffre, appointed in 1911 as a moderate republican, rock-like in appearance, stolid and unemotional in manner. The son of a cooper, he was evidence of the reality of *la carrière ouverte aux talents* even in the army. Not lacking in the intellectual qualities needed to gain a place in the École Polytechnique, he was endowed with a peasant shrewdness that was to enable him to meet and often beat the politicians at their own game. Above all he was a man who gave the impression of being reliable. He shared, of course, the views on the nature of the coming war and the correct policy for the French Army that prevailed in the General Staff. Something more than the normal decline of a peace-time army is needed to explain the thrice repeated – in 1870, 1914, and 1939–40 – failure of the great French General Staff to judge correctly the nature of the war which each time it believed to be coming and for which it was preparing. In 1914 it calculated, as also the Germans did, on a short war, which could be won by a sharp, decisive offensive. It was launched in Lorraine, a wooded, hilly, unsuitable terrain for an advance, and gained a minute patch of German-held territory. At the same time the German right wing under Von Kluck was sweeping through Belgium and into Northern France.

Faced with invasion, Viviani strengthened his government by calling Delcassé to the Ministry of Foreign Affairs, Millerand to the Ministry of War, Briand to Justice, and bringing in Guesde and another socialist. The government needed all the strength it could get. Kluck was approaching so close to Paris that, to avoid a repetition of 1870, on 1 September the government left for Bordeaux, where it was to stay for some three months. There was no suggestion of yielding. If any defeatists existed in France they were silent and there were no pro-Germans, so different was the situation from what it was to be in 1940. Again unlike the later campaign, the armies maintained their cohesion, and the General kept his head and never lost control of the situation. On 5 September Gallieni, in command of the troops defending Paris, saw the opportunity to counter-attack. Joffre let him loose on the right flank of the advancing Germans and the battle of the Marne saved Paris. There followed the 'race to the sea', the consolidation of the front on both sides from the sea to the Alps, and the beginning of what no one knew was to be four years of exhausting trench warfare. France, in the first four months, had lost in dead, missing, wounded, or prisoners some 850,000 men, and had yielded up one of her most important industrial and agricultural areas to enemy possession.

Despite the experience of 1914 the French General Staff continued to be dominated by the *mystique* of the offensive. In 1915 the 'young Turks' of Joffre's headquarters pursued what was called a 'war of attrition' by launching continual petty attacks on the enemy. Since the offensive was invariably more costly than the defensive, it is fairly clear which army was being worn down by this policy. Governmental nerves also were becoming frayed, and in October 1915 internal differences of opinion, and criticisms from outside, brought about the fall of the Viviani cabinet. Briand took over the premiership, still at the head of a broad coalition preserving the *union sacrée*.

The next year, 1916, was the year of Verdun. In February a great German attack on the Verdun salient was launched. It was a cleverly worked out strategic move. The great fortress was in an exposed situation and would be expensive to defend; but the Germans had studied history and knew that Verdun had a particular meaning for France. Moreover, by making it their main objective they could practically force the French army to defend it because of the moral value of its retention and the pessimism that would be engendered by its loss. In spite of this the French High Command had not taken the steps that seemed called for if Verdun were to be treated as a vital position. Joffre, with his usual common sense, was probably prepared to abandon it and shorten the French line when the Germans had paid a sufficient price. Briand, however, knew that the fall of Verdun would not only seriously affect French morale it would also be fatal to his government. He gave the order to defend Verdun at all costs, and the defence was conducted with a skill, stubbornness, and heroism that made the reputation of General Philippe Pétain. However, the German High Command had perhaps achieved its object of enticing the French to sacrifice their man-power for the purpose of holding a fortress of mainly symbolic value. It was the war of attrition in reverse, applied with Teutonic thoroughness. France was to be 'bled white' at Verdun. German losses were also heavy but, starting the war with a population of 66 millions against the French 39 millions, the German Command doubtless thought it could better afford extensive blood-letting. By the time the German attack had worn itself out each army had lost about a quarter of a million men in the fighting. In July, Joffre began a counter-offensive on the Somme, which gained a little territory: the allied and German armies lost another half-million men between them in this sector.

The continuous and calamitous loss of life, to no apparent gain, inevitably had its effect on the national spirit. By the end of 1916 disillusionment was widespread. A change of leadership was psychologically necessary and a veiled press campaign was launched against Joffre, who for all his cunning was no match for Briand. The responsibility for the carnage of Verdun was gently but firmly placed on the General's shoulders. When his prestige was sufficiently undermined he was promoted chief military adviser to the government, in which post he was ignored and from which he soon resigned. The new Commander-in-chief of the French armies on the Western Front was Nivelle, who had achieved a number of tactical successes and was affable and popular with the politicians. He was believed, and probably believed himself, to have the secret, which had evaded Joffre, of breaking the enemy line.

Briand's victory over Joffre did not enable his government to hold out much longer. He fell in March 1917 and was replaced by an elderly, conservative nonentity, Ribot. The first measure of the new government was to approve a great offensive projected by Nivelle. The previous War Minister, Lyautey, the great colonial administrator, whose political maladroitness had in fact brought Briand's ministry down, had not concealed his belief that Nivelle's plans were mad. Lyautey's successor in the War Ministry, the mathematician Painlevé, was himself profoundly sceptical; but Nivelle, asked to modify or postpone his offensive, threatened to resign. Ribot, who saw that this would involve the fall of his government, and Poincaré, who believed in generals, supported him. Although every sane calculation was against it and Nivelle's plan was, in the words of Lyautey, only suitable for the army of the Grand Duchess of Gerolstein, he was allowed to go ahead with it and walk into the trap laid by the Germans, who by now, after all the discussions between politicians and generals, knew the details of the coming offensive almost as well as the French themselves. They withdrew their main forces to prepared positions in the Hindenburg line. On 16 April, having been delayed for a week because of the rain, which should in itself have led to a change of plan, the fated offensive, mis-conceived and mis-conducted, began. It was a disaster from the outset.

Painlevé, who was struggling to remove the amiable, incompetent, obstinate general from his command and bring the offensive to an end, found himself opposed on all sides. The anti-clerical Minister of the Interior, Malvy, supported Nivelle because he was a Protestant and likely to be succeeded by a Catholic, the British General Haig because the offensive helped to concentrate the fighting on the Western front where Haig was in command and avoid 'side shows', Poincaré because he had committed himself, in the face of warnings, to the Nivelle plan. But in the end the evidence of continued and useless slaughter was irresistible and on 15 May Painlevé succeeded in removing Nivelle.

He was replaced by Pétain, who was known to prefer the defensive, with Foch as Chief of Staff. The team had been found that, after waiting while waiting was necessary, until France's allies had filled the gaps left by a death roll of well over a million men since 1914, was in due course to win the war.

Despite military mistakes, the Third Republic had stood the test of the most appalling of wars with remarkable cohesion and constancy. Even Verdun and the Somme had not produced more than a demand for a change in leadership. After the pointless massacres of Nivelle's offensive the crack came. In May 1917 scattered mutinies broke out. Pétain dealt with a critical situation with intelligence, tact, firmness, and humanity. He established personal contact with as many units as he could, improved the troops' conditions so far as was possible, limited the military operations that had to be undertaken, minimized losses, and restored discipline at the cost of no more than twenty-three executions of mutineers.

Equally dangerous unrest, developing in civilian quarters, was exposed to the public gaze in a series of political scandals. A campaign against the alliance with Great Britain, against the President, and surreptitiously against the war, was appearing in the press. A minor left-wing journal called *Le Bonnet rouge*, which was particularly marked by the violence of its language, was found to be receiving subsidies from Germany. The Minister of the Interior, Malvy, who had laxly tolerated the campaign of defeatism, was driven from office. This brought down Ribot's government and his place as premier was taken by Painlevé. Trouble did not end there. A deputy was discovered with a large packet of Swiss francs, for the possession of which he could give no explanation. There followed the cases of an absurd adventurer named Bolo, supplied with German money to spread defeatist propaganda, and the dramatized woman spy Mata Hari. In November the Painlevé cabinet, tarred with all these scandals and in its turn charged with weakness, was overthrown.

Something more serious was at issue than the machinations of petty German agents and spies. The belief had begun to spread, especially among the parties of the left, that a negotiated peace was the only alternative to endless, meaningless slaughter. The idea of a common humanity and unity among the workers of the world, roughly shaken when the German Socialists wheeled into line behind their Government's aggression in 1914, was reviving. The Russian Revolution had aroused an idealistic echo in the West. The concrete expression of this tendency was the calling of an international conference of Socialists at Stockholm. The French Socialists, refused passports to attend the conference by their government, now left the Sacred Union and gave up participation in the government. Industrial strikes, which had hitherto been conspicuously absent, began to develop. Caillaux, re-emerging into political life, with characteristic lack of tact prematurely envisaged the possibility of a compromise peace. Even Briand was not unsympathetic to the idea of eventual negotiations with Germany. Reason and humanity suggested that at least the possibility should be explored, though passion and politics prohibited it. The age of slogans had come upon the warring world – the war to end wars could not be abandoned half-won; the propaganda-mongers were caught in their own toils. It must also be recognized that German policy now brought its nemesis: what trust could be put in a régime that had launched a World War by flagrant aggression and justified it by blatant mendacity? Moreover, the recovery of Alsace-Lorraine had now become a war aim for France and only total defeat would bring a German government to envisage this. It might be said that, in spite of all this, nothing would have been lost by allowing the enemy to expose his intransigence, but any willingness to contemplate a compromise peace was interpreted as weakness. Pétain, asked by the President if he could keep his troops under control should there be discussions with the Germans at Stockholm – a loaded question – replied firmly, No. The *Action française* began to resume its characteristic activity with a charge by Léon Daudet that the ex-Minister of the Interior, Malvy, had betrayed French battle-plans to the Germans.

The lead among those who were determined that there should be no negotiated peace was taken by the old 'tiger' of French politics, Clemenceau, now aged seventy-six. He was an isolated figure, cut off from all the parties by temperament and the bitter struggles of the past, and belonging to a different generation. His incessant attacks on the conduct of the war, in the Parliament and in the pages of his paper *L'Homme libre*, renamed under war censorship *L'Homme enchaîné*, marked him out in the public mind as the man who could put things right. Poincaré, with his usual clear-sightedness, saw that a choice had to be made, either Caillaux or Clemenceau, and though he hated Clemenceau, he hated Caillaux and the idea of peace without victory even more. He called Clemenceau to office. The prospect of a compromise peace was at an end, though it is impossible to believe that the German General Staff, now on the eve of its greatest victory in the East, would have contemplated such a peace in the West.

The new premier turned on the would-be negotiators – defeatists to use the language of the time – savagely. Briand received a fright which sent him into retirement until the war was over; Malvy was put on trial; Caillaux, arrested and charged with intelligence with the enemy, was to stay in prison for two years. Many lesser actual or alleged 'pro-Germans' experienced attacks in which personal enmities were given ample scope and accusations of treachery were flung about wildly. The right wing welcomed these steps, which provided what was now effectively a war dictatorship with the needed temporary unity, but also introduced a cleavage into French politics more permanent and deeper than had been known since the struggle over Dreyfus.

So far as winning the war, or not losing it, was concerned, Clemenceau had not come to power too soon. In December 1917 an armistice was signed on the Eastern Front and the German Command was free to concentrate

its forces on the West, where American reinforcements
were only slowly arriving. In March 1918 the Ludendorff
offensive drove deep into the Allied lines. An attempt,
earlier in the year, to take the first step towards a badly
needed unity of command over the allied armies, by putting
the most widely respected French general, Foch, in charge
of a Reserve Force for the whole front, had been frustrated
by an unholy alliance between Haig and Pétain, more
concerned with their own prestige than the efficient conduct
of the war. When the German break-through came, Pétain's
deep temperamental pessimism seemed likely to prohibit
a vigorous reaction; but the situation was now so obviously
critical that the political leaders were able to impose Foch
as supreme commander over both the jealous generals.
From March to July Ludendorff desperately let loose
offensive after offensive, penetrating as deep into the allied
lines as Château-Thierry and the Marne. Foch bided his
time, stoically supported by Clemenceau. At last, on 18
July, he began the counter-offensive, which was not to stop
until the German army had been driven back to its own
frontier and on 11 November accepted an armistice.

It was, or at least it seemed to be, the most glorious hour
in the history of the Third Republic. France had borne the
brunt of the struggle against the military power of the
German Reich and had survived with her national life, her
ideals, and her institutions intact. The Republic had
emerged triumphant from the severest of all tests, though at
a cost that in the moment of triumph was hardly realized.
Part of the price of victory had already been paid in some
million and a quarter military, and half a million civilians,
dead or soon to die, and three-quarters of a million permanently injured, in the invaded departments looted and
devastated, and in a national debt of colossal proportions.
The price was to continue to be paid for another generation
in the loss of the high hopes which might reasonably have
been held in the opening decade of the twentieth century.

In 1918, on the morrow of victory, such pessimism would
have seemed absurd. Looking back one can see that a good

peace was inconceivable. That the peace was as bad as it proved to be may partly be attributed to the degradation of the public spirit in all the belligerent countries that resulted from the punitive death roll of the war and the vicious and mendacious propaganda that had been used as a major weapon on all sides; partly to the fact that the common purpose which had united the Western allies inevitably failed to survive victory.

The Peace Conference at Paris revealed their divergent aims and ideals. France, in the person of Clemenceau, knew what she wanted – first the return of Alsace-Lorraine, and on this there was no dispute; secondly, security; and thirdly, reparations. Even with Alsace-Lorraine, France would remain weaker in population and resources than Germany. The main aim of Clemenceau was to redress this balance. He secured the reduction of the German army to a maximum of 100,000 men, without air force or heavy artillery, though, contrary to French wishes, it was, on mistaken British ideas, to be a long-service force, and therefore capable of rapidly providing the trained cadres for a conscript army. To counter-balance the loss of resources in the French devastated areas, the great mining basin of the Saar was put under international control; but this was only for fifteen years, after which it was to decide its future affiliations by plebiscite. As a military precaution the right bank of the Rhine was demilitarized, and the left bank, with bridgeheads on the right, to be occupied by France for fifteen years. The demilitarized zone was perhaps the most valuable safeguard of peace created in 1919, but of course only on condition that it remained demilitarized.

Foch and the nationalists had been demanding far more than this and they condemned Clemenceau for his failure to secure the left bank of the Rhine for France. The internationalists, such as Léon Bourgeois, put their faith rather in an international army. Great Britain and the United States were unwilling to contemplate either road to security. They frustrated one French plan after another. What remained in the end of the French search for security, apart from the demilitarized zone, was a joint Anglo-American guarantee of assistance to France if Germany should make an unprovoked attack. Even this commitment was to be repudiated subsequently by the United States and the repudiation used as an excuse for cancelling her obligation by Great Britain. Clemenceau was certainly no Talleyrand and he tried to make obstinacy do the work of finesse, but given the American misjudgement of the European situation, and the shiftiness of British policy, it is difficult to see what more he could have rescued from the wreck of the alliance.

Thrown back on her own resources, France reverted to her traditional policy of alliances in Eastern Europe. Close relations were established with the successor states to the Austro-Hungarian Empire – Czechoslovakia, Yugoslavia, and Rumania, grouped in the Little Entente. Poland was rescued from a Bolshevik invasion with the aid of a French military mission under Foch's chief of staff, General Weygand, in 1920, and subsequently a Franco-Polish treaty was concluded. It was hoped that in this way a *cordon sanitaire* might be established to prevent communism from penetrating into Europe, and at the same time allies against Germany be found to fill the void left by the collapse of Russia. What France had obtained from victory was much less than she had hoped for, but in fact the terms of peace were sufficient to guarantee French security on the simple condition of being kept in operation.

The other great aim of the French negotiators was one which she shared with all her allies – to make somebody else pay for the war; the only difference was that whereas Great Britain and the European allies were determined to make Germany pay, the Americans were determined to make their allies pay. Every war cost that could be thought of was added to the bill for reparations in a frantic competition to draw up an astronomical total. In this way it was hoped to avoid the painful necessity of raising money by taxation. The result was that further borrowing was added to the already huge French war debt and the budget was balanced on the promise of German reparations. The inflation that was the inevitable result was to be a powerful factor in undermining the stability of French society.

By the end of the peace negotiations tempers were frayed and the victorious alliance was dead, but somehow a document was produced which was called the Treaty of Versailles and signed in the Hall of Mirrors on 28 June 1919.

6. THE INTER-WAR YEARS, 1919–39

PEACE having been restored after a fashion, normal political life was resumed in France. The Chamber of Deputies, elected in 1914, was dissolved and a new Chamber elected in November 1919. For this election a system of multi-member constituencies was adopted. Supposed to give a fairer proportional representation, in fact it exaggerated the swing which would have occurred in any case away from the left-wing and pacifist chamber of 1914. The right had many advantages in 1919. It gained from the accusations of defeatism launched against the left, from the fear of Bolshevism, and from the nationalist exaltation which accompanied victory. Grouped in the Bloc National, supported by the great reputation of Clemenceau, the parties of the right won 433 seats, against a mere 86 Radicals and 104 Socialists.

The first act of the victorious Bloc was to rid itself of the presence of the formidable old man under whom the war had been won by electing as President against him, on the conclusion of Poincaré's term, a distinguished nonentity who had to retire to a home for mental cases within eighteen months. This unfortunate episode perhaps encouraged the politicians to risk next the choice of a stronger president in the form of Millerand. Weak governments followed the fall of Clemenceau. Reparations proved difficult to extract. Finally Poincaré was called back to make Germany pay, in January 1922. In January 1923, German payments still being in default, French troops were sent in to occupy the industrial and mining district of the Ruhr and collect reparations in kind. This was an isolated venture, for Anglo-French relations were now as bad as they could be, and the Americans strongly condemned the French for attempting to collect reparations from Germany. The Ruhr experiment was a disastrous failure: it merely provided an excuse to put off still longer the unpleasant necessity of paying adequate taxes. By 1924 the flood of inflation was in full spate, and, reflected in these muddy waters, the colour of the 'sky-blue' Chamber elected in 1919 looked a good deal less attractive. In the elections of May 1924 the Radical Socialists and Socialists combined in a Cartel des Gauches and obtained 289 seats against 211 to the Bloc National; there was a middle group of 44, and 25 communists found their way in.

The first aim of the victorious Cartel was to drive Millerand, who had identified himself with a strong nationalist policy, out of the Élysée, by the simple device of refusing to form a government under him. Though it succeeded in doing this, the Cartel failed to replace him with its own candidate, Painlevé, and had to see the moderate President of the Senate, Doumergue, elected President. The leader of the Radicals, Édouard Herriot, then formed the first of the Cartel governments. Herriot, solid and conscientious, who was the invariably re-elected *maire* of Lyon for a generation, was a man of unshakeable patriotism; he had a genuine desire for the well-being of the ordinary Frenchmen, of whom he was so obviously one. He had a pipe and a friendly smile, humble origins, intellectual and artistic tastes, and a sentimental turn of mind which only partially concealed real political shrewdness.

The time was ripe for a government of the left such as a moderate reformer like Herriot could provide: it was what the balance of social forces in France seemed to call for. Unfortunately the left now proved what it was repeatedly to demonstrate – that it could only hold together during an election; in office ideological divisions made it difficult for Radicals and Socialists to co-operate. Politically closest to the Socialists, in fundamental political ideas the Radicals were far removed from them. Both the strength and weakness of the Radicals can be seen in the writings of their favourite spokesman, the teacher of philosophy who wrote under the name of Alain. Our only programme, Alain declared in his *Éléments d'une doctrine radicale* in 1925, 'is to have no other ideal than government in conformity with the will of the majority'. 'The *élite* is worthless. . . . Because it is destined to exercise power, the *élite* is destined to be corrupted by power.' 'What I call liberty is the close dependence of the elected on the elector.' 'In a democracy, not only does no party have power, but even better, there is no power properly speaking.' Basically, radicalism believed in reducing government to a minimum; it was a recipe for failure at a time when political and social problems were urgently demanding positive action; but it suited the peasant proprietors, small employers, and shopkeepers who voted Radical and who represented a great vested interest in economic backwardness.

The partners of the Radicals in the Cartel, the Socialists, naturally had a much more positive attitude towards the economic functions of government, though they shared the faith of the Radicals in political democracy. But they were in a weak position because, since the Russian revolution of 1917, they had to face the growing threat of a Communist party, always ready to outbid them and taking full advantage of the traditional republican *mystique de gauche*, the principle of 'no enemies on the left'. At a Congress of the Socialist Party at Tours in December 1920, those who accepted the directives of Moscow and the method of the dictatorship of the proletariat won a three to one majority over the supporters of democratic socialism. The former constituted the French Communist Party and the latter the S.F.I.O., in bitter political rivalry with one another. A year later the trade union confederation also split, the democratic section remaining in control of the C.G.T. (Confédération Générale du Travail) and the Communists forming the C.G.T.U. (Confédération Générale du Travail Unitaire). The latter won a majority of the trade unionists, some 500,000, as against 370,000 who remained faithful to the C.G.T.; and the latter were largely lower officials, teachers, railwaymen, postmen, and black-coated workers. About a million workers were lost to organized labour altogether in the course of the struggle. Henceforth the presence of the Communists on their left prevented the Socialists from cooperating whole-heartedly with the Radicals, for fear of losing their own clientele to the former. The Communists could always employ the emotional appeal to the tradition of revolution, and there was an ample supply of social grievances and injustices in French society to provide motivation for a revolutionary party. In pursuance of well-considered Russian policy they concentrated their fire on the Socialists.

The division of Socialists and Radicals, with the guerrilla attacks of the Communists on their left, provide the fundamental reason for the failure of the Cartel des Gauches. In addition it had inherited major problems in the colonies, and was to create problems in France for itself, which precipitated its collapse. The political difficulties arose through an attempt to recement the left by the old and rather dried-up glue of anti-clericalism. Rather unnecessarily, it was decided to withdraw the French ambassador to the Vatican, and apply French religious legislation to the regained provinces of Alsace and Lorraine, where the laws of separation, of course, had never been operative. Both these measures proved difficult to apply and aroused much opposition.

The colonial problem was represented first by Morocco, where a rebel chief, Abd-el-Krim, who had been in arms since 1921, was only to surrender in 1926. A revolt broke out in Syria in 1925, Damascus was bombarded, and the struggle dragged on until 1936 when the French promised eventual independence. Agitations of an as yet less formidable nature also appeared in Indo-China, Tunisia, and even Algeria.

The crucial problem for the Herriot government was finance. The illusion that the gap in the French budget would be filled by reparations died hard. The wealthier classes, represented by the parties of the right, resisted any increase in direct taxation; the parties of the left opposed increases in indirect taxation. The only alternative was inflation. As the national debt rose the value of the franc sank. By 1926 the pound sterling, which itself had not preserved its 1914 value, stood at 243 francs. The parties of the right and the big financial interests, which had no desire to see the Cartel overcome its difficulties, waged a violent campaign to discredit its financial policy. The millions of small property owners and investors saw their savings vanishing, and employees their real wages shrinking. The Herriot cabinet, incapable of agreeing on any policy to meet the crisis, broke up. Caillaux, brought back from political ostracism as the former financial genius of the left, found himself out of touch with post-war politics; Briand employed his skill at building bridges in vain; and the franc continued to fall in value. The public was increasingly restive. There were demonstrations before the Chamber of Deputies. The Cartel, it began to be felt, had shown itself incapable of governing. At last the Chamber turned to Poincaré, who, in July 1926, formed a government of national union with power to govern by decree-laws. It was the first admission that the French parliament might now be unworkable in a crisis. The new government, of the centre and right, was a strong one, with a galaxy of leading politicians – Herriot, Briand, Barthou, Painlevé, Tardieu, Louis Marin – under a former President, and confidence at once began to return. The franc rose by December to 125 to the pound and was stabilized at this figure.

The Cartel des Gauches reunited temporarily in 1927 to pass a new electoral law, restoring single-member constituencies with a double ballot, which was expected to be more favourable to the left; but the elections of 1928, held under the influence of the financial success of the Poincarist experiment, proved a disappointment. The Communist Party had received instructions from Moscow that there were to be no electoral alliances; it consequently maintained its candidates at the second ballot, securing only 14 seats with over a million votes, but handing over some 60 or 70 seats to the parties of the right, which won 330 seats out of 610.

There was now open war between Socialists and Communists. The latter summoned all workers to unite under their lead, while the Socialist leader, Léon Blum, proclaimed that the unity of the workers had as its necessary condition the destruction of the Communist cadres. In fact neither Communists nor Socialists were likely to make much headway in the late twenties, when economic prosperity and progress were at last returning to France. International tensions also were beginning to relax under the careful diplomacy of Briand, who, becoming Foreign Minister in April 1925, was to continue in the same post, apart from a gap of two days, until 1932. The climate of Versailles had now passed away. The belief in total victory no longer survived. French military predominance would evidently not last for ever, and the need for another basis of French security was beginning to be felt. Briand looked to the League of Nations for the machinery of a peaceful consolidation of the status quo. After the Ruhr episode France did not wish to find herself again, in peace or in war, *tête-à-tête* with Germany. It was therefore necessary to bring back Great Britain into the European balance. The first attempt to do this, the Geneva Protocol of 1924 and the consequent disarmament plan, was wrecked by the British government of Baldwin; but the Locarno agreements of 1925 led up to the admission of Germany to the League of Nations in 1926. Briand devoted his last years to the noblest work of his life – the attempt at a genuine reconciliation with Germany and the creation of a peaceful international order. The greatest difficulty, the fog of reparations which had spread like a miasma over the international scene, seemed at last to be dissipated when the plan named after the American banker, Young, was accepted by both France and Germany in 1930. It was followed by the French evacuation of the Rhineland, five years before the appointed time.

But already at this high noon of inter-war hopes ominous clouds were gathering. In October 1929 occurred the Wall Street crash, from which all the disasters of the following decades date. This destroyed the recently-arrived-at reparations settlement. Under pressure from the American President Hoover, a moratorium was imposed on the payment of reparations by Germany, while at the same time Hoover insisted on the payment of the war debts that France owed to the United States. The other cloud darkened the prospects of Franco-German reconciliation. In 1930, hard on the heels of the last French soldier leaving the Rhineland, 107 Nazi followers of Hitler took their seats in the Reichstag. The failure of Briand's efforts was already written in the realities of the international scene and nothing he or France could have done would have prevented it. Early in 1931 when Doumergue's term as President ended, Briand expected to crown his long service to the state with the highest of its offices. Once again the most distinguished was rejected. Paul Doumer, who was chosen, was to be assassinated by a mad Russian in May, but Briand, disappointed, worn out, and ill, was already dead. He was replaced at the Quai d'Orsay by Pierre Laval.

In the elections of May 1932 the Communists, still faithfully following the order of *poing brandi contre le parti socialiste*, fell from some 1,000,000 votes in 1928 to 800,000 and elected only 10 members, while the Socialist vote increased by almost exactly the number that the Communists lost. The Radical, Socialist, and lesser partners in the Cartel gained in representation with 334 seats against 259 to the right. The misfortune of the left in inter-war politics was that it achieved a clear electoral victory three times, in 1924, 1932, and 1936, each time on the eve of a grave financial or economic crisis which was to present it with decisions that almost inevitably ruined its cohesion. France had resisted the effects of the economic crisis that began in 1929 longer than most countries, but by 1933 there were 1,300,000 unemployed and both industry and agriculture were distressed. After the election the President Lebrun, a worthy political hack who had replaced the assassinated Doumer, called on Herriot to form a government. His position, as in 1924, rapidly proved an impossible one: an attempt at a policy of economy and retrenchment split the Cartel. There followed a period of weak and changing governments, beginning in 1932 and extending right through 1933. Economic distress and political incapacity, along with a steadily deteriorating international situation, produced a general feeling of insecurity and a heightening of hostilities within the nation. Left-wing papers and politicians denounced their opponents as Fascists, the right-wing could retaliate with the charge of Communism. Both extremes concentrated their attack on the incompetence and alleged corruption of the republican politicians. The calendar seemed to be turning back to the days of Boulanger and Panama.

At the appropriate moment, late in 1933, the Stavisky affair burst, a gift to the factions of the right. This shady financier, who had evaded the law time and time again by the collusion of influential friends, found that his frauds had finally caught up with him. In January 1934 he committed suicide. The papers of the right alleged that he had been murdered to prevent him from betraying the corruption of his protectors. Ministers who had been connected with him were hounded from office, and the premier Camille Chautemps, not the purest of the pure, was himself forced to resign. His place was taken by the Radical Daladier, whose Napoleonic cast of features and stocky build created the illusion that he was a strong man. One of his first acts was in fact reasonably strong: it was to dismiss the Paris Prefect of Police, the Corsican Chiappe, who had sinister connexions with the Fascist leagues. Whether with Chiappe's collusion or not, this proved the signal for a co-ordinated push against Daladier's government which was due to meet the Chamber on 6 February. On that day the right-wing groups and the leagues called out their forces, the Action Française perhaps taking the lead as its long history of disorder entitled it to do. Colonel de la Roque's

Croix de Feu, the Solidarité Française financed by the perfumer Coty, the Jeunesses Patriotes, the anti-semitic (as indeed all these groups were) Francistes, added their forces, along with a number of ex-servicemen's associations. Assembling at different points, they converged on the Chamber of Deputies. Armed police and *gardes mobiles* held them off, and in scattered firing killed fourteen of the demonstrators. If the affair had been intended to effect a *coup d'état* it was a very badly organized one. It succeeded, however, in forcing Daladier, acting on the advice of the weak President Lebrun, to resign.

The ex-President Doumergue was now called in, at the head of a government of national union which the country greeted with relief. The economic crisis, however, continued, and the classic financial and economic ideas of Radicals and the right prohibited any positive policy of economic revival. Doumergue rapidly proved that he was not another Poincaré. He discontented the parliamentarians by direct appeals to the people in wireless speeches. The assassination of the Foreign Minister, Barthou, helped to promote the disintegration of the Cabinet, which Doumergue's own action in putting forward proposals for constitutional reform completed.

Weak and transient governments followed for the rest of the life of the parliament, but the threat of 6 February was not renewed. Indeed, the wind was now blowing from another quarter. It is tempting to say that the shock delivered by the attempted *coup* had brought the parties of the left to their senses and forced a broad collaboration on them; but this is not the true explanation of what happened. At any time after the 'sky blue' elections of 1919 France ought, if the balance of social forces and political opinion had been properly represented, to have had a government of the left. The conflicting ideas of Radicals and Socialists and the wrecking policy of the Communists prevented it. Now the triumph of the Nazis in Germany had belatedly aroused the Communist International to the consequences of its policy, and under instructions from

Moscow the French Communist Party suddenly reversed its propaganda-line and held out the hand of friendship to Socialists, Radicals, and even to Catholics.

The Popular Front thus created issued its manifesto in January 1936. This demanded, rather pathetically, the defence of peace by international disarmament and action through the League of Nations, and more realistically by the consolidation of the Franco-Soviet pact, and the dissolution of the Fascist leagues. It added a call for a new deal inside France – long needed social reforms, a reduction in the hours of work, the introduction of national pensions, paid holidays, national control of the banking and financial system. The enemy, since it was necessary to have one, was the 'two hundred families' – a reference to the Regents of the Bank of France who were taken to represent the power of organized wealth. On this programme an alliance of Radicals, Socialists, and Communists entered the elections of April 1936, maintained remarkable electoral discipline, and obtained some 380 seats, against 237. It was significant that the Radicals dropped from 159 to 116, while the Socialists rose from 97 to 146, and the Communists from 10 to 72. The effect of the Popular Front was in fact to polarize opinion to the left and the right and weaken the centre, to which the Radicals really belonged. The question was whether the new alliance of the left would prove any more stable than the earlier Cartel des Gauches. One ominous sign was the presence of ten dissident Communists under the future collaborator Doriot, and twenty-six Neo-socialists under Marquet; both sets were to find their future in alliance with the Nazis.

The first reactions to the elections were not promising: they were the occupation of the factories by militant workers and the refusal of the Communist Party to share in the responsibility of government. The Socialist leader, Blum, in charge of the cabinet, coped with the situation with diplomacy and strength. He called representatives of employers and workers together at the Hotel Matignon, where they reached a settlement. By this the employers recognized collective negotiation, conceded an immediate increase of between seven per cent and fifteen per cent in wages, and agreed to open discussions on general conditions of labour. In the subsequent agreements France attempted to catch up almost overnight with generations of neglect of social legislation. Recognition of workers' delegates in factories, the forty-hour week, paid holidays, nationalization of munition factories, the extension of government control over the Bank of France, were enacted. The Fascist leagues were outlawed and leaders of a secret revolutionary organization called the Cagoule put on trial.

These measures were not taken without arousing feeling on the right, already excited by the international situation, to fever pitch. The campaign in press and meeting against Blum and his government reached an almost unprecedented degree of violence. From the left, the failure of the government to intervene in the Spanish civil war also brought bitter attacks. Once again, however, what was to be fatal to a government of the left was its finances. The actions of the Front Populaire, and the propaganda of its enemies, brought a flight from the franc, and this in turn led to a sudden devaluation in October 1936. This did not stimulate the revival of the economy that was expected. Slump conditions continued. The index of industrial production, 140 in 1929, was 101 in 1937. Unemployment remained at the high level it had reached in 1934.

In the face of this situation, Blum, early in 1937, announced a 'pause' in his social programme, which gave the Communists an excuse for attacking his government, without tempering the opposition of the right. In June 1937 he asked for power to issue decree-laws. The Radicals of the Senate, now risen from its early political insignificance to a position in which its powers equalled and its prestige surpassed those of the Chamber, took the opportunity to overthrow his cabinet. The traditional pattern had repeated itself once more. Weak radical governments under Chautemps followed until, in April 1938, the radical leader Daladier brought in the conservative Paul Reynaud to take charge of finances. With the forces of organized wealth thus conciliated, the financial and economic sky at once brightened and by 1939 France seemed at last to be emerging from the prolonged slump of the thirties.

Unfortunately finance was no longer what mattered most. The thundercloud across the Rhine, which had first appeared when a large body of sinister Nazis sat in the Reichstag in 1930, had steadily darkened. When, after Hitler became Reich chancellor in January 1933, he did not declare war immediately, the French right began to feel that it had been unnecessarily alarmed. It had ideological sympathies with Fascists and Nazis, and welcomed the Four-Power pact that the British prime minister, MacDonald, brought back from Rome in June 1933, uniting in a hypocritical and transient condominium France, Italy, Germany, and Great Britain. The pact was killed a few months later when, in October, Germany quitted the disarmament conference and the League of Nations.

The sudden shock, after being lulled into quiescence by Nazi reassurances, temporarily reinvigorated French policy. A foreign minister of the old school in the Doumergue cabinet, Louis Barthou, author of the three years law of 1913, was ready to put a stronger policy into practice. He was supported in the ministry by Clemenceau's former lieutenant Tardieu, and by Herriot. In a diplomatic tour through Eastern Europe, Barthou revived the Little Entente and began negotiations for an alliance with Russia. In October 1934 King Alexander of Yugoslavia paid a state visit to France and was met at Marseille by Barthou. There the two were assassinated and the hope of a revived French foreign policy ended.

The successor to Barthou at the Quai d'Orsay was Laval, a former left-wing socialist who had devoted himself to a single-minded pursuit of wealth and power. He belatedly and reluctantly signed the Franco-Soviet pact in May 1935, but only in a weakened form, and refused to follow it up with military conversations. Already, earlier in the same year, the Saar had voted to return to German rule and Germany had re-established universal military service. All that the Western Powers could do was to build up a paper barrier at Stresa which the British government broke almost immediately by concluding a naval agreement with Germany. The Italian invasion of Ethiopia completed the ruin of Stresa, which was never really viable. When the Hoare-Laval pact was repudiated, Laval, whose one idea at this moment seems to have been the alliance with Mussolini, fell from office, as a result of what he regarded as a British betrayal, in January 1936. A caretaker government took office to see out the last few months of existence of the parliament, and it was this weak government that was faced with the most vital decision France had to take between 1919 and 1939. In March 1936 Hitler denounced the Locarno treaties, proclaimed the remilitarization of the Rhineland, and sent in a token force of German troops.

Confronted with this challenge the premier, Albert Sarraut, a typical professional politician of the Radical party, surprisingly was in favour of a military reaction by France. The Foreign Minister, Flandin, was intelligent enough to appreciate the real nature of the crisis, but also to see that internal and external factors practically prohibited a successful opposition by France. The opposition of the parties of the right to intervention could of course be taken for granted; they had now joined a section of the left in a policy of peace at any price. Given a strong lead by the government, which Sarraut and Flandin were unlikely to give, a majority might have been obtained in the Chamber for action against Germany, but there would have been a formidable opposition both there and in the country. Even more alarming was the attitude of the French General Staff, the dominant influence over which had for some time been that of Marshal Pétain. The lessons of the First World War, and the temperament of Pétain, both seemed to dictate a defensive policy, which had been given concrete form by the constitution of the great and almost invulnerable Maginot line from the Alps to the Belgian frontier. The French army in 1936 could only have taken offensive action against the remilitarization of the Rhineland by a necessarily slow readjustment of its plans and redeployment of its forces. The government might have ordered this, and there is little doubt that France still had sufficient military superiority over Germany for a successful intervention, but for the second and ultimately fatal obstacle. It knew only too well that such action would meet, not only with no support from its British allies, but even with positive disapproval and an attempt to stop the conflict, for Anglo-French relations were now – as a result of the British naval agreement with Germany, conflicting attitudes towards the Italian war in Ethiopia, and the repudiation of the Hoare-Laval agreement – very strained. Sarraut and Flandin were therefore helpless and knew it; though they have had to bear the blame for their weak reaction, the greater responsibility lay with the British government, and with the decisions taken years before by the French General Staff.

The result of the remilitarization of the Rhineland was the crumbling of the whole French system of security. Her eastern allies drew the logical conclusion that France could do nothing to aid them in the event of a German attack, and tried to come to terms with the Nazis. Belgium tried to escape the coming storm by a declaration of neutrality. France had passively to watch the Germans and Italians aid a new Fascist dictator to establish himself on her Spanish frontier, with the sympathy of her own right-wing parties. Mussolini, who had flirted with Laval while it seemed advantageous, now joined in the Berlin-Rome axis. The pattern of forces, both domestic and foreign, that had paralysed French action in January 1936 continued to have the same effect, while Hitler steadily pursued his path of successful aggression. In September 1938 the ultimate humiliation was reached at Munich by Daladier, who had all the bitterness of knowing what he was helplessly being forced to do, and by the British Prime Minister, Chamberlain, in a state of blissful and imbecile innocence.

Many on the right wing in France were now, partly

through sympathy with Fascist and Nazi ideas, and partly through hatred of Communism, committed to the idea of cooperation with Germany; on the left many, including an important section of the Socialists, were won over to the idea of pacifism at any price. The real puzzle of 1939 is how the weak government of Daladier, with a country behind it torn by bitter feuds, a right-wing – represented in the highest places – that sympathized with Hitler and Mussolini, widespread pacifist views on both left and right, and a massive Communist Party committed, as a result of the Hitler-Stalin pact, to a policy of alliance with the Nazis, came to follow Great Britain into war with Germany, as after the Nazis invaded Poland it did on 3 September 1939.

7. THE SECOND WORLD WAR

THE minister under whom France entered the Second World War, Daladier, was conscientious and intelligent, but like his country for the last five years, he had been following events without the power to control them. His vice-premier, Chautemps, a typical political middleman, had not emerged unscathed from the Stavisky scandal. The Foreign Minister Georges Bonnet had clung to appeasement as long as he could; he was moved to another ministry but remained in the cabinet. From the beginning it can hardly be said that the government was united on the conduct of the war, and the absurdly optimistic propaganda with which it concealed its own doubts did little to prepare the country for the trials to come. The pro-Nazi opposition on the right was comparatively subdued at the beginning, though biding its time. The Communist Party also, somewhat discredited by the Hitler-Stalin pact, was not able to take strong action against the war at first; and after the Soviet armies had joined the Nazis in mopping up Polish resistance, Daladier dissolved it. The Communist leaders went underground to prepare for the day when they would take over the country.

The French and British armies meanwhile, which had done practically nothing to assist the Poles, passively sat on the defensive waiting to be attacked. It was indeed a *drôle de guerre* all that winter. There was more enthusiasm for aiding the Finns against the Russian attack than for fighting the Germans, and when the Finns, after a stubborn resistance, capitulated in March 1940, the outcry against Daladier brought his ministry down. He was replaced by Paul Reynaud, a dapper, dynamic, optimistic little man; but Daladier, with the Radical-Socialist party behind him, clung to the Ministry of Defence and saved the Commander-in-chief, Gamelin, in whom he had implicit faith.

On 10 May 1940 the German army invaded the Low Countries. The French and British, abandoning their prepared positions, moved into Belgium to meet them. Reynaud took the opportunity to broaden his government by taking in representatives of the right. It was the beginning of a trend that was to go much farther than he expected. In spite of the lesson of the Polish campaign and the warnings of a French officer named de Gaulle, the *blitz* campaign that now descended on the allied armies took them by surprise. The German offensive developed on the Meuse, where the nature of the ground was supposed to prohibit it. By 15 May the debris of the French army of the Meuse was everywhere in retreat, the defences of France had been breached, and the Panzer columns were ranging the French countryside. The disaster gave Reynaud the chance at last to eliminate his enemy Daladier from the Ministry of Defence, though, conducting a stubborn retreat, the Radical leader only moved to the Ministry of Foreign Affairs. Reynaud, who took over the Ministry of Defence, at once removed Gamelin, who in the depth of his bureaux had progressed from slow motion to almost total inaction. Weygand was called back from Syria to assume command of the lost battle, and Pétain joined the government as chief military adviser to Reynaud.

In calling back these distinguished if aged figures from the past, Reynaud was aiming to restore the morale of the

country, and in this he had a momentary success; but more
than morale was needed to hold back the German onrush.
The military situation was already out of the control of any
general. Politically, disillusionment was degenerating into
recrimination and despair. The Western alliance was
breaking up: the Belgian armistice let loose a flood of
bitter invective against the Belgian king; the Dunkirk
evacuation opened the door to anti-British feeling. On 9
June the Council of Ministers moved from Paris to scattered
châteaux in the Tours area; on 14 June the German army
marched into Paris.

Weygand and Pétain were without hope from the
beginning; they had come in as liquidators of a bankrupt
army to bring hostilities to an end. The defeat of France, it
must be emphasized, was a military defeat. The French
army had been launched into a war it was quite unprepared
to fight, against a weight of armour and an air force that
outclassed it and tactics it did not know how to cope with,
and under a passive leadership. The military disaster gave
their chance to the defeatist and pro-Nazi elements –
Georges Bonnet and the 'Munichois', Faure and the
Socialist pacifists, the Fascist and Germanophile groups,
strong in Paris and among the journalists, and the Communists, openly demanding the end of an imperialist war.
The new Minister of the Interior, Mandel, who had
worked with Clemenceau and inherited some of his spirit,
for the first time took strong action against the Communist
saboteurs and the Germanophiles. But it was clear that the
military defeat of France was total. The only question before
the cabinet was how and by whom the fighting in France
should be brought to an end.

Weygand was determined that France should leave the
war and that the government and not the army should have
the onus of concluding an armistice. Reynaud, and those
who supported him in the cabinet, wanted the military
command to take the responsibility for the armistice, and
were prepared to remove the government to North Africa
and continue the struggle from there. Weygand, like

Bazaine in 1870, was concerned above all to preserve an army in France to maintain law and order and repress the anticipated Communist rising. Both he and Pétain were determined that the government should not leave the soil of France, and this was undoubtedly the view of the majority in both official and political circles. It would probably have been shared by the great masses of the people if, bewildered, harassed, overwhelmed, pouring in endless streams along the roads of France or despairingly awaiting the next blow and not knowing from which direction it would come, they had been capable of having an opinion. Their one hope was in the man who had been summoned in the extremity to save France. Pétain, with the aloofness from immediate concerns and the impassive reaction to misfortune of extreme old age, was already thinking of the future, and the task, to which he believed himself called, of regeneration of a France weakened and corrupted by the ideologies of the left. Defeat was almost to be welcomed if it could bring about this.

On 14 June the government moved to Bordeaux, where the last scene in the tragedy was enacted. Relations with Great Britain, in a state of mutual misunderstanding and general confusion, were steadily deteriorating as the pressure for a separate peace increased. A group of ministers behind Chautemps now joined in the demand for an armistice. Outside the cabinet, Laval and his clique, including many who had belonged to the pro-German propagandist organization *France-Allemagne*, were intriguing. Reynaud yielded to the pressure and resigned on 16 June. Pétain was the obvious successor, and the next day the old Marshal broadcast to the nation a message in which he said that it was necessary to end hostilities and seek an honourable peace with Germany as between soldiers. This completed the demoralization of the army.

It had still not been quite settled whether the government should transfer itself to North Africa and continue the struggle from there. Twenty-four deputies including Daladier and Mandel sailed in the *Massilia* with the intention of doing so, only to be prevented from landing in North Africa, sent back ignominiously and condemned as *fuyards* by official propaganda. Reynaud's Under-Secretary for War, General de Gaulle, more successfully made a dramatic escape to England and appealed for continued resistance, but only a handful joined him. On 22 June the armistice was signed with Germany, and on 24 June with Italy, which had entered the war on 10 June when it was quite clear that France was safely beaten.

There was yet one more tragic episode to be enacted. The future of the French fleet had been left, to British minds, in doubt. Knowing that the French government was now composed of ministers whose varying degrees of Anglophobia had been intensified by the circumstances of the French defeat, and knowing nothing of the secret plans of its commander Darlan for keeping the fleet under French control, the British government determined to prevent at least those units that were not in French metropolitan ports from falling into German hands. The last blow, it seemed to most Frenchmen, was to see their fleet bombarded and sunk with heavy loss of life at Mers-el-Kebir, by their recent allies.

Whatever the price, France, it was thought, was now out of the war. After a brief initial hesitation all the French Empire, with only one or two minor exceptions, recognized the authority of Pétain. It was hardly to be expected that they would do otherwise. Control was monopolized everywhere by the army and the bureaucracy, and officers and officials were conditioned, by long training and tradition, to accept the authority of whatever government was *de facto* at the head of the official hierarchy. The Armistice terms were accepted everywhere with passive resignation, though they cut off and put under German control the whole of the north and west of France. All French military equipment was to be handed over to the Germans for use against France's former ally. All warships were to be brought back to France, and the French fleet demobilized under German or Italian control. Any Frenchman who continued the fight in the British forces was to be treated as a *franc-tireur*. And to ensure that the Germans kept a strangle-hold over France, the cost of maintaining the German occupying forces – to an indefinite figure – was to be borne by the French government, and the prisoners of war were to remain as hostages in German hands until the conclusion of peace. Bad as these terms were, the way in which they were to be carried out made them far worse. But Pétain and his ministers thought it was an honourable peace between soldiers, and had more hatred for their former ally than their former enemy.

After leaving Bordeaux the French government moved to Clermont-Ferrand, but this town lacked suitable accommodation for the ministries; Lyon was next thought of, but there the presence of a large urban population, in the very fief of Herriot, was liable to produce undesirable pressures. Pétain and his ministers therefore fixed their capital at Vichy, where the hotels offered an ample supply of rooms for their accommodation.

The first act at Vichy was to convoke the Chambers in extraordinary session. By 229 votes out of 230 the Senate, and by 395 out of 398 what was left of the Chamber, voted in favour of the revision of the constitutional laws. To secure this nearly unanimous verdict Pétain had relied on the feverish activity of Laval. '*Il sait prendre les gens,*' commented Lebrun; and Pétain, '*Laval a été inouï.*' On the next day, a proposal presented by Laval to give Pétain full constitutional powers was passed by the two Chambers voting together, as was laid down in the conditions for constitutional revision, by 569 votes to 80. Pétain's first use of his new powers was to abrogate Article 2 of the constitutional law of 25 February 1875, the famous *amendement Wallon* providing for the election of the President. Secondly, he constituted himself Head of the State and Head of the Government, with full legislative and executive powers. Thirdly, the Senate and the Chamber of Deputies were adjourned *sine die*. The government of Vichy was henceforth to rest in the hands of the bureaucracy; its political idea was loyalty to Pétain. Its work has been presented by its advocates in terms of the devoted service of its officialdom under the Marshal to the survival of France and its re-emergence from almost total chaos. On the other hand, the American Ambassador, Leahy, far from a hostile witness, described Pétain, fifteen months later, as 'a feeble, frightened old man, surrounded by self-seeking conspirators'.

If this was what the régime was to become, it was not yet evident. Vichy had been born by intrigue out of defeat, its politics were those of personal ambition and faction; but at the beginning, it is only fair to recognize, there was also an ideal, inspired by the campaign which the men who in the hour of defeat had obtained the appearance of power had been waging for so long against the Third Republic. At last the men of the revolutionary right, descendants of Barrès and Déroulède, supporters of the Action Française and the Fascist leagues, reactionaries of the Army and Church and the higher bureaucracy, had the chance to put their ideals into practice. The Pétainists experienced something like a masochistic pleasure in a defeat which they regarded as a punishment for the sins of the Third Republic, for its corruption, materialism, and desertion of the political and spiritual ideals of traditional France. Suffering, they thought, would purify; Pétain was the new saviour of society. In the words of the Archbishop of Lyon, he was the incarnation of suffering France. The leaders of Catholic and Protestant churches alike proclaimed that Frenchmen had only one duty, to follow the Marshal with implicit faith.

Pétain had some of the qualities necessary to fill the rôle for which he was cast. As the hero of Verdun he had a great military reputation which his age had prevented him from losing in the Second World War. His disastrous influence between the wars on the French General Staff was not yet appreciated. In restoring the French armies to discipline in 1917 he had combined firmness with humanity. He was old – eighty-four in 1940 – and France habitually reverts to gerontocracy in a crisis. He was honest, unpretentious in life and manner, dignified, with something of the calm and fatalism of great age. Above all, there was nobody else who could possibly have acted as an acceptable figurehead for the new régime which was to introduce the 'National Revolution'. Time was to reveal less attractive characteristics in the old man: his secretiveness, which could be regarded as political astuteness and which was to be used later to justify the theory of the *'double jeu'*, was often pursued, one feels, for its own sake; his vanity, which was all the stronger because it was exhibited in none of the ordinary forms of pomp and ceremony, fed on popular adulation; the mediocrity of his mind, filled with the ordinary ideas of a man of his training and environment, gave him no understanding of the problems of the contemporary world; he had little grasp of principles; and for all his remarkable state of preservation his age robbed him of the capacity for concentration needed to control the government, or even to manage his own cabinet. His policy was therefore the policy of whatever ministers or advisers happened to predominate at any moment, though, given his secretiveness, it is not always possible to know which influences these were.

The first task of the National Revolution was one of destruction. The belief that local self-government was the key to democracy in France is confirmed when we find that it was one of the first things to be pulled down by Vichy. Elections were ended in communes of over 2,000 inhabitants. Next, the confederations of trade unions were dissolved and an attempt made to organize industry and agriculture on a corporative basis. The *écoles normales* for training teachers were abolished and religious teaching was brought back into the schools. The Church was one of the bases of Pétain's new régime and Roman Catholics looked forward to the triumph of their social and political ideals. A purge of officials was directed mainly against Freemasons, Jews, and persons of non-French parentage. The anti-semitism of the French right now had its opportunity: quotas were established for Jews in the professions, from some of which they were totally excluded. Arrangements were made for the trial of members of the pre-war government, who were taken into custody.

A more immediate problem was that of the future international alignment of France. There was a general desire to have done with the war and a widespread belief that, apart from a mopping-up operation in Great Britain, it was over. The traditional Anglophobia of the upper classes had been accentuated by the events of the war, and a body of opinion led by Laval was in favour of France entering the German orbit. The French people as a whole preferred a policy of neutrality, but Laval was able to engineer the interview of 24 October between Pétain and Hitler in a railway carriage at Montoire, where the principle of collaboration was announced. For the success of this policy German moderation in the use of victory was required. Instead, the occupying forces, after a brief period during which they were on their best behaviour, began to use their victory ruthlessly. The economic exploitation of France was systematically organized; Alsace and Lorraine were cut off from the rest of the country and the process of germanization started with the expulsion of large numbers of Lorrainers. Despite such obstacles Laval devoted himself to the task of Franco-German reconciliation. By taking the lead in offering concessions he hoped to establish himself firmly in the favour of the Nazis. A scheme was concocted for getting Pétain to Paris to be present at the reburial of the remains of Napoleon I's son in the Invalides. The other members of the Vichy government rightly suspected that once there Pétain would not be allowed to return, and joined in collective pressure on him. Not very unwillingly perhaps, on 13 December he removed Laval from his cabinet.

After a period of confusion, Laval was succeeded, early in February 1941, as the leading influence at Vichy, by Admiral Darlan, who, having the undoubted allegiance of the French navy, controlled the one card in the French hand that was capable of taking a trick. Darlan was an able administrator, an intensely ambitious politician, and a complete opportunist. To keep in power it was necessary for him, as it had been for Laval, to produce results for the Germans. He therefore concluded the May Protocols, giving the Germans valuable military facilities in Syria and North Africa. The result was that by July Vichy had lost Syria and the Lebanon, where General Dentz had accepted the Darlan policy. On the other hand Weygand, who had been pushed off to rule North Africa to get him out of France after the Armistice, refused to apply it. He hated the Germans even more than he hated the British. Under pressure from Weygand, therefore, Vichy refused to ratify the May Protocols and the German government did not react immediately, because it had more important business on hand.

In June 1941 the whole world situation, including the problems of the Vichy régime, was changed by the German invasion of Russia. This at once brought the two extremes of political opinion in France into action. At one extreme were the ultra-collaborationist factions of Paris, including some of the wilder spirits of the pre-war Cagoule, a number of former socialists, communists, and pacifists under the trade unionist Dumoulins, the anti-militarist agitator Suarez, the relics of the Parti Populaire under Jacques Doriot, the former socialist Marcel Déat with a new Fascist organization called the Rassemblement National Populaire, an insignificant bonapartist Ligue Française, and a miscellaneous collection of journalists and politicians from both left and right. They greeted the invasion of Russia with wild excitement and founded a Legion of French Volunteers against Bolshevism, which seems never to have managed to recruit more than about 3,000 volunteers, allegedly of poor quality.

At the other extreme were the Communists, opponents of the war against the Nazis from the moment of the Hitler-Stalin pact. For them the defeat of France by Hitler had been a victory of one imperialism over another; they held out the hand of friendship to the occupying Nazis and proclaimed their readiness to collaborate with them on the basis of the German-Soviet pact. The Nazis showed themselves more than cold to these advances and the French Communists had to retire underground again, but faithful to the party line they continued in their clandestine publications to denounce the imperialist war being waged by Great Britain, and the efforts of de Gaulle to involve France in it again. The outbreak of war between Germany and Russia changed all this and brought them into the war overnight, with all the advantages of being already an underground organization. They began acts of sabotage and the assassination of members of the occupying forces straight away. The Germans retaliated by seizing and shooting hostages. From now to the end of the war resistance and repression were to grow till in the end they had reached major proportions; but in 1941 both were still only in their beginnings.

Darlan was probably prepared for active collaboration in the war against Communist Russia. A group of pre-war Germanophile financiers and industrialists, particularly connected with the Banque Worms, which had now obtained control of practically all the departments of government dealing with economic matters, was promoting economic collaboration with the Germans. Pétain, and the isolated little circle round him at Vichy, still held back. Their one positive act was, early in 1942, to put Blum, Daladier and a few others on trial. Instead of saddling the accused with war guilt as the Germans intended, the trial turned into a debate on the reasons for the French defeat, and since it was casting more discredit on Pétain and the General Staff than on the politicians it was hurriedly abandoned and the accused returned to custody unsentenced. By now the Germans were becoming discontented with Darlan, Pétain was jealous of his predominance and the pomp which he affected, and many of the other ministers were hostile to him. In April 1942, therefore, Laval, who had been negotiating with Göring, was able to return to power with German support, while Darlan moved down to the position of Commander-in-chief. Laval was now head of the government with the effective authority, leaving Pétain as merely nominal head of the State.

Laval's policy was what it had been from the beginning of the war or even earlier. He had the obstinacy, the perverse clinging to a few fixed ideas, and the rigidity in ends, that are apt to go with extreme flexibility in the use of means and a mastery of successful intrigue. He had made up his mind, long before the war, that the countries of Western Europe must draw together, as the only means of defence against the Communist menace, which as an ex-member of the extreme left he perhaps understood. This meant that France must collaborate with Fascist Italy and Nazi Germany at any price, and he was not worried by any moral objections to this. From the inter-war experience, and particularly the fate of the Hoare-Laval agreement, he had acquired intense anti-British sentiments. He prided himself on his realism, and was convinced of the military superiority and ultimate triumph of Germany and he was determined that a Laval should not be found on the losing side. It was natural, given his undoubted courage, that he should have been ready to broadcast, in June 1942, the notorious sentence, '*Je souhaite la victoire de l'Allemagne.*' In this Laval was going beyond the overwhelming majority of Frenchmen, who certainly did not wish, and who after the entry of the United States and Russia into the war had even begun to doubt, the ultimate victory of Germany. For the same reason, and because of the increasingly oppressive and brutal behaviour of the occupying forces, sympathy in France with the small Gaullist movement, which had only been growing slowly, received considerable impetus.

The Free French movement headed by de Gaulle, after gaining the allegiance of French Equatorial Africa and the Cameroons, had failed in an expedition off Dakar in September 1940. A small Free French contingent gave distinguished service in the desert campaigns of the British army in North Africa. In the Syrian campaign for the first time Frenchmen fought against Frenchmen. As the Free

French forces and territories slowly grew it became necessary to have something more like a government to control them, and in September 1941 a National Committee was set up. Complications between the Free French and the Allies continued, in December 1941 over the seizure of the islands of Saint-Pierre and Miquelon, in 1942 over the British move against Madagascar. However, persistent wireless propaganda to France made the name of de Gaulle familiar, and when Resistance movements grew up it was natural that they should look towards him, even if, in the earlier stages in particular, with some hesitation.

The British government, while welcoming de Gaulle and his followers, had found his disposition to regard himself as an independent power, and negotiate as an equal, inconvenient. To the American government, which had put its hopes on winning over Vichy, he seemed an intolerable nuisance. Hence the plans for an Allied landing in North Africa in the autumn of 1942 paid no attention to de Gaulle. It is true that sympathy with the Free French hardly existed there. Weygand, recalled in November 1941 because the Germans distrusted him, had been replaced by General Juin, who was also a faithful supporter of Vichy. The American representatives in North Africa believed that they had established contacts which would prepare the way for an Allied invasion, and thought that in General Giraud, who had escaped from a German prison, they had a leader whose name would rally the population against Vichy. Both beliefs were profoundly mistaken. What saved the situation was the accidental presence of Darlan in Algiers. Given full powers, or so it seems, in a secret telegram from Pétain, he used them with typical opportunism to bring North Africa back into the war. The negotiation with Darlan and the Pétainist authorities in North Africa aroused strong resentment among the Free French, but Darlan's support had been invaluable. He did not live long to enjoy his transfer of allegiance for he was assassinated in a very mysterious episode, in which the small monarchist movement may have been implicated. His death left Giraud and de Gaulle to compete for control of North Africa. Finally, after joining in a Committee of National Liberation, Giraud showed a lack of political capacity which was responsible for his elimination from the scene, leaving de Gaulle as the undisputed leader in March 1944. Meanwhile there had been great changes in France.

The Allied invasion of North Africa was followed by a German occupation of the whole of France. The last French fleet, at Toulon, sank itself to avoid capture by the Germans. November 1942 saw the real end of Vichy. For the remainder of the war three themes dominate the story – the desperate attempts of the Germans to exploit the economic resources and man-power of France, the growing Resistance, and the increasingly ruthless repression.

The economic difficulties of France during the Second World War began with the chaos at the moment of the Armistice. They were intensified by the legalized looting of French resources that was facilitated by a huge and inflated bill for occupation costs, an artificial rate of exchange which enabled German troops to go through the shops like a plague of locusts, and the requisitioning by the occupying forces. The barrier between Occupied and Unoccupied Zones increased the economic difficulties. Complete breakdown was only averted by the introduction of a complicated system of controls and rationing, but in a country of small producers these could have only limited success: the black market became omnipresent, under both French and German auspices.

As the war continued, the greatest need of the Nazis came to be for labour, and the pressure for French recruits, voluntary or compulsory, steadily increased. Up to June 1942 the number of French workers transferred to Germany was officially 150,000, in fact probably half this number. To keep in German favour Laval had to increase the supply. By the autumn of 1943 it was estimated that the French labour force in Germany amounted to 605,000 men and some 44,000 women. In January 1944 the Reich Plenipotentiary General for Labour called for a million more, to be dispatched at the rate of 90,000 a month. This fantastic demand was beyond the bounds of possibility, and Laval, by playing off one German department against another, was able to keep the increase in 1944 down to relatively small proportions. He was clever enough to realize that the greater the concessions he had to make to the Germans the less the support he could count on in France.

Labour conscription was the most dangerous of all the German policies because those who fled to escape it were directly added to the strength of the Resistance. The small Resistance movements of 1940 to 1942 gradually amalgamated and grew in size. An extensive clandestine press was developed. After the liberation of Corsica from North Africa, in September 1943, the Corsican term of the *maquis* was given to the armed groups of resisters who took refuge in the more wooded and mountainous areas. The two dominant influences in the Resistance, Communist and Gaullist, formed a tacit and temporary alliance against the Germans.

German repression mounted with the growth of the Resistance, though it was still to an important degree diverted from its true objects by the insane German pre-occupation with persecuting the Jews, a pastime in which the French extremists enthusiastically joined. The official services of Vichy were employed, more or less unwillingly, in the process of repression and persecution. Maurras, in the pages of the *Action française*, was conducting a private war against the Gaullists. Special brigades of French police were created for hunting down members of the Resistance, but the most effective French aid in the task of repression came from the Militia formed by the French war-hero Darnand. The conflict between the Resistance and the German repressive services, with their French adherents, became increasingly atrocious. From 1943 onwards attacks on individuals are said to have amounted to 100 a day. The German forces, the Nazi organizations, the French special police, the Militia, the Communists, and the non-

Communist *maquis* all took their turn in the competition at clandestine massacre. The Nazis certainly won, with achievements such as the burning of some six hundred women and children by the SS division *Das Reich* in the church of Oradour-sur-Glane on 10 June 1944. Among individual assassinations were those of the Radical politician Zay and of Mandel, and on the other side of the pro-Nazi journalist and broadcaster, Philippe Henriot.

Pétain and his group of intimates at Vichy had long since ceased to exercise any influence over the course of events. The German authorities were increasingly discontented with the little assistance they provided and more inclined to favour the Paris collaborationists, who had throughout the war been struggling for the government of France. Although the Nazis were not unaware how little support these extremists commanded in the country, in January 1944 they decided to make use of them in the government and Pétain and Laval gave way. When the Allies landed in Normandy in June 1944, the Paris collaborationists were attempting to oust Laval, but without success until, on 17 August, the Germans ordered Pétain and Laval to withdraw to Belfort. When they refused they were taken there and thence into Germany by force. As the German armies retreated into the Reich, they were accompanied by Darnand and the nucleus of the Militia, and the shadow government of the collaborationists.

Meanwhile de Gaulle had sent his representatives to France in the wake of the invading forces. The American authorities, who had never accepted the idea that the Gaullist movement represented France and still hankered after an arrangement with the now non-existent authority of Vichy, had made plans for an allied administration. They found to their surprise that a Gaullist régime was springing up everywhere in the liberated territory under their feet. This was just as well, for where, as in the South-west, there was a gap between the withdrawal of German forces and the establishment of the new national authority, the Communist partisans were able to seize control and institute a local reign of terror. A Communist attempt to seize Paris by a rising before the Germans had withdrawn or Allied forces had arrived might have led to the destruction of the city. Fortunately the German commander, von Choltitz, against his orders concluded a truce, and the Allied Supreme Command yielded to Gaullist pressure by allowing a French division to advance to take over Paris. On 26 August, de Gaulle entered Paris and set up a government combining representatives of the Resistance inside France and the Committee of National Libération from without.

It remained to be decided whether, when a new and properly constituted government was formed, it should revive the constitutional arrangements of the Third Republic. In October 1945 the people of France were summoned to elect an Assembly, and at the same time to decide, by popular vote, if it should have the constituent power, in other words whether it was to have the duty of framing a new Constitution or whether the institutions that France had lived under from 1875 to 1940 should remain in force. By an overwhelming majority they repudiated the Third Republic: those who were not allowed to vote – the collaborationists of various shades and depths – had already repudiated it. The régime under which France had lived since 1871, with its pettiness and its greatness, its triumphs and its disasters, was ended. The Fourth Republic was to make a clean break with the corruption, misery, and defeats of the recent past, its political leaders to abandon the ways to which they were long habituated, and France to escape from its history.

If anyone believed this, they were living in a world of illusion. France was to exhibit once again her remarkable power of recovery, but the ills that had afflicted her since 1919 were not to be cured so easily. The Fourth Republic came into an inheritance that was to prove fatal to it; 1945 was neither an end nor a beginning, and only dimly, in the subsequent years, could it be seen that a new society was indeed being born, painfully, out of the travail of the twentieth century.

CHRONOLOGICAL TABLE

1799 November. Coup d'état of 18 *brumaire*
December. Constitution of year VIII. Bonaparte First
    Consul
1800 February. Foundation of Bank of France
Law of 28 *pluviôse* year VIII establishes prefectoral system
Pacification of the West
June. Marengo
December. Hohenlinden
Royalist bomb plot
1801 Armed Neutrality
February. Treaty of Lunéville
April. Copenhagen
August. French army in Egypt capitulates
1802 Chateaubriand's *Le Génie du Christianisme*
March. Peace of Amiens
April. Concordat promulgated
May. Bonaparte Consul for life
1803 April. British ultimatum
May. Renewal of war with Great Britain
Sale of Louisiana to United States
1804 March. Civil Code promulgated
Cadoudal plot
Execution of duc d'Enghien
May. Proclamation of Empire
Camp at Boulogne
2 December. Coronation of Napoleon
1805 August. Third Coalition
15 October. Ulm
21 October. Trafalgar
2 December. Austerlitz
1806 January. Peace of Pressbourg
June. Confederation of the Rhine formed
July. Maida
October. Jena
Auerstädt
November. Berlin decrees
1807 February. Eylau
June. Friedland
July. Treaty of Tilsit

1807 October. Invasion of Portugal
     November, December. Milan decrees
1808 Establishment of the University
     May. Joseph Bonaparte King of Spain
     July. Capitulation of Baylen
     August. Vimiero
     Convention of Cintra
     December. Napoleon invades Spain
1809 January. Corunna
     March. Invasion of Portugal
     April. Austrian offensive
     Disgrace of Talleyrand
     May. Annexation of Papal States
     Imprisonment of Pius VII
     July. Wagram
     October. Peace of Schönbrunn
1810 Divorce of Josephine
     April. Marriage of Napoleon to Marie-Louise
     Disgrace of Fouché
     Mme de Staël's *De l'Allemagne*
     September. Lines of Torres Vedras
1811 Economic crisis
1812 24 June. Grand Army crosses the Niemen
     September. Borodino
     14 September–14 October. Occupation of Moscow
     October. Malet plot in Paris
     27 November. Crossing of Beresina
     14 December. Ney recrosses Niemen
1813 May. Lützen
     Bautzen
     June. Vittoria
     August. Dresden
     October. Leipzig
     Wellington crosses the Pyrenees
1814 January. Allied invasion of France
     February. March. Negotiations at Châtillon
     31 March. Capitulation of Paris
     6 April. Abdication of Napoleon
     10 April. Toulouse. Defeat of Soult by Wellington
     11 April. Treaty of Fontainebleau
     1 May. First Treaty of Paris
     2 May. Declaration of Saint-Ouen

1814 4 June. Constitutional Charter of Louis XVIII
      September. Congress of Vienna meets
1815 1 March. Napoleon lands at Fréjus
      20 March. Napoleon enters Paris
      16 June. Ligny and Quatre-Bras
      18 June. Waterloo
      22 June. Second abdication of Napoleon
      8 July. Second Restoration
      Government of Talleyrand-Fouché
      White Terror in Midi
      August. Election of *Chambre introuvable*
      September. Talleyrand and Fouché resign
      Richelieu ministry
      November. Second Treaty of Paris
      December. Execution of Marshal Ney
1816 September. Dissolution of *Chambre introuvable*
      Election of new Chamber
1818 November. Occupation of France ended
      December. Richelieu replaced by Decazes
1819 de Maistre's *Du Pape*
      Géricault's *The Raft of the Medusa*
1820 February. Assassination of duc de Berry
      Recall of Richelieu
      September. Birth of comte de Chambord
1821 Death of Napoleon
      Revolutionary movement of the Charbonnerie
      December. Fall of second Richelieu ministry. Ultras take
         over government
1822 March. Plot of four sergeants of La Rochelle
      September. Villèle President of the Council
1823 April. Expedition into Spain
1824 March. Elections return an ultra Chamber
      June. Dismissal of Chateaubriand
      Delacroix's *The Massacres of Scio*
      September. Death of Louis XVIII
      Succession of Charles X
1825 Law against sacrilege
      Indemnity to *émigrés* voted
      May. Coronation of Charles X at Reims
1827 Victor Hugo's *Cromwell*
      October. Battle of Navarino
      November. Elections

317

1827 December. Fall of Villèle
1828 January. Government of Martignac
1829 August. Polignac government
1830 Victor Hugo's *Hernani*
     Berlioz's *Symphonie Fantastique*
     June. Elections
     July. Capture of Algiers
     25 July. Four Ordinances
     28-30 July. Revolution in Paris
     31 July. Duke of Orleans accepts lieutenant-generalcy of
         France
     2 August. Abdication of Charles X
1831 Victor Hugo's *Notre-Dame de Paris*
     Stendhal's *Le Rouge et le Noir*
     February. Anti-clerical riots
     March. Casimir-Périer ministry
     August. French expel Dutch from Belgium
     October-November. Revolt in Lyon
1831-32. Cholera epidemic
1832 Death of duc de Reichstadt
     May. Attempt of duchesse de Berry to rouse Vendée
     Death of Casimir-Périer
1833 Guizot's education law
1834 Revolt in Lyon
     Massacre in rue Transnonain
     Lamennais' *Paroles d'un croyant*
     Balzac's *Le Père Goriot*
     Louis Blanc's *L'Organisation du travail*
1835 July. Fieschi bomb plot
     Gautier's *Mademoiselle de Maupin*
     Vigny's *Chatterton*
1836 Attempt of Louis Bonaparte at Strasbourg
     September. Government of Molé
1838 Rachel plays in Racine
1839 Revolt of Abd-el-Kader
     March. Fall of Molé
     Louis Bonaparte's *Les Idées napoléoniennes*
1840 Re-burial of Napoleon in the Invalides
     Attempt of Louis Bonaparte at Boulogne
     March. Government of Thiers
     Mehemet Ali crisis
     October. Fall of Thiers

1840 Ministry of Guizot
     Proudhon's *Qu'est-ce que la propriété?*
1841 Entente cordiale of Aberdeen and Guizot
1842 Comte's *Cours de philosophie positive* completed
     Sue's *Les Mystères de Paris*
     Death of duc d'Orléans
     Guizot's railway law
1842–6 Railway mania
1844 Pritchard affair in Tahiti
     Dumas' *Le Comte de Monte-Cristo*
1846 Escape of Louis Napoleon Bonaparte from Ham
     October. Spanish marriages
1847 Economic crisis
     Capture of Abd-el-Kader
     May. Teste trial
     August. Murder by duc de Praslin
     July–December. Campaign of banquets
1848 23 February. Revolution in Paris. Resignation of Guizot
     24 February. Abdication of Louis-Philippe
     Provisional Government set up
     Proclamation of Universal Suffrage
     Abolition of slavery
     16 March. Demonstration of *bonnets à poil*
     17 March. Left-wing demonstration
     23 April. Election of Constituent Assembly
     15 May. Demonstration of the clubs
     22-26 June. June Days
     Government of Cavaignac
     4 November. Constitution of Second Republic
     10 December. Election of Louis Napoleon Bonaparte as
         President
     Government of Odilon Barrot
1849 April. Expeditionary corps sent to Rome
     May. Election of Legislative Assembly
     13 June. Attempted rising in Paris
     July. Fall of Roman Republic
     October. Dismissal of Barrot Ministry
1850 March. *Loi Falloux* on education
     Left-wing victories in by-elections
     May. Law restricting franchise
1851 July. Legislative Assembly fails to accept constitutional
         reform

1851 2 December. *Coup d'état*
    14 December. Plebiscite
1852 January. Constitution
    20-21 November. Plebiscite on Empire
    1 December. Proclamation of Empire
    Foundation of Crédit Foncier and Crédit Mobilier
1853 January. Marriage of Napoleon III and Eugénie
1854 March. War with Russia
    September. Siege of Sebastopol
1854-65 Faidherbe in Senegal
1855 Paris Exhibition
    September. Fall of Sebastopol
1856 Peace Congress in Paris
1857 Prosecution of *Madame Bovary* and *Les Fleurs du Mal*
    Port of Dakar founded
1858 January. Orsini bomb plot
    July. Conference of Napoleon III and Cavour at Plombières
    Vision at Lourdes
1859 Construction of Suez Canal begun
    Amnesty
    April. War of Italian Unification
    June. Magenta
    Solferino
    July. Armistice of Villafranca
1860 Annexation of Savoy and Nice
    Free-trade treaty with Great Britain
    Anglo-French occupation of Pekin
    Expedition to Syria
    First Constitutional changes
1861 October. Expedition to Mexico
1862 Annexation of Cochin-China
    French troops remain in Mexico
1863 Revolt of Poland
    Renan's *Vie de Jésus*
    Salon des refusés
    Manet's *Le Déjeuner sur l'herbe*
    May. Legislative elections
    Fall of Persigny
    Rouher Minister of State
1864 Schleswig-Holstein War
    Maximilian proclaimed Emperor in Mexico
    Papal Syllabus of Errors

1865 Death of Morny
     Educational reforms of Duruy
1866 Austro-Prussian War
     French troops evacuate Mexico
1867 January. Letter of Napoleon III announcing constitutional
          changes
     February. Proposals for rearmament
     Crisis of Crédit Mobilier
     June. Execution of Maximilian
     November. Garibaldi repelled at Mentana
1868 May. Press laws relaxed
1869 Flaubert's *L'Éducation sentimentale*
     Suez Canal opened
     May. Elections
     Election of Gambetta on Belleville programme
     Government of Ollivier
1870 May. Plebiscite on constitutional changes
     June. Hohenzollern acceptance of throne of Spain,
          subsequently withdrawn
     14 July. Ems telegram
     19 July. French declaration of war on Prussia
     August. French defeats
     Fall of Ollivier
     1 September. Surrender of Napoleon III and MacMahon
          at Sedan
     4 September. Government of National Defence set up
     19 September. Paris besieged
     10 October. Gambetta arrives at Tours
     27 October. Capitulation of Bazaine at Metz
     November. Victory at Coulmiers
     Reoccupation of Orleans by French
1871 19 January. Failure of *sortie en masse* from Paris
     28 January. Armistice
     8 February. Election of Assembly
     Government of Thiers
     1 March. Terms of peace ratified by National Assembly
     18 March. Troops fail to remove guns from Montmartre
     28 March. Election of Commune
     10 May. Treaty of Frankfort
     21 May. Versaillais enter Paris
     28 May. End of the Commune
     5 July. Manifesto of comte de Chambord

1871 July. Supplementary elections
1873 Death of Napoleon III
     May. Resignation of Thiers. Appointment of MacMahon
     September. End of German occupation
     October. Letter of comte de Chambord
     November. Law of the *Septennat*
1875 February. Amendement Wallon
     Constitutional laws
     December. Dissolution of National Assembly
1876 Mallarmé's *L'Après-midi d'un faune*
1877 16 May. Dissolution of Chamber
     De Broglie government
     September. Death of Thiers
     October. Legislative elections: republican victory
1879 Republican majority in Senate
     Resignation of MacMahon
     Grévy elected President
     Death of Prince Imperial
     Parliament returns to Paris
1879–82 Educational reforms of Ferry
1880 Amnesty to the exiles of the Commune
     Les Soirées de Médan
     September. First ministry of Ferry
1881 May. Protectorate over Tunisia
     November. Fall of Ferry
     Ministry of Gambetta
1882 January. Union Générale crash
     February. Fall of Gambetta
     Death of Gambetta
     Anglo-French demonstration at Alexandria
     Foundation of Ligue des Patriotes
1883 February. Ministry of Ferry
     Death of comte de Chambord
1884 Trade unions legalized
     Municipal reform
1885 Tonkin reverse
     Fall of Ferry
     Legislative elections: revival of Right
     December. Grévy re-elected President
     Protectorate over Madagascar
1886 January. Boulanger Minister of War
1887 Formation of Indo-Chinese union

1887 Foundation of Bourses de Travail
   November. Wilson scandal
   December. Resignation of Grévy
   Sadi Carnot elected President
1887–9 Building of Eiffel Tower
1888 Boulangist campaign
1889 January. Election of Boulanger at Paris
   April. Flight of Boulanger
   Paris exhibition
1890 November. Cardinal Lavigerie starts the Ralliement
1891 May. Encyclical *Rerum Novarum*
   French fleet visits Cronstadt
1892 November. Panama scandal
1894 Franco-Russian defensive alliance
   June. Assassination of Sadi Carnot
   Casimir-Périer President for six months
   December. Condemnation of Dreyfus
1895 January. Félix Faure elected President
   Establishment of Confédération Générale de Travail
   November. Radical cabinet of Léon Bourgeois
1896 April. Cabinet of Méline
   Annexation of Madagascar
1897 Barrès' *Les Déracinés*
1898 January. Zola's *J'accuse*
   June. Resignation of Méline
   June 1898 – June 1905. Delcassé Foréign Minister
   September. Marchand at Fashoda
1899 Death of Faure
   Election of Loubet as President
   June. Government of republican defence under Waldeck-
      Rousseau
   Foundation of *L'Action française*
   September. Court martial finds Dreyfus guilty of high
      treason with extenuating circumstances
1901 July. Law on Congregations
1902 Debussy's *Pelléas et Mélisande*
   May. Legislative elections: victory of Bloc Républicain
   June. Resignation of Waldeck-Rousseau
   Government of Combes
1903 Edward VII and President Loubet exchange visits
1904 April. Anglo-French Entente

A History of Modern France

1904 November. Law for separation of Church and State
  introduced
1905 January. Resignation of Combes
  March. Wilhelm II at Tangier
  June. Resignation of Delcassé
  December. Law of Separation
1906 Conference at Algeciras
  Amiens Charter
  Presidency of Armand Fallières
  October. Government of Clemenceau
1907 Bergson's *L'Évolution créatrice*
1908 Anatole France's *L'Île des pingouins*
  Affair of German deserters in Morocco
1909 Wave of strikes
1910 November. Railway strike broken by Briand
1911 July. Government of Caillaux
  The *Panther* sent to Agadir
1912 January. Fall of Caillaux
  Government of Poincaré
  French protectorate over Morocco set up
1913 Proust's *Du côté de chez Swann*
  January. Poincaré elected President
  August. Law of three years military service
1914 April-May. Legislative elections: victory of left
  Government of Viviani
  28 June. Assassination of Archduke at Serajevo
  16-23 July. Visit of Poincaré and Viviani to Russia
  23 June. Austrian ultimatum to Serbia
  28 July. Austrian declaration of war on Serbia
  30 July. Russian mobilization
  31 July. German ultimatum to Russia
  Assassination of Jaurès
  1 August. German declaration of war on Russia
  French mobilization
  3 August. German declaration of war on France
  4 August. British declaration of war on Germany
  22 August. French defeated in the Ardennes
  23 August. Viviani government re-formed
  1 September. French government leaves for Bordeaux
  5-12 September. Battle of the Marne
  December. French government returns to Paris

1915 October. Fall of Viviani
     Briand ministry
1916 21 February. Battle of Verdun begins
     1 July–September. Battle of the Somme
     December. Nivelle appointed commander-in-chief
1917 March. Fall of Briand government
     Ribot ministry
     16 April. Nivelle offensive
     15 May. Dismissal of Nivelle
     Appointment of Foch and Pétain
     Mutinies in French army
     Trouble among workers
     Bonnet rouge affair
     Fall of Ribot government
     13 September. Ministry of Painlevé
     Bolo Pasha affair
     13 November. Fall of Painlevé
     Clemenceau government
1918 March–July. Ludendorff offensive
     18 July. Counter-offensive of Foch
     11 November. Armistice
1919 28 June. Signature of Treaty of Versailles
     November. Election of Assembly: Bloc National
1920 Valéry's *Le Cimetière marin*
     January. Paul Deschanel elected President
     Resignation of Clemenceau
     Government of Millerand
     Weygand mission to Poland
     September. Resignation of Deschanel
     Millerand elected President
     December. Socialist Congress at Tours
1921 Trade Union split
1922 January. Government of Poincaré
1923 January. Occupation of Ruhr
1924 May. Election: Cartel des Gauches
     June. Resignation of Millerand
     Doumergue elected President
     Government of Herriot
     September. Geneva Protocol
1925 April. Fall of Herriot
     July. Revolt in Syria

1925 Defeat and exile of Abd-el-Krim
July. Evacuation of Ruhr begins
October. Locarno Agreements

1926 July. Government of Poincaré

1928 Military service reduced to one year
Decision to build Maginot line

1929 July. Retirement of Poincaré
October. Wall Street crash

1930 French evacuation of Rhineland
Election of 107 Nazis to Reichstag

1931 May. Paul Doumer elected President

1932 May. Assassination of Doumer
Lebrun elected President
Election of Chamber: success of Cartel des Gauches
Government of Herriot

1933 January. Hitler becomes Reich chancellor
June. Four-power Pact
Stavisky affair

1934 6 February. Attempted *coup d'état* of the Leagues
9 February. Government of Doumergue
9 October. Assassination of Barthou and King Alexander
Laval becomes Foreign Minister
November. Fall of Doumergue

1935 January. Saar votes for reunion with Germany
May. Franco-Soviet pact
September. Italian attack on Abyssinia
December. Hoare-Laval agreement

1936 January. Fall of Laval
Manifesto of Popular Front
March. Remilitarization of Rhineland
April, May. Election of Chamber: victory of Popular
   Front
Government of Blum
October. Devaluation of franc

1937 January. Léon Blum announces 'pause'
June. Fall of Blum government

1938 April. Government of Daladier
September. Munich

1939 April. Lebrun re-elected President
23 August. Hitler-Stalin Pact of non-aggression and for the
   partition of Poland
1 September. Invasion of Poland

1939 3 September. Great Britain and France declare war on
      Germany
1940 20 March. Reynaud succeeds Daladier
      10 May. German invasion of Low Countries
      15 May. French front broken on Meuse
      18 May. Reynaud becomes Minister of National Defence in
      place of Daladier
      Pétain enters government
      20 May. Gamelin replaced by Weygand
      29 May–4 June. Dunkirk evacuation
      9 June. French government moved to Touraine
      10 June. Italy enters war
      14 June. Germans enter Paris
      Government moves to Bordeaux
      16 June. Resignation of Reynaud. Succeeded by Pétain
      18 June. General de Gaulle calls from London for continued
      resistance
      22 June. Armistice with Germany
      24 June. Armistice with Italy
      1 July. French government moves to Vichy
      3 July. Mers-el-Kebir
      10 July. National Assembly votes full powers to Pétain
      11 July. Vote of constitutional laws
      Ministry of Laval
      September. Free French expedition to Dakar fails
      Japanese forces enter Indo-China
      24 October. Hitler-Pétain interview at Montoire
      13 December. Dismissal of Laval
1941 February. Darlan in control of government
      May. Protocols
      June. Syrian campaign
      June. German invasion of Russia
1942 April. Trial at Riom of Blum, Daladier, etc., abandoned
      Laval returns to power
      8 November. Allied landing in North Africa
      11 November. Germans move into unoccupied France
      27 November. French fleet sunk at Toulon
      24 December. Assassination of Darlan
1943 June. Committee of National Liberation formed at Algiers
      under de Gaulle and Giraud
      September. Liberation of Corsica
1944 January. Paris collaborationists enter government

1944 6 June. Allied landing in Normandy
20 August. Pétain transferred to Belfort
26 August. De Gaulle enters Paris
1945 21 October. Election of Constituent Assembly
Referendum votes end of Third Republic

FURTHER READING

THE fullest general history of France in the nineteenth century is still Lavisse, *Histoire de France contemporaine* (1920–22); reference to specific volumes will be made later. There are useful bibliographies in these, in the volumes of the *Peuples et civilisations* series, and in *Clio*: L. Villat: *La Révolution et l'Empire, ii. Napoléon* (1936); *L'Époque contemporaine*, i. Droz, Genet et Vidalenc: *Restaurations et révolutions 1815–1871* (1933), ii. Renouvin, Préclin et Hardy: *La paix armée et la Grande Guerre 1871–1919* (1939. 2nd ed. 1947). Excellent general histories, in less detail than Lavisse, are J. P. T. Bury: *France 1814–1940* (2nd ed. 1951); *Histoire de la France pour tous les Français*, G. Lefebvre: *de 1774 à 1815*, C. H. Pouthas: *de 1815 à 1878*, M. Baumont: *de 1878 à nos jours* (1950); and M. Reinhard's finely illustrated *Histoire de France ii. de 1715 à 1946*; J. Vidalenc: *Le Premier Empire, la Restauration*; L. Girard: *Le Règne de Louis-Philippe, La Révolution de 1848, Le Second Empire*; M. Sorre: *La Troisième République*; L. Genet: *La France au XXe siècle* (1954). A selection of works on special aspects of French history since 1799 follows.

The best short account of French constitutional developments is given in the Introduction to the earlier editions of Duguit, Monnier et Bonnard: *Les Constitutions et les principales lois politiques de la France depuis 1789*. M. Deslandres: *Histoire constitutionelle de la France depuis 1789 jusqu'à 1870, ii* (1932); *iii. L'Avènement de la IIIe République, la constitution de 1875* (1937) is long and rather arid but it contains useful material that cannot easily be obtained elsewhere. An interesting sketch of right-wing movements, perhaps unduly schematized, is R. Rémond, *La Droite en France de 1815 à nos jours* (1954). An essential book for understanding the operation of parliamentary institutions in France is D. W. S. Lidderdale's *The Parliament of France* (1951).

French historians are only now beginning to work on the economic history of nineteenth-century France. J. H. Clapham's *Economic Development of France and Germany 1815–1914* (4th ed. 1936) is an able survey on the basis of the material available when it was written. The trade policies of France are traced by S. B. Clough in *France, a History of National Economics, 1789–1939* (1939), a useful book though written to a theme which does not necessarily command acceptance. An account of religious developments is given by C. S. Philips in *The Church in France, 1789–1907* (2 vols. 1929,

1936), and more recently in the series edited by Fliche and Martin, especially *La Crise révolutionnaire 1789–1846* (1949) by J. Leflon. The study of the interaction of Church and State in France by P. H. Spencer in *The Politics of Belief in Nineteenth-Century France* (1954) is thoughtful and illuminating. Concise and impartial summaries of foreign problems and policies, with bibliographies, are given in the *Histoire des relations internationales*, edited and in these volumes written by P. Renouvin – *Le XIXe siècle: i. 1815–71 L'Europe des nationalités et l'éveil de nouveaux mondes, ii. 1815–71 L'Apopée de l'Europe* (1954–5); *Les Crises du XXe siècle* (2 vols. 1957–8). On French colonies a competent survey with sufficient detail for the non-specialist is the *Histoire de la colonisation française* (1946) by H. Blet, while the ideas behind French colonization are described in H. Deschamps' *Méthodes et doctrines coloniales de la France du XVI siècle à nos jours* (2 vols., 1953). R. Girardet's *La Société militaire dans la France contemporaine 1815–1939* (1953) has interesting *aperçus* on the history of the army but is rather slight. A more scholarly work, containing much new material, is P. Chalmin, *L'Officier français de 1815 à 1870* (1957). In place of various rather dull histories of education may be mentioned G. Duveau's *Les Instituteurs* (1957), slight and opinionated but also lively and realistic. A well-documented study of the press laws is *The Government and the Newspaper Press in France 1814–1881* (1959) by Irene Collins. It is difficult to pick out a single book on French art for mention, but a stimulating general history of architecture is P. Lavedan's *French Architecture* (1944, trans. 1956). The *Oxford Companion to French Literature* (1959) is a useful work of reference. R. Soltau's *French Political Ideas in the Nineteenth Century* (1931) is a helpful if uninspired survey. Selections from a number of leading French social and political thinkers, with introductory notes on their authors, are edited by A. Bayet and F. Albert under the title, *Les Écrivains politiques du XIXe siècle* (1907).

Turning to special periods, we find the nineteenth century very unevenly served by secondary works. The literature on Napoleon I is immense. The best life in English is J. M. Thompson's *Napoleon Bonaparte: his Rise and Fall* (1952), though the arrangement is a little confusing. F. M. H. Markham's *Napoleon and the Awakening of Europe* (1954) is a well-written and judicious short account. In French may be mentioned G. Lefebvre's *Napoléon* (1935) in the *Peuples et Civilisations* series, and the brief survey by F. Ponteil, *Napoléon Ier et l'organisation autoritaire de la France* (1956). The changing views on Napoleon during the subsequent century are

summarized by P. Geyl in *Napoleon For and Against* (trans. 1949).
A well-presented collection of contemporary verdicts which takes
some of the gilt off the Napoleonic gingerbread is J. Savant's
Napoleon in his Time (1954, trans. 1958). Works on special aspects
of the meteoric career of the Emperor from one little island to
another, and on all those who impinged on it from his marshals
to his mistresses, are so many and so detailed that the effort to pick
out particular volumes for mention here has had to be abandoned.
The histories already referred to will provide an introduction to the
voluminous Napoleonic bibliography.

The counter-revolution and the opposition to Napoleon has
been served much less well, but its importance for the future
intellectual development of France is indicated in F. Balden-
sperger's *Le Mouvement des idées dans l'émigration française, 1789–1815*
(1924). There is now an excellent history of the evanescent but
unduly depreciated régime that followed the catastrophe of
Napoleon, in G. de Bertier de Sauvigny's *La Restauration* (1955).
Sympathetic to the Catholic and royalist ideals of the Restoration,
it is therefore perhaps a little hard on parliamentarians like
Decazes and Villèle.

The July Monarchy lacks any good recent general history and
even specialized studies are comparatively rare. Competent
accounts of the reign of Louis-Philippe are the volume in Lavisse
by S. Charléty, *La Monarchie de juillet* (1921) and P. de la Gorce,
Louis-Philippe 1830–1848 (1931). A useful light on the politics of
the reign is thrown by S. Kent in *Electoral Procedure under Louis-
Philippe* (1937). The economic and social problems of a still mainly
pre-industrial society have not been adequately studied, but indi-
cations are to be found in C. H. Pouthas, *La Population française
pendant la première moitié du XIXe siècle* (1956), L. Chevalier's
authoritative *La Formation de la population parisienne au XIXe siècle*
(1950), the same author's stimulating *Classes laborieuses et classes
dangereusès à Paris pendant la première moitié du XIXe siècle* (1958), and
J. B. Duroselle's *Les Débuts du catholicisme social en France 1822–70*
(1951).

With the Second Republic and the Second Empire we come to
a period in which our problem is not to find titles to include, but
rather to know what to omit. The best history of the Second
Republic is the volume in Lavisse by C. Seignobos, *La Révolution
de 1848 et l'Empire* (1921), which reflects a great deal of archival
research, unfortunately – for lack of references – all to be done
again. One traditional misinterpretation was eliminated by D. C.

MacKay in *The National Workshops, a study in the French Revolution of 1848* (1933); and something to rescue the reputation of Ledru-Rollin from excessive contempt was achieved by A. R. Calman's *Ledru-Rollin and the Second French Republic* (1922). Karl Marx's *Class Struggle in France 1848–50* was a brilliant analysis for its time but is naturally inadequate by the standards of modern economic history. F. A. Simpson's *Louis Napoleon and the Recovery of France 1848–56* (1930. 3rd edition 1956) is well written but lacks the research that might have given it more lasting value. The same author's *Rise of Louis Napoleon* (1909) is brilliantly written and amusing but very slight, and H. A. L. Fisher's *Bonapartism* (1914) is somewhat misleading. Louis Napoleon's own *Des idées napoléoniennes* (1839) is essential for the understanding of the Second Empire. Karl Marx's *The Eighteenth Brumaire of Louis Bonaparte* is a brilliant piece of contemporary history.

Among general histories of the Second Empire the volumes by Seignobos in Lavisse are probably still the best. A. L. Guérard's *Napoleon III* (1943) is a bright account and J. M. Thompson's *Louis Napoleon and the Second Empire* (1954) is of value as a study of the personality of Napoleon III. A thoughtful introduction to the economic policy of the Second Empire is H. N. Boon's *Rêve et réalité dans l'œuvre économique et sociale de Napoléon III* (1936). There is a thorough and well-documented study of the Chevalier-Cobden commercial negotiations in *The Anglo-French Treaty of 1860* (1930) by A. L. Dunham. D. H. Pinkney's *Napoleon III and the Rebuilding of Paris* (1958) is a well-balanced account based on original sources. A competent life of the rebuilder of Paris, derived from printed materials, is *The Life and Times of Baron Haussmann* (1957) by K. M. and Brian Chapman. L. Girard's *La Politique des travaux publics du second empire* (1952) is authoritative. On the other side of the medal is the detailed but impressionistic *La Vie ouvrière en France sous le second empire* (1946) by G. Duveau. The membership of the legislative assemblies is sketched by T. Zeldin in *The Political System of Napoleon III* (1958), which combines the brilliance and the narrowness of the Namier approach. A revealing picture of political life under the Second Empire can be obtained from biographies, such as R. Schnerb's thorough and penetrating *Rouher et le Second Empire* (1949). There are many studies of the foreign policy of Napoleon III. One of the most illuminating, which uses the reports of the procureurs, is L. M. Case, *French Opinion on War and Diplomacy during the Second Empire* (1954). The Franco-Prussian War belongs as much to European as to French history and has an extensive literature. A detailed though rather anti-French account of *The Siege of Paris 1870-1871* (1950) is by M. Kranzberg. The attempt of France to fight back after the collapse of the Empire is well described by J. P. T. Bury in *Gambetta and the National Defence* (1936). F. Jellinek's *The Paris Commune of 1871* (1937) is lively but to be used with caution. A scholarly account of the ideological conflicts among the Communards is given by C. Rihs in *La Commune de Paris* (1955).

The most useful single book on France since 1870 is D. Thomson's *Democracy in France* (3rd ed. 1958). This is analytical in treatment. A narrative history of the Third Republic, packed with detail, is D. W. Brogan's *The Development of Modern France 1870– 1939* (1940). F. Goguel in *La Politique des partis sous la IIIe République* (1946) makes an interesting study of the conflict of left and right under the labels of 'Mouvement' and 'Ordre établi'. J. Barthélemy's *Le Gouvernement de la France* (ed. of 1939) is a clear and penetrating analysis of the political institutions of the Third Republic. *The Beginnings of the Third Republic in France* (1940) are described by F. H. Brabant in a witty account with sympathetic pictures of the personalities involved. The historical value of a scholarly piece of electoral analysis is shown by J. Goualt's *Comment la France est devenue républicaine* (1954). The classic in this field is A. Siegfried's *Tableau politique de la France de l'Ouest sous la IIIe République* (1913). A broader picture, but also a classic in its way and for its period, is J. E. C. Bodley's *France* (revised ed. 1902). Among many political biographies may be named *Clemenceau* (1943) by G. Bruun and a lively short life, *Clemenceau and the Third Republic* (1946) by J. Hampden Jackson. On the famous affair we have G. Chapman's *The Dreyfus Case* (1955), a very careful survey, though perhaps a little limited in its references to the background.

The literature on the period since 1914 is a mixture of contemporary history and journalism. Some of it will be of value as source material for future historians and some may escape the limitations of a purely contemporary view, but such a discrimination is at present too difficult a task to be attempted here.

In a different sense contemporary writings are, of course, very enlightening to the historian, perhaps particularly so in France where literature has so often been 'engagé'. The list that follows represents merely a sample of the riches that French literature holds for the historian. Chateaubriand's *Mémoires d'outre-tombe* is better for conveying atmosphere than facts. In *Choses vues* Victor Hugo gives us a series of political and social vignettes, largely of the period of the July Monarchy. De Tocqueville's *Souvenirs* contain a penetrating study of the social and political errors, in which the author shared, of the Second Republic. The comte de Falloux's *Mémoires d'un royaliste* reveal the limitations of the clerical and conservative mind. In *L'Éducation sentimentale* Flaubert sets the gradual disillusionment of a young bourgeois, haunting the Paris boulevards with no end in life, against the tragic events of revolution and class war. Zola wrote, under the Third Republic, the *Rougon-Macquart* cycle of twenty novels, portraying in lurid detail a Second Empire society made up almost wholly of an amalgam of luxury, crime, misery, and vice. The *Journal* of the Goncourts describes literary and artistic society in the second half of the nineteenth century. The outburst of nationalist feeling is illustrated by the novels of Maurice Barrès, such as *Les Déracinés*. Anatole France's *L'Île des pingouins* is a satiric history of the Third Republic. Nor should the kind of literature with no apparent political reference be forgotten. Balzac's novels were deliberately conceived as a many-faceted reflexion of the *Comédie humaine* in the first thirty years of the nineteenth century. In a more subtle way Marcel Proust in *À la recherche du temps perdu* not only looks back on the apparently stable society of the eighteen-nineties and the early years of the twentieth century, but prophetically forward to an age of decay and disaster.

INDEX

Some Pelicans on history and literature
are described on the
following pages

Geoffrey Brereton

A SHORT HISTORY OF
FRENCH LITERATURE

A 297

This compact history deals in outline with the whole of French
literature, from the *chansons de geste* to the theatre today. While
the chief works of the Middle Ages are described briefly, the
great writers since the beginning of the Renaissance receive ful-
ler treatment, and almost half the book is devoted to the nineteenth and twentieth centuries. Over eight hundred years of
rich and varied writing are treated on a scale which makes
clear the great general movements of thought and taste without
neglecting the characteristic qualities of individual authors and
their works. These are approached primarily as literature, to be
read as the personal expressions of particularly interesting
minds, but they are related to the social history of their time
and, on occasion, to the literatures of countries other than
France. The book is intended both for the general reader and
for the student who wishes to take his bearings before special-
izing in any one particular field. Based on modern scholarship
and reflecting modern critical opinion, it is a concisely informa-
tive as well as a companionable work.

William C. Atkinson

A HISTORY OF SPAIN
AND PORTUGAL

A464

This book attempts to show as a whole the Peninsula made up
of Spain and Portugal. Through its varied history a characteristic pattern of social life has emerged. The successive
occupations of Roman, Visigoth, and Muslim span between
them more than a thousand years. The Peninsula's great contribution to the modern age was the opening up of the New
World in the west by Spain, and of new routes to the east by
Portugal. 'And were there more lands still to discover,' wrote
Camoens, 'they would be there too.' Over the last century and
a half the history of both peoples provides a case-study in the
essential relativity of forms of government. The reader will find
here, too, a commentary upon great Spanish and Portuguese
literary and artistic figures: Camoens, Cervantes, Lope de Vega,
Calderón, Velázquez, Goya, and many more.

G. R. Storry

A HISTORY OF MODERN JAPAN

ᴀ475

The rise, fall, and renaissance of Japan, within the space of less than a hundred years, is one of the most curious and dramatic stories of our time. The first part of this book gives the historical background to Japan's emergence as a modern state in the sixties of the last century. It then discusses in detail the stages of Japan's advance as a world power up to the tragedy of the Pacific War. This struggle and its aftermath – the Occupation – are vividly described and analysed. The last chapter, bringing the account right up to the present day, is a fascinating study of the new Japan that has come into being since the San Francisco Peace Treaty of 1951.

DATE DUE
